THE ASIAN AMERICANS:

Changing Patterns, Changing Needs

THE ASIAN AMERICANS:
Changing Patterns, Changing Needs

BOK-LIM C. KIM

UNIVERSITY OF ILLINOIS

AKCS

ASSOCIATION OF KOREAN CHRISTIAN SCHOLARS IN NORTH AMERICA, INC.

Montclair   *New Jersey*

This volume may be ordered from
AKCS/Publication Services
204 W. Pennsylvania Ave.
Urbana, IL 61801

Library of Congress Cataloging in Publication Data

Kim, Bok-Lim C., 1930–
    The Asian American, changing patterns,
changing needs.

    (The Association of Korean Christian Scholars
in North America publication series; 4)
    Bibliography: p.
    Includes index.
    1. Social work with minorities—United States.
    2. Asian Americans—Illinois—Chicago metro-
politan area. I. Title. II. Series: Association of
Korean Christian Scholars in North America. The
Association of Korean Christian Scholars in America publication series; 4.

HV3198.A2K55   362.8'4   78-23599
ISBN 0-932014-03-8

TABLE OF CONTENTS

LIST OF FIGURES

LIST OF TABLES

ACKNOWLEDGMENTS

Many persons deserve a measure of heartfelt thanks for their assistance and support in the long process of gathering the data and writing this book. In particular, I would like to acknowledge:

—The thirty-six bilingual interviewers who conducted the 726 interviews upon which the study is based. Without their commitment to the project, and their extra efforts in locating the respondents, the study would not have been possible.

—The Survey Research Laboratory of the University of Illinois at Chicago Circle. This organization acted as the data collection agent for the project. In particular, Ron Czaja provided valuable assistance in developing the sampling procedure and constructing the questionnaire. Theresa Silva handled the sprawling task of coordinating the data collection activities, working with four supervisors and 36 interviewers from several different Asian ethnic backgrounds.

—Dr. Kee Whan Choi of Georgia State University. Dr. Choi provided essential help with the selection of statistical analysis procedures, as well as with computer programming.

—Dr. Mary Harper of the Center for Minority Group Mental Health Programs at the National Institute of Mental Health. While serving as project officer of the research project upon which this book is based, Dr. Harper's understanding and helpfulness were deeply appreciated by everyone involved with the project. I would especially like to acknowledge her assistance in securing the changes and extensions in the research grant which made the writing of the book possible.

—Dr. Ford Kuramoto, formerly of the National Institute of Mental Health, who provided much advice and encouragement during the initial phase of the research project.

—Dr. Margaret E. Condon, co-principal investigator of the research project, who contributed heavily to the analysis of data and the preparation of the interim study report. She has been a valuable partner in sharing the inevitable ups and downs of a long and complicated project, a valuable collaborator in the process of seeking insights and sounding out ideas.

—Dr. Michael R. Sawdey and Dr. Barbara C. Meihoefer of Publication Services, for their extensive work in reorganizing the interim report and providing editorial assistance in the preparation of the manuscript of this book. They have provided much helpful advice on the organization and presentation of the study findings.

—Community leaders of the four ethnic communities in which the study was conducted. The cooperation and assistance of these persons was essential in planning and conducting the study.

—The 726 respondents who found time in their busy schedules to participate in this study. It goes without saying that without their cooperation this research would have been impossible: I extend to all of them my heartfelt gratitude.

—Special thanks go to my two devoted children, Stanley and Mary Ann Kim, who cheerfully bore the extra burden of family chores and responsibilities while I was engaged in—and often preoccupied by—this project.

—Finally, my sincerest appreciation and gratitude go to my husband, Chin, for his unfailing support, encouragement, and guidance throughout the course of the study—especially for his unwavering faith in my ability to finish what often appeared to be an interminable project. Without his help, both tangible and intangible, this book could not have been written: in many ways it is truly a result of his support.

—B.-L.C.K.

FOREWORD

Having just coauthored an annotated bibliography on Asian-American mental health literature, I have become keenly aware of the inadequacies in our knowledge of Asian Americans. Myths and stereotypes still exist with respect to the social, economic, educational, and mental health status of Asians in the United States. Very few systematic empirical studies have been conducted on Asian Americans in various communities. Thus, policy makers, mental health practitioners, and service deliverers have had to rely upon personal experiences and intuition in planning for the needs of Asian Americans.

For a long while, I have felt that the field is in desperate need of a systematically conducted survey of the needs and status of various Asian-American groups. In *The Asian Americans: Changing Patterns, Changing Needs* Professor Bok-Lim Kim has taken that giant step in contributing to our knowledge. Her review of the existing literature, careful reporting of the survey research on various Asian groups, and thoughtful analysis of the data provide a good model for those wishing to conduct clinical and community research with applied and policy implications. It is not that her research design and methodology are without limitations. Rather, Professor Kim systematically and thoughtfully confronts research problems encountered by Asian–American investigators: finding meaningful examples of respondents, gaining cooperation from Asian Americans, including diverse Asian groups, interviewing respondents in their own ethnic languages, collecting comprehensive information, and drawing from the data implications for each group as well as for Asian Americans as a whole. All of this was accomplished in a sensitive and insightful manner.

Readers not familiar with Asian Americans will certainly have their eyes opened by the consistency of the findings that demonstrate the pressing needs and problems of Asian Americans. There are also surprises for researchers and practitioners who have worked in Asian–American communities. Students, practitioners, researchers, policy makers, and the general public will gain much from reading this book. It contains information on social, economic, educational, and mental health needs; on utilization patterns of social service organizations and cultural resources; and on attitudes and beliefs.

After reading this book, I feel disturbed over the immensity of the unresolved and inadequately addressed issues facing Asian Americans, as revealed by Professor Kim; and yet, I also feel optimistic. Solutions can only come when we fully appreciate the magnitude of the problems and when we develop a realistic and sensitive understanding. Bok-Lim Kim has made a truly unique and significant contribution to our understanding of Asian Americans, a major achievement that will stand for many years to come.

— Stanley Sue
University of Washington

PREFACE

Soon after Bok-Lim Kim joined the faculty of the School of Social Work of the University of Illinois at Urbana-Champaign she began a series of research studies about Asian Americans. She has assessed their characteristics, individually and in groups, their social service needs, and the adaptations in the social service delivery system that are necessary to enable the nation's newer immigrants to use their strengths in their adopted country. The recommendations Professor Kim makes for improved social services to Asian Americans reflect an emphasis upon the cultural diversity of these peoples—the key to the richness of the contributions that immigrants have always made to American society.

If the equality of cultural diversity is not to be an obstacle, but rather an enhancing influence in communities where Asian Americans have settled, then, as Professor Kim points out, social services must be, among other variables, based on a sensitive understanding of the particular immigration history of individuals and groups, the effects of generational differences, and the characteristic ways by which these strong people have solved problems earlier in their lives. The need for bilingual communication between service-giver and client is imperative, as are advocacy-oriented referral services, the use of law, adaptations in government's regulatory authority, and other influences for social action to change the conditions creating the problems.

The label "Asian American" is a broadly inclusive semantic umbrella so that the nature and strengths of cultural diversity and the demands it places upon those who supply social services tend to be obscured. Even more serious is the readiness of most persons in this country to view Asian Americans as a "safe" or "model" minority, one that takes care of its problems without the need for community-planned services. Such a view retards progress toward an understanding of the diverse characteristics and needs of Asian Americans, and denies the serious impact of the American society on the Asian immigrant. It is, in fact, an attitude that rests on a discrimanatory base—a willingness to ignore these new residents' right to community services and to depress their potential for important contributions to American life.

This country has grown rich from the work of its immigrants. The earliest non-European immigrants, those most discriminated against, were the involuntary ones from the coasts of Africa whose racial difference was so pronounced and unaccepted as to make their enslavement possible. Only the "first wave" of immigrants was easily received—those who came before the late 1860s from Great Britain and the countries of northern Europe. Their heritage and racial identity, perceived by Americans as like or very similar to their own, and the new nation's need to settle and develop the sweeping agricultural lands to the west, greatly lessened adverse feelings towards those newcomers. The second wave of immigration between 1860 and 1915 aroused much suspicion and resentment. Twenty-eight million foreigners from the countries of eastern and southern Europe poured into the cities of the eastern seaboard and west to Chicago. They came to escape poverty, religious persecution, militarism, or political tyranny—and because of the lure of promised opportunity. Yet Italian immigrants from the southern provinces and from Sicily, Slavic peoples from Austria-Hungary and Rumania, Jews from Russian Poland, and Russia were welcomed only because of the Industrial Revolution and the nation's great need for unskilled labor. Fear was common that the new foreigners would weaken its institutions and dilute the fabric of American society. A movement grew to restrict immigration from countries viewed as racially different.

Asian Americans, in turn, have come to America for some of the same reasons as the earlier immigrants from Europe. In turn they have felt their share of overt and latent discrimination because of their "differences"—the very qualities that have the inherent power to enrich the productivity of a newly adopted environment.

One means of weakening the discrimination which present-day Asian Americans experience is to correct the deficiencies of the social service delivery system, to address the problem of inadequate communication between service-giver and recipient, and to provide education to social workers about the individual characteristics and needs of the various Asian groups and the strategies these persons can be enabled to employ in their own behalf. Thus their true strengths and potentialities for enriching the life of this country can become more clearly woven into the character of American society. Professor Kim's book will be enormously helpful in bringing about essential changes in the social service system.

Members of the social work profession, planners and policy makers in the social welfare system, and Asian Americans whom Professor Kim so well represents are all indebted to her for a carefully constructed and insightful line of research.

— Lela B. Costin
University of Illinois at
Urbana-Champaign

CHAPTER I

INTRODUCTION

Historical Stereotypes

Since the passage of the Immigration and Naturalization Act of 1965 (PL 89-236) most of the publicly held stereotypes about the social condition and composition of Asian-American minorities have lost whatever limited validity they may have once possessed. Over the years the American public has most often based its conceptions of Asian Americans on the perceived condition of the West Coast Japanese and Chinese populations. To the outsider, the Asian American has generally been perceived as either a person who immigrated prior to the Immigration Act of 1924,[1] or a first or second generation descendant of such an immigrant.

For nearly forty years there was a certain amount of truth to this perception. In fact, the mass of Chinese immigration took place between 1850 and 1882,[2] followed by a later wave of Japanese immigration from about 1890 to 1908. It is these Asian Americans, and their descendants, who are perceived as having entered the mainstream of American life by dint of perseverance, sobriety, intelligence, and cultural accomodation. As has been revealed in numerous studies over the last two decades, the stereotype of these Asian Americans as "model minorities" and the "quiet Americans," is in many respects erroneous.[3] Among these groups, socioeconomic success is often meager when compared against the standard of the white majority, assimilation into the mainstream[4] is largely tokenistic, and severe personal problems frequently lurk behind a facade of apparent quiet contentment.[5]

Beyond these considerations, however, there is a more basic way in which the public perception of Asian Americans is generally in error: fully a third of all Asian Americans have arrived in the United States since 1965.[6] Who are these new Asian Amerians? What sort of social and economic success have they achieved in the United States? More realistically speaking, what problems of adjustment and integration are they encountering—and how well is the American system of social services responding to their problems and consequent service needs? It is questions of this sort that the present study seeks to answer, both through the presentation and critical consideration of existing research in this area, and through analysis of the results of research conducted by the author and the coinvestigator on Asian Americans of four national origins in the Chicago area. The groups specifically considered in this study are Americans of Chinese, Japanese, Pilipino, and Korean origin or descent. They are discussed in a chronological order based upon the time periods when the greatest numbers of each group began to arrive in the United States: (1) Chinese (1850s–1882); (2) Japanese (1890–1908); Pilipinos (1900–1930); Koreans (1902–present).

The data presented in this study were collected in 1973–74 with the assistance of a grant from the Center for Minority Group Mental Health Programs, National Institute of Mental Health. As in all cases where data have been collected during a single time period and from a single location—in this instance the metropolitan area of Chicago—it has been necessary in this study to set the findings in a global perspective. I have attempted to do this by providing, where necessary, a comparison of the characteristics of the Chicago Asian-American communities with those of their counterparts elsewhere in the country. In this way, the study findings can provide a useful starting point for exploring and evaluating local conditions and, subsequently, for implementing policies and programs.

Early Asian Immigration

Although the immigration of Asians since 1965 has proceeded under a system of quotas and priorities more nearly like that applied to immigration from other parts of the world, the earlier immigration of these people was often controlled and determined by the labor market and the social whims of the white majority.[7] The first to arrive in substantial numbers were the Chinese, many of whom came to California in the 1850s as sojourners seeking their fortunes in the gold fields.[8] Although they proved to be industrious miners, few Chinese became wealthy from their efforts. In part, they were bankrupted by the infamous Foreign Miners' Tax, which was in practice collected only from the Chinese, and in part they went the way of all small-time miners, of whatever nationality: the surface deposits were quickly exhausted and the deep mining operations were monopolized by the mechanized, corporate mining industry.

Those Chinese who stayed on after the initial rush turned to service industries, such as the laundry or restaurant trade, or entered small-scale manufacturing of such items as brooms and sandals, or performed unskilled labor of various sorts for meager wages. Of particular importance, some 12,000 Chinese laborers provided the chief manpower for the construction of the Central Pacific end of the transcontinental railroad, while thousands more were employed in the reclamation of the land upon which much of present-day San Francisco rests.[9] During the '80s and '90s, some Chinese entered truck farming and fishing, but restrictive legislation quickly drove them from these occupations.[10] As a result of anti-Asian agitation in the period from 1870 onward, numerous Chinese left California and established themselves in midwestern and eastern cities.[11]

By 1890 Chinese immigration had effectively been halted, first as a result of unilateral U.S. revision of treaties with China, and finally by acts of Congress.[12] In their quest for cheap labor, agricultural contractors turned to the importation of Japanese laborers, first to Hawaii and later to the west coast.[13] Many Japanese settled into truck farming with considerable success, and immigration continued until 1908 when it was halted by the so-called Gentlemen's Agreement, which was an exchange of diplomatic notes between the U.S. and Japan, declaring their policy in the Far East.[14] In reality, this was hardly a "gentlemen's agreement" since it was a case of U.S. foreign policy being dictated to a nation which was in no position to resist it.

Beginning about 1900, agricultural operators in Hawaii experimented with importing Korean contract laborers as cheap field help. It was only a matter of time before some Koreans reached the West Coast. Although Korean immigration never reached the proportions of that of the Chinese or Japanese, about 10,000 Koreans had entered Hawaii, and another 1,000 had reached the mainland, before emigration was forbidden by the Korean government in 1905.[15]

The Pilipinos* present a somewhat different historical situation. The Philippine Islands became a U.S. territory after the U.S. defeated the nationalist forces in 1902.[16] Although Pilipinos were not allowed to become naturalized citizens, neither were they under the control of the immigration laws. They were permitted to enter the United States on a U.S. passport, and many took advantage of this to seek work as field hands in California. Growers in California encouraged this practice since the cheap labor of the Pilipinos helped them undercut competing producers in other states who were dependent on the more costly labor of Mexicans or poor whites.[17] The laborers who were competing with the Pilipinos took quite a different view of the situation, and the resulting tensions erupted in riots as the economy contracted with the coming of the depression. By 1930 there were some 45,000 Pilipinos in California. Thereafter immigration was slowed by economic conditions, and virtually halted by the Philippino Exclusion Act of 1934, which limited immigration to 150 persons per year.[18] Under the U.S. Repatriation Law of 1935, Pilipinos then in the United States were given the option of returning to the Philippines at government expense. With the granting of Philippine independence in 1946, the Pilipinos became subject to the severe immigration restrictions then prevailing for other Asian groups.

The Immigration Act of 1924, generally known as the Exclusion Act, essentially ended immigration from China, Japan, and Korea since it denied admission to the United States of all persons ineligible for citizenship, a category which at that time included Asians and other "non-whites." During World War II, the combination of anti-Japanese feeling and the alliance with China led to the granting of token immigration quotas for Chinese.[19] While these quotas, as well as those for Koreans, were stretched somewhat in the post-war era through the admission of "non-quota" immigrants such as refugees and spouses of U.S. citizens, one can,

---

*The spelling "Pilipino" has been adopted for this study because it more nearly reflects the actual native pronunciation of the word. There is no soft "f" sound in the Pilipino language.

for all practical purposes, divide Asian immigration into two eras: pre-1924, and post-1965.

Pre-1924 immigration, as outlined briefly above, consisted primarily of laborers, sojourners, and others seeking expanded economic opportunities—miners, businessmen, and farmers among them. Some, such as Syung Man Rhee, later president of the Republic of Korea, came as students or exiles, but they are so few as to be insignificant.[20] In general, the early immigrants brought little with them in the way of educational or professional attainments, although some, such as the Chinese masons, were skilled or semi-skilled laborers.[21] For the most part, their process of survival involved exploiting areas of the economy—running all the way from ditch-digging to sandal-making—where the white majority either would not or could not compete with them. Lacking diplomatic or treaty protection and systematically denied the usual rights of naturalization, these early waves of Asian immigrants achieved some measure of economic success, but generally found themselves excluded from most forms of social participation.

Throughout the twentieth century, shifting public opinion and the slow process of judicial redefinition and review have gradually removed the legal barriers to both naturalization and legal protection of Asian Americans,[22] as well as to the handling of Asian immigration on an equal footing with that from the rest of the world. Court decisions determined quite early that American-born children of Asian parents could not be denied American citizenship by birth.[23] However, it was not until 1952 that the last legal impediments were removed to the naturalization of foreign-born Asian Americans.[24] In California, where the largest concentration of Asian Americans was (and is) located, state laws restricting the economic activities of Asian immigrants were gradually struck down by the courts or repealed by the state legislature.[25] As noted earlier, limited Chinese and Korean immigration was permitted after 1943, and when the Philippines received independence in 1946 a small Pilipino quota was established.

The ultimate result of this long, and often willy-nilly, process was the amended Immigration and Naturalization Act of 1965 which has subsequently controlled immigration to the United States from all parts of the world. Technically, the Act is itself an amendment of the Immigration and Nationality Act of 1952, but the 1965 law represents such a radical departure from previous immigration policies that it will be considered separately here.

Although there were virtually no restrictions in the earliest days of U.S. immigration law, the general principle later was to provide certain annual quotas for each nation of the world from which immigrants might come to the United States. In general, the pattern of quotas was established by the ethnic preferences of the white majority: relatively high limits for the countries of northern and western Europe, substantially lower ones for the southern and eastern countries. By and large, African and Asian immigrants were in an anomolous position since they were forbidden to become naturalized citizens under the provisions of legislation dating back to 1790.[26] While immigration by persons ineligible for citizenship was not finally forbidden until 1924, this restriction had a depressing effect on immigration from Asia and Africa. Even when token immigration of the Chinese was permitted in 1943, they were handled differently from other immigrant groups: all other quotas were expressed in terms of nationality (country of citizenship) of the immigrant, while "Chinese" was defined in terms of ancestry, regardless of actual nationality.[27] Thus, for instance, a Russian who had acquired French citizenship would be considered under the quota of French, but a Chinese from Hong Kong who was a British subject would still come under the Chinese quota.

The New Asian Immigration

This and other discriminatory provisions of the immigration law were eliminated by the amendments of 1965. Under the amended law, individual national quotas were eliminated. Instead, an annual quota of 170,000 immigrants was established for the entire eastern hemisphere, with no country to contribute more than 20,000. Within these limits, certain priorities were established for the granting of visas, beginning with the relatives of current U.S. citizens and running on down through professionals and skilled laborers to refugees and unskilled laborers.[28] These preferences have, as we shall see, played a significant part in the current plight of thousands of Korean and Pilipino immigrants from the upper socioeconomic strata.

The new provisions have had a profound effect on the level of immigration from the Asian countries. Prior to 1965, for example, the Chinese immigration quota was 105 persons annually. In actual practice the number of Chinese (and other Asians) admitted was always a good deal above the quota, since certain categories—such as refugees, expellees, and spouses of American citizens—were not charged against the quota. In 1964, for example, the total Chinese immigration was 2,978.[29] Still, even these totals of quota and nonquota immigrants were always far below the levels subsequently permitted under the 1965 act.

As can be seen from Table 1, immigration from Korea, the Philippines, Japan, China, and Hong Kong has increased very rapidly since 1965. When these immigration figures are used to extrapolate the 1970 census figures to show growth through immigration over the decade from 1964-1974, the results are as shown in Table 2. For all groups except the Japanese the overall growth due to immigration has been quite dramatic. In the case of Japanese Americans it must be remembered that they were, by a considerable margin, the largest Asian-American population group in 1964. This, coupled with modest immigration figures, leads to the low (7%) growth of the Japanese-American population due to immigration. Taken in absolute numbers, however, even the Japanese immigration (42,110) is substantial. The percentage increases for Pilipinos (85%) and Chinese (62%) are quite large indeed, and the 261% increase for Korean Americans belongs to yet another order of magnitude.

The Needs of Asian Americans

Figures such as these give some indication of the influx of Asian Americans since the passage of the Ammendment to the 1965 Immigration and Naturalization Act. What becomes of these Asian immigrants when they arrive in the United States? The first—and perhaps most definite—conclusion is that nearly all of them settle in urban population centers. The 1970 census figures indicate that, depending on national origin, from 86% to 97% of Asian Americans are urban residents. For recent immigrants it is fair to assume that the percentages will be even higher, since new arrivals are more likely to be dependent on relatives, ethnic enclaves, and the concentration of job opportunities in the urban setting. By comparison, only about 75% of the general U.S. population lives in urban areas.

The distribution of Asian Americans in the U.S. urban centers is far from uniform. As might be expected from the historical

Table 1
Overall ranks in world emigration to U.S. and actual totals of Asian immigration to U.S., 1965–1974

	Korean rank	Total	Philipines rank	Total	Japan rank	Total	China rank	Total	Hong Kong rank	Total	Annual totals
1965	28th	2,165	17th	3,130	16th	3,180	13th	4,057	52nd	712	13,244
1966	25th	2,492	13th	6,093	20th	3,394	8th	13,736	16th	3,872	29,587
1967	18th	3,956	11th	10,865	19th	3,946	6th	19,741	15th	5,355	43,863
1968	21st	3,811	7th	16,731	24th	3,613	10th	12,738	22nd	3,696	40,589
1969	17th	6,045	3rd	20,744	22nd	3,957	8th	15,440	19th	5,453	51,639
1970	14th	9,314	2nd	31,203	21st	4,485	8th	14,093	25th	3,863	62,958
1971	9th	14,297	2nd	28,471	20th	4,457	7th	14,417	23rd	3,205	64,847
1972	5th	18,876	2nd	29,376	21st	4,757	6th	17,339	22nd	4,391	74,739
1973	4th	22,930	2nd	30,799	17th	5,461	6th	17,297	22nd	4,359	80,846
1974	—	28,028	—	32,857	—	4,860	—	18,056	—	4,629	88,430
Totals by country		111,914		210,269		42,110		146,914		39,535		550,742 Grand total, 1965–74

Table 2
Population increase of Asian Americans due to immigration,
1964–1974

	Korean	Pilipino	Japanese	Chinese*	Total
1964 population	42,815	247,965	565,749	328,827	1,185,356
1974 population	154,729	458,234	607,859	533,276	1,754,098
absolute increase	111,914	210,269	42,110	204,449	568,742
percentage increase	261%	85%	7%	62%	48%

*Includes immigration from China, Taiwan, and Hong Kong.

patterns of migration, the states of Hawaii and California together account for about half of the total. And, while the geographic pattern varies from one national origin group to another, the remaining half of the Asian-American population outside of California and Hawaii tends to be concentrated in a relatively small number of large cities. For instance, in 1970, of 3,855 foreign-born Koreans residing in the state of New York, 2,665, or about 70%, were living in New York City. Of 2,506 foreign-born Koreans in Illinois, 1,333 were living in Chicago.[30] Concentrations of this sort are typical of all the groups considered here.

The overall picture, then, is that the Asian American population has increased substantially since 1965 due to immigration, and that this influx of population has tended to concentrate itself in a relatively small number of urban areas.

Therefore, the social service needs of the current Asian-American population may be expected to stem from an aggregate of new and old problems. On the one hand, there are the problems of incomplete structural assimilation common to a visible minority group which has coexisted uneasily for several generations with a white majority which has never totally accepted it. On the other, the large influx of new immigrants leads to problems arising from a lack of cultural assimilation. The new immigrant may not know how to read road signs; the second generation Asian American may still be asked when he immigrated.

The existence of these general problem areas can be hypothesized from the bare facts of the immigration figures. However, when the researcher, community planner, or provider of social services attempts to move beyond stereotypes and generalizations, there are often few reliable guideposts to follow. For instance, it is a disconcerting fact of life to Asian-American community leaders that the 1970 U.S. census probably undercounts the Asian-American population by a substantial margin.[31] Unfortunately, there is no way of knowing how inaccurate the figures are because only part of the probable error is systematic: the remainder is based on such intangibles as the reluctance of older Asian Americans to respond to government inquiries, the high residential mobility of new immigrants, the number of census forms filled out incorrectly or discarded altogether because of the respondent's difficulties with English, or the failures of mail delivery arising from the dense and complicated structure of living arrangements in ethnic enclaves.

Many of the difficulties facing the census-taker also plague the researcher who attempts to gather reliable data, free from sampling bias, among Asian Americans. The Immigration and Naturalization Service files, which are a logical starting point for most sampling procedures, present special difficulties in and of themselves. For example, the files are not arranged according to the exact status of the alien registration sufficiently stringent to guarantee the completeness of the sample pool. Then, once a sample has been arrived at, response rates are often poor. Finally, those who are actually contacted may prove reluctant respondents unless the interviewer is not only an Asian American, but also a member of the same national group as those interviewed. Ironically, when all these conditions have been met, some researchers have had the experience of having respondents answer "yes" to nearly everything in order to be gracious to the interviewer as a fellow ethnic person![32] Nevertheless, certain pieces of the Asian-American puzzle have emerged from previous research. In the next chapter we will systematically review the literature of the subject; for now, a topical summary of the current state of knowledge will serve to develop a picture of the information needs which the present study attempts to fill.

Existing studies of the socioeconomic condition of recently-arrived Asian Americans point to a pattern of downward mobility, under-employment, and status incongruity.[33] When viewed in absolute terms, the income levels of these immigrants often do not appear to be unusually low. Family income levels are frequently reported to be at, or only slightly below, the median levels for the general population.[34] However, certain types of indirect evidence point to problem areas which may not be revealed by a superficial examination of income levels. For one thing, the educational levels of the Korean and Pilipino immigrant groups are conspicuously higher than that of the general U.S. population.[35] Whether this is brought about by the preference categories of the current immigration law, socioeconomic conditions in the donor countries, or a combination of these factors, is not altogether clear. What is clear is that the educational level of these immigrants is not fully reflected in their income levels. It has also been suggested that family income levels may be a misleading measure of success since it is common in Asian-American families to have several family members working and contributing to the total income figure. Thus a single family income figure may conceal the substandard earnings of several persons.

In addition it has been reported that most Asian-American immigrants are working at jobs which are one or more strata below the sorts of jobs they held in their home countries. That is, the professional class Asian-American immigrant is more likely to be found working at the white collar level, and the white collar immigrant at the blue collar level.[36] Given the state of flux in the American economic system it is not always clear whether or not these status changes represent real socioeconomic downward mobility. Furthermore, the psychological impact of this status incongruity is likely to be difficult to isolate and measure because recent immigrants are typically undergoing social and psychological stresses from so many other sources. Thus, one aim of the present study is to measure, and assess as objectively as possible, the degree of downward mobility, underemployment, and status incongruity experienced by Asian Americans in a fairly typical urban setting.

Because of the large proportion of recent immigrants among most Asian-American groups, it is important that we have a clear picture of the immigration experience of these people. In addition to the length of time since immigration, it is important to know as much as possible about the preimmigration demography of the population. As noted earlier, status incongruity and downward mobility are suspected to be common among Asian-American immigrants: information on preimmigration socioeconomic status is necessary in order to measure these conditions.

Once the immigrant arrives in America, what is the nature of his social support system? It has been assumed for many years that Asian-American immigrants have a comprehensive support system waiting for them in the form of extended family structures, ethnic community enclaves, and ethnic self-help organizations.[37] Does such a support system exist, and if it does, has it managed to remain viable with the great influx of immigration since 1965? Can the experience of Asian-American communities (such as the Japanese) which do have well-established ethnic self-help organizations be generalized to the more recently arrived groups? It is also important to know what effect the new immigration has had upon the self-help structures of the older Asian-American communities. This may affect the overall service needs of these communities.

There is a perennial suspicion among social service providers that Asian Americans underuse social services, when compared to the general population.[38] In many cases, however, this suspected underuse has been rationalized or dismissed with such statements as, "Asian Americans don't have problems," or "they take care of their own." The first of these statements is of dubious validity if one considers the large proportion of Asian Americans who are recent immigrants, are probably underemployed, and have settled in decaying neighborhoods of densely populated urban centers. Whether or not Asian Americans solve problems by "taking care of their own" is very difficult to determine objectively: in part this is a stereotype generated by the white majority, but it also has a definite basis in the outlook and social mores of many Asian peoples. It is perhaps more appropriate to ask whether Asian Americans "take care of their own" to a greater extent than the white American majority does, or whether what they can do on their own is adequate to the problems they face. In this connection, very little work has been done on the use of social services by the general population, although some research indicates that, at least in the area of mental health problems, the American population as a whole is much less inclined to rely on outside professional help than mental health service providers would like to believe.[39]

The present study seeks to explore both the degree and kind of services utilized by Asian Americans in the urban setting. How important are the family and the ethnic community in providing help? Do Asian Americans fail to utilize social services provided by the majority community, and if so does this failure result because Asian Americans do not wish to utilize such services, because the services are inappropriate, or because they do not know how to locate and utilize them?

The service needs of a population can be defined in two ways:

in terms of the services which the people perceive themselves to need, or in terms of those services which seem important to the service provider, based on the problems he perceives among the service population. There are obvious shortcomings to either approach taken alone. Thus the present study seeks to evaluate the respondents' expressed service needs in relation to the demographic facts of the population involved. It is of course impossible to evaluate all possible service needs of a population or to elicit all the perceived service needs desired by a respondent group. However, it is possible to evaluate the prime areas of need if one has accurate demographic information and reasonably uninhibited respondent replies to work from, and it is these materials which the present study attempts to supply for certain populations of Asian Americans.

Answers to all such questions about the service needs of Asian Americans depend upon the availability of certain types of basic demographic data about the population group. These data are not generally available, in part because they are not collected through the regular channels of demographic information in the United States, that is, through the decennial census and related government surveys.[40] Independent researchers, on the other hand, frequently find the ethnic enclaves to be a "closed book" unless they are fluent linguists and are themselves members of the group under study.[41] As a result, there is a paucity of hard data on Asian Americans, especially with respect to recent immigrants. For almost all areas of social demography we need to know more about Asian Americans—and we need data that are not usually collected by such means as the decennial census. In addition to family income, we need to know how many family members are contributing to this income, in what proportion, and from what sources. In addition to present income and job status level, we must know what socioeconomic standing these persons enjoyed before coming to America. In addition to years of education, we need to know the relevance of that education to the person's present employment. In part, this study attempts to collect this kind of basic demographic information for one urban population of four Asian-American groups.

The Approach of the Present Study

In conclusion, when scrutinized, most knowledge of the current problems and service needs of Asian Americans is revealed to be an empirical collection of mutually contradictory intuitive statements. As noted earlier, social service workers tend to perceive that Asian Americans either have no problems, or handle their problems within the family and ethnic group context. If, on the other hand, an outsider questions Asian Americans directly about their problems and service needs, the answer will almost always be, "I have no problems," or, "I need no services."[42] On both sides, these statements may be quite sincere, but taken together they give an improbably idealistic picture of the inner life of a visible minority which is known to suffer from economic and social discrimination. The approach adopted for the present study is to obtain information on the problems and service needs of Asian Americans by working from the inside out, as it were. To this end, interviewers from each national origin group were used to administer specially-designed questionnaires translated into the subjects' ethnic languages.

From this overview of what we need to know about Asian Americans in order to assess their problems and service needs realistically, it should be clear that there are several tasks to be performed by this study. The first is the synthesis and organization of existing information. This is no simple task in itself since this information has been collected by workers in several disciplines operating under a variety of constraints. There are problems of subjectivity, stereotyping, and special-pleading which must be considered. The existing literature in this area will be discussed and evaluated in Chapter II.

The second area of emphasis in this study is the survey research on Asian Americans in Chicago performed by the present writer and her coinvestigator. This research attempts to answer the questions raised about the demography and service needs of this Asian-American population. The study itself is discussed in Chapter III, while the results are presented as composites of the various ethnic groups in Chapters IV through VII, and an overall composite in Chapter VIII. (For those who have a technical interest in the construction and administration of the survey, details of the statistical and sampling techniques are presented in Appendix A.) Finally, Chapter IX draws conclusions from the data and presents recommendations based on an evaluation of existing practices in the light of the results of the study.

NOTES TO CHAPTER 1

1. The title of the act can only be regarded as a euphemism; it is often referred to as the "Exclusion Act of 1924." This act effectively barred Asian (and African) immigration by declaring that immigration was not open to any person ineligible for citizenship, a category which included "Mongolians" and other "nonwhite races."

2. For detailed figures, see B.L. Sung, *The Story of the Chinese in America,* New York: Collier Books, 1971, Table 4-1.

3. See, for instance, H.H.L. Kitano, *Japanese Americans; The Evolution of a Subculture,* Englewood Cliffs, N.J.: Prentice-Hall, 1969, 100–101. M.K. Maykovich, *Japanese American Identity Dilemma,* Tokyo: Waseda University Press, 1972, Chapter 4. R. Homma-True, "Characteristics of contrasting Chinatowns: 2. Oakland, California," *Social Casework,* 57(3):155 (1976). A.I. Mass, "Asians as individuals: The Japanese community," *Social Casework,* 57(3): 160 (1976).

4. In most cases, when the term "assimilation" is used in this study it will be qualified to indicate social (structural) or cultural assimilation. My usage largely follows that of Gordon: social or structural assimilation refers to the assimilation of an ethnic group into the existing social groups and institutions of the majority society. If a member of a given minority group can attain membership in the local country club (on the basis of his/her qualifications, not as a token gesture), then it may be said that this person's group has achieved social or structural assimilation into the majority society. On the other hand, cultural assimilation (or acculturation, to use Gordon's terminology) means simply that the members of a minority group have learned to deal with the cultural apparatus of the majority society: how to do the grocery shopping, file income tax forms, apply for a driver's license. While a person or group may be culturally assimilated without being socially assimilated (this is in fact often the case), it is unlikely that a person or group will manage to be socially or structurally assimilated without achieving prior cultural assimilation: it is more or less assumed that the country club only admits people who can be counted on not to drink from the finger bowls.

5. For a striking—and only partly fictional—portrayal of these hidden tensions, see Frank Chin's play, "The Year of the Dragon."

6. Extrapolations from the 1970 census figures are provided in Tables 1 and 2, below. For projections to 1980, see, T. Owan, *Asian Americans: A Case of Benighted Neglect,* Chicago: Asian American Mental Health Research Center, Occasional Paper 1, n.d., 8–12. Briefly, Owan projects the total Asian-American population to be over 3 million in 1980, or about twice that in 1970, with most of the increase resulting from immigration.

7. European immigration was, for instance, virtually unlimited until 1965, with the present system of controls finally taking full effect only in 1968.

8. See B.L. Sung, 1971, Chapter 3.

9. Ibid., 29–36.

10. B. Hosokawa, *Nisei: The Quiet Americans.* New York: William Morrow, 1969, 44–57. B.L. Sung, 1971, 42–57.

11. See, for instance, J.W. Loewen, *The Mississippi Chinese: Between Black*

and White, Cambridge, Mass.: Harvard University Press, 1971, 21-31, T.-C. Fan, *Chinese Residents in Chicago,* Chicago: University of Chicago thesis, 1926. Reprinted, San Francisco: R and E, 1974, 13-14.

12. Ibid., 1974, 1-4.

13. For a detailed account of the early stages of Japanese immigration, see R. Daniels, *The Politics of Prejudice,* New York: Atheneum, 1973, 1-11.

14. B. Hosokawa, 1969, 110-111. H.H.L. Kitano, 1969, 28.

15. L. Shin, "Koreans in America: 1903-1945," in *Roots: An Asian American Reader,* ed. A. Tachiki and others, Los Angeles: Asian Studies Center, University of California at Los Angeles, 1971, 200-206. Shin, in turn, is quoting C.-Y. No, *Chae Mi Hanin Saryak (A Short History of Koreans in America),* Los Angeles: 1951, 1-4, 30.

16. The events leading up to U.S. control of the Philippines are a classic case of history as "one damn thing after another." The tacit assumption underlying the U.S. takeover seems to have been that the United States could do as it pleased by right of conquest—even though Dewey's fleet was originally sent to Manila on the pretext of aiding the Philippine independence movement! Several general histories of this period are available (e.g., Keesing, 1937; Chapman, 1950), but the flow of events is probably clearer in condensed treatments such as that provided by the *Encyclopedia Britannica* entry, "Philippines."

17. H.A. DeWitt, *Anti-Filipino Movements in California,* San Francisco: R and E, 1976, 33, 38.

18. The Tydings-McDuffie Act of 1934, which provided for Philippine independence in 1946, was the end product of considerable pressure from various politically powerful groups in the U.S., among them the sugar industry and organized labor. To these pressure groups, the granting of Philippine independence was the most expedient means of eliminating a source of unwanted competition. It is surely significant that the immigration barrier was to be instituted at once, rather than upon the actual granting of independence.

19. B.L. Sung, 1971, 77-81.

20. H.-C. Kim, and W. Patterson, *The Koreans in America: 1882-1974,* Dobbs Ferry, N.Y.: Oceana, 1974, 1-65.

21. B.L. Sung, 1971, 31.

22. C. Kim, and B.-L. C. Kim "Asian immigrants in American law," *American University Law Review,* 26: 1977, 373-407.

23. The matter was supposedly settled by the Supreme Court in the case of United States v. Wong Kim Ark (169 U.S. 649) in 1898, although there was some obfuscation of the issue in later decisions.

24. C. Kim, and B.-L.C. Kim, 1977.

25. B.L. Sung, 1971, 43-57. T.-C. Fan, 1974, 3-4, 8, 10.

26. C. Kim, and B.-L.C. Kim, 1977, 390.

27. B.L. Sung, 1971, 79.

28. T. Owan, n.d., 6.

29. B.L. Sung, 1971, 81, 83. From U.S. Immigration and Naturalization Service figures.

30. H.-C. Kim, "Some aspects of social demography of Korean Americans," *International Migration Review,* 1974, 8: 23-42.

31. Evidence of the rising concern over the inaccuracy of census data for

Asian Americans may be found in Senator Matsunaga's Senate Joint Resolution 47.

32. Homma-True, 1976, 157–158.

33. W.M. Hurh, H.C. Kim, and K.C. Kim, *Cultural and Social Adjustment Patterns of Immigrants in the United States: A Case Study of Korean Residents in the Chicago Area,* Washington: Department of Health, Education and Welfare, Grant R03 MH 27004, Final Report, 1976, 10, 19.

34. T. Owan, n.d., 30–33.

35. This is reflected in the relatively large numbers of professional persons among the Korean and Pilipino groups, many of whom find themselves unable to practice their professions because of licensure restrictions, the language barrier, or outright discrimination. See U.S. Commission on Civil Rights, *Asian Americans and Pacific Peoples: A Case of Mistaken Identity,* Washington: Author, prepared by the California Advisory Committee to the Commission, 1975, 40–42.

36. W.M. Hurh, H.C. Kim, and K.C. Kim, 1976, 19.

37. See, for example, *U.S. News and World Report,* "Success story of one minority group in the U.S.," 61(26):73–76 (1966).

38. For some investigations in the area of mental health, see G. Gurin, J. Veroff, and S. Feld, *Americans View Their Mental Health,* New York: Basic Books, 1960. For a more general investigation, see, B.A. Gutek, D. Katz, R.L. Kahn, and E. Barton, "Utilization and evaluation of government services by the American people," *Evaluation,* 2(1): 41–48, 1974. These authors have also made a complete presentation of their data in, D. Katz, B.A. Gutek, R.L. Kahn, and E. Barton, *Bureaucratic Encounters: A Pilot Study in the Evaluation of Government Services,* Ann Arbor: Institute for Social Research, The University of Michigan, 1975. See also, S. Sue and H. McKinney, "Asian Americans in the community mental health care system," *American Journal of Orthopsychiatry,* 45: 111–118, 1975.

39. G. Gurin, J. Veroff, and S. Feld, 1960.

40. T. Owan, n.d. 4. U.S. Commission on Civil Rights, 1975, 16–18.

41. D.W. Sue, and S. Sue, "Ethnic minorities: Resistance to being researched," *Professional Psychology,* 3: 11–17, 1972b.

42. R. Homma-True, 1976, 156. This theme permeates the *U.S. News and World Report* article cited in note 35, above. Although the provenance of the direct quotations in this article is not detailed, one suspects that these responses were given by Chinese Americans to Caucasian reporters who were strangers in the community. Under these circumstances, it is not surprising that the respondents denied having either personal or community problems severe enough to require outside help.

CHAPTER II

EXISTING LITERATURE

There has been little direct study devoted to the service needs of Asian Americans, or to consideration of the problem-solving strategies of this population. However, in many studies the question of service needs has received peripheral attention, and in some areas of concern—notably mental health—there has been a certain amount of empirical and historical observation. In other areas, such as demography and the socioeconomic consequences of immigration, available data, though scanty, can provide important contextual information for consideration of the results of the present study. Therefore, this chapter is devoted to a presentation of the existing knowledge in the study area.

It may come as something of a surprise to the reader, given the awakening interest in ethnic studies over the past decade and the various bibliographies which have appeared on Asian American studies,[1] that we should here be reduced to collecting peripheral and fragmentary materials. For the most part, however, this chapter excludes the general studies which make up any bibliography on Asian Americans (including the one at the end of the present study). An obvious exception to this rule is that portions of general studies are considered here when they shed any new light on the problem of Asian American service needs. As was noted in Chapter I, specific data on the service needs of Asian Americans are difficult to come by, and even when they are available it is difficult to draw meaningful conclusions for lack of useful comparative data on the general population. In part, then, the problem is a larger one: the social sciences have simply not done a thorough job of determining the comprehensive picture of service needs for any group. In consequence, the delivery of social services must often be planned and accomplished on the basis of the "best guess" of those responsible. When the service population is composed of Asian Americans the problem is simply compounded because those who are doing the guessing, planning, and providing are likely to be culturally isolated from the persons they must serve. This is an especially pressing problem in the case of newly-arrived groups, such as the Indo-Chinese refugees, who have never before been represented in the American population.

In order to condense the amount of peripheral data presented on the general condition of Asian Americans, this chapter is organized by topical areas: mental health, cultural factors in service usage, demography, the immigration experience, health care and problems of the aged, previous findings directly related to service needs, and materials important in the design of the present study. This series of topics covers the bulk of the existing literature which is relevant to considering the conditions under which Asian Americans experience service needs and—sometimes—receive the help they need.

Mental Health

This area has received considerable attention from investigators, perhaps because the raw data (mental hospital admissions and clinical records) are not subject to the accessibility problems which confront any study utilizing either the Census or the Immigration and Naturalization Service files.[2] Furthermore, there is perhaps no area in which the stereotypes about Asian Americans are more blatant. As Berk and Hirata observe, "Stereotypic notions still prevail that the Chinese family system and their segregated position in the larger society have successfully insulated them from the stresses and anxieties of modern life, and whatever insignificant amounts of deviance there were, were taken care of by the Chinese community itself."[3] To a large extent, this stereotype may be said to prevail with respect to every Asian-American group in the U.S. In consequence, those studies which have been

conducted have largely been the work of Asian-American investigators, and demonstrations of need have been difficult to bolster
with hard facts.[4] Those facts which are available, such as hospitalization rates for mental illness, often seem to indicate either a
low rate of usage or a low incidence of need for mental health
services among the Asian-American service population.

Studies based on hospitalization records have been conducted
by Jew and Broady,[5] with further analysis of the same data by
Berk and Hirata.[6] In both cases, records covering the period from
1855 to 1955 were used, and in both cases the target population
was Chinese Americans in California. The conclusion of these
studies is that, although the admission rates for Chinese Americans
in California have generally been lower than for the total population, the Chinese-American rate has increased steadily over the
past century, and for the years 1925–1945 it actually exceeded
that for the population as a whole. While this finding does not
indicate extraordinary mental health problems on the part of the
Chinese Americans, it does suggest that, at least in recent times,
there is little to support the stereotype that this group is "self-
contained" in the area of mental health. It is also true that admission rates may be only a dim reflection of total mental health
needs, and that the increase in Chinese-American rates may only
indicate increased acculturation and, with it, greater acceptance
of American mental health services.

In dealing with the problem of mental illness among Japanese
Americans, Kitano makes some use of admissions rates,[7] but is
largely forced, by lack of hard data, to structure his discussion
around anecdotal materials. He does note that, based on available
hospitalizatin figures, (1) the Japanese-American rate is lower
than for the general population, (2) however, while the rate per
100,000 population has dropped quite sharply for other groups in
the period 1950–64, it has declined only moderately for Japanese
Americans, and (3) once hospitalized, the Japanese American is
likely to remain longer than the Caucasian American.

Kitano's interpretation of these trends raises some intriguing
implications concerning Asian-American attitudes toward mental
health and service utilization. The minimal decline relative to
other groups and the longer average hospitalization for Japanese
Americans may indicate, according to Kitano, that the Japanese
American who is hospitalized may well have been rejected by his
family and community. If this is true, it would tend to suggest
that, whatever the current level of usage, there is considerable

need for social service intervention, since rejection by family and community is almost certain to be a difficult situation for a disturbed person to face. Most importantly, such rejection would indicate that the existing community and family structure in some Asian-American groups may be inadequate to cope with the detection and prevention of mental health problems.

A perusal of Kitano's hospitalization figures also provides a good example of the limited usefulness of such data in assessing underlying patterns of need. Although the Japanese-American figures are lower than those for Caucasian Americans, the rates for Mexican Americans (who are often stereotyped as marginally stable) are lower still! Then too, the rates for Chinese Americans (who are stereotypically lumped with Japanese Americans) are markedly higher, in Kitano's data, than those for any other group. It is beyond the scope of this study to deal with the discrepancies between the data bases established by Kitano, and those used by Jew and Broady, and Berk and Hirata. Among other things, the historical periods only partially overlap, and Kitano counts hospital population, rather than admissions, thus introducing a time factor which is not present in the admissions data alone. One thing that is clear, however, is that, while the hospitalization data used in these studies are neither comparable nor consistent, they do suggest, quite uniformly, that the stereotypes surrounding the mental health service usage of Japanese and Chinese Americans bear little relation to reality.

Studies of actual case-by-case usage of mental health facilities by Asian Americans sometimes show patterns which do not differ markedly from those for the general population. For instance, Brown, Stein, Huang, and Harris,[8] in a study of mental illness in the Chinatown area of Los Angeles, found little data to support the idea that the Chinese-American service population either was unaware of the existence of mental health facilities, or waited inordinately long to use them. On the other hand, there were some important differences in use patterns. Seventy percent of the Chinese-American patients were male, while only 40% of all mental patients from the general population were male. Also, the symptoms exhibited by the Chinese-American patients tended to be more pronounced.[9] These facts led the investigators to hypothesize that the practice among Chinese Americans may be to seek help only for a wage-earner who is so severely disturbed that he can no longer work. Overall, mental health service usage among the Chinese-American population was only about half of what would have been expected. Brown, et al., concluded that there is a definite need for increased bilingual/bicultural services in the mental health area, especially since Chinese-American patients proved reluctant to return to the clinic for follow-up treatment on an outpatient basis. In this connection, Sue and McKinney (1975) found that the drop-out rate for Asian-American patients receiving mental health services was extremely high (52%, compared to 29.8% for white patients).[10]

Among the more recently arrived Asian-American groups such as the Koreans and Pilipinos there has been little work done in the area of mental health service needs. This may stem, in part, from the lack of historical and census data, and in part from the fact that these groups have simply received less study, generally, than have the more established Chinese and Japanese Americans. For these groups it has generally been necessary to collect original data. Because of the pioneering nature of such studies, they have often been quite general, as, for instance, in the case of Park's study of three generations of Korean Americans in the Los Angeles area.[11]

Quite clearly, for all Asian groups we need to know more about group attitudes toward mental illness, actual rates of service usage, coping and adaptive behaviors, levels of knowledge about service availability, and the interrelation of the cultural concepts of shame and family honor with service usage. Since few mental health services are provided to Asian Americans in a bilingual/bicultural context, it is difficult, if not impossible, to determine the degree to which these services meet the needs of the service population.

Cultural Factors in Service Usage

Asian cultural attitudes toward personal problems and the seeking of help are particularly important because there is much circumstantial evidence to indicate that mental illness is the object of considerable shame among Asian Americans. Kitano notes, for instance, that Japanese Americans have sometimes come to tolerate a high level of "crazy" behavior within the family situation in order to avoid seeking outside help.[12] The question of "shame" and "face-saving" generally has been considered an important one for all Asian-American groups when it comes to utilizing available social services.

These cultural concepts (Haji, or shame among the Japanese, Hiya, among the Pilipinos, Mentz, or face-saving among the Chinese, and Chaemyun among the Koreans) have been recognized by several investigators as being important factors in Asian-American use of many types of social services. Kaneshigi,[13] and Sue and Sue,[14] for instance, suggest that the feeling of shame may prevent Asian American students from seeking counseling and guidance services. Having a problem which one cannot solve is regarded as a reflection on one's resourcefulness and will power, and may also be regarded as bringing dishonor upon the family. Kaneshigi also notes that certain cultural traits, such as lack of verbal assertiveness, may handicap the Asian-American counselee in the traditional counseling situation—particularly if the counseling is done in a group.

Kitano[15] notes that the extremely strong and cohesive Japanese family structure (at least among the Issei and Nisei) reinforces the desire to solve problems without reference to outside sources of assistance. The result is described by a Japanese-American psychiatrist, quoted by Kitano:

> Every time I give a public lecture (usually sponsored by a church or service club) on family problems, sexual information, or child rearing, the place is packed, and they ask all kinds of questions. Some of the questions are remarkably naive and others appear to indicate quite a bit of conflict, but I'm sure the questioners will never go for professional advice.[16]

The experience of this psychiatrist is indicative of one of the major problems facing providers of social services to Asian Americans: lack of expressed desire for help *cannot* be taken as a reliable indication of lack of need.

There is in fact a whole collection of culturally-based Asian-American behavior patterns which ought to lead—if we are to accept the tenets of Western psychiatry—to wholesale mental disorders.

Subordination of self to family, disapproval of emotional expression, enforced deference to the vertical authority structure of the family, and disapproval of self-assertion or expression of desires presumably do not lead to mental disorders in the Asian societies of which they are integral and essential cultural elements. To the Asian American, however, they may well be not only sources of psychological stress, but may also serve as impediments to seeking professional help.

Duff and Arthur,[17] for instance, hypothesize that the Pilipino concept of *Hiya* (shame) may be responsible for certain mental disorders often observed among Pilipino stewards in the U.S. Navy. Having "made good" by securing a coveted position in the Navy, the Pilipino steward is often under unbearable pressure not to "fail" and thereby dishonor his family. At the same time, like an immigrant, he is cut off from the tacit support systems in his native culture which would otherwise ameliorate some of this pressure. Similar patterns of conflict can be observed in other Asian-American groups where survival in the outside—non-Asian—world often dictates patterns of behavior which sharply conflict with those approved by the individual's traditional culture.

The principal problem in approaching the service utilization patterns of Asian Americans through these cultural paths is that no direct data base is available. On the one hand, we have a few statistics indicating underuse of social and mental health services by Asian Americans, and on the other, a set of cultural expectations which would seem to inhibit the use of such services. The connection is anecdotal and circumstantial, although, as Thoreau pointed out, circumstantial evidence can be quite strong—as, for instance, when one finds a trout in the milk! Unless the connection can be examined empirically rather than circumstantially, however, it is difficult to prescribe any but very general remedies for the problem. While the present study does not purport to unravel all of the interconnections between cultural norms and service usage, it does seek to define and describe the problem-solving strategies of Asian-Americans, which are an important link in this causal chain.

Asian-American Demography

In collecting the necessarily circumstantial evidence for a picture of our current knowledge of Asian-American service needs, it is important to make use of available demographic knowledge. As noted earlier, information from the decennial census is of limited use because, until recently, many Asian-American groups have been lumped with "others," a category including a wide variety of unrelated minority groups.[18] It is only with the 1970 census, for instance, that Korean Americans were finally disaggregated from the "others" category. Attempts are being made by minority group researchers to improve the data collection techniques to be used in the 1980 census, but informational benefits from these changes lie, of course, far in the future.[19]

Various investigators have, however, collected and analyzed available demographic data on Asian Americans, one of the most complete studies being that of Owan.[20] In studying the geographical distribution of Asian Americans, Owan concludes that, although Asian Americans constitute only a very small proportion of the U.S. population (about 1% in 1970), their distribution is wildly uneven. In the following cities, for example, the proportions of Asian Americans in the total population are far above the national average:

San Francisco	13.3%
Los Angeles–Long Beach	3.0%
Honolulu	85.0%
Boston	2.0%

Nor are these areas by any means the only ones which show concentrations above the national average. Because of these concentrations of Asian Americans in a few urban areas, the service needs of this group may well be greater than would be indicated by their share of the total national population.[21] This arises from the nature of urban life: increased concentration of population tends to go hand in hand with poverty, crime, and health and housing problems.[22] We may assume that this situation will not alleviate itself automatically: Owan projects that the 1980 Asian-American population will exceed three million, or double the population of this group in 1970, and the historical trend has been for this population to concentrate itself in a relatively small number of urban centers.

Income figures for Asian Americans may be as misleading as population figures when it comes to indicating actual levels of need. For example, the 1970 U.S. median family income was $9,596. Figures for the most numerous Asian American groups were as follows:[23]

Japanese Americans	$12,515
Chinese Americans	$10,610
Pilipino Americans	$9,318

However, several other factors must be taken into account. For example, restricting one's view to urban areas, and considering only individual rather than family income, reveals that Chinese-American males in New York City had a median income in 1970 of only $4,352, and in Boston, only $3,823 per year. These are the lowest income figures for *any* group covered by the decennial census.[24] Owan concludes that the economic success of some Japanese males, primarily West Coast Nisei, is sufficient to distort the overall picture for all Asian Americans. Even among Japanese Americans, numerous aged Issei live in extreme poverty. Taking another extreme case, half of all Samoan families in California live below the poverty line. A further distortion is introduced by the fact that fully a fourth of all Asian Americans live in the state of Hawaii, where the high cost of living makes national median income figures relatively meaningless.

Demographic data tend to suggest that Asian Americans considerably underuse available social services. For instance, they receive the lowest level of social security benefits of any group in the U.S. population, and their public assistance income is the lowest of any U.S. urban group.[25] This is particularly significant given the low income levels of Asian Americans in many urban areas.

Although health data on Asian Americans are scanty and incomplete, it is known that in San Francisco the incidence rate for tuberculosis among Pilipino Americans is four times that for the general population, and for Chinese Americans it is twice the general rate.[26] On the other hand, while the Japanese-American incidence rate for tuberculosis is quite low, the *death* rate from tuberculosis for this group was the highest for any group studied. This may indicate a very high incidence rate for the disease among aged Issei, who would be expected, because of their age and poverty, to show a high death rate relative to incidence. In any case, high tuberculosis incidence and death rates can generally be taken as a good indicator of nutritional and sanitary deficiencies, as well as of overcrowding and generally inadequate levels of health care.

We have already discussed Asian-American mental health needs, but a few observations are in order with respect to the demographic information in this area. The first is that, as noted by Berk and Hirata,[27] hospitalization rates for aged and foreign-born Chinese Americans are particularly high, suggesting that cultural factors may be at work: those who succumb to mental illness are apparently those least able to cope with the American social system. However, these figures apply directly only to Chinese Americans and at present there are so many gaps in the data for other groups that generalizations for Asian Americans as a whole must be made at a high level of speculation. One speculation which is worth making, however, is that if the foreign-born are more likely to require mental health services, then we can certainly expect a vast increase in service needs in this area, given the massive immigration since 1965.

Demographic considerations of Chinese-American ethnic enclaves by Jung,[28] Homma-True,[29] and Fong-Torres[30] suggest that the "self-help" network in Asian-American communities may be inadequate to cope with the social problems of a dense urban population. For instance, the population density of the Oakland (California) Chinatown is 885.1 persons/acre, which is no less than ten times that for the rest of the city. In this dense area, 67% of the housing is legally substandard, compared with 19% for the rest of the city. The Chinatown unemployment rate is twice that for San Francisco generally, and the suicide rate is three times the national average.[31]

For the same area, Homma-True found that 22% of the population were living below the poverty level, but that only 13% were receiving public assistance. By contrast, only 13% of the general population of Oakland were living below the poverty line at the time of the study, but a surprising 44% were receiving public assistance. In conducting her survey, Homma-True experienced a substantial rejection rate (24%) from prospective respondents, and a large number of "no response" replies to personal questions on the questionnaire.[32] She takes this as an indication of the general level of Asian-American suspicion of confiding problems to strangers. Jung found a similar suspicion and reticence among the population of the Philadelphia Chinatown, characteristics which he attributes to a historically based distrust of all governments, and government agencies, among the Chinese.[33] If this is a general phenomenon, it is also indicative of the problems involved in both need assessment and service delivery among Asian-American populations.

The Demographics of the Immigration Experience

A major consideration of any study of contemporary Asian Americans must be the influence and consequences of the massive immigration which has taken place from the Eastern Hemisphere since the implementation of the 1965 amendments to the Immigration and Nationality Act. Not only has the sheer volume of immigration been a factor in altering the composition of existing ethnic communities—and entirely creating others—but the provisions of the act have had important effects on the composition of the immigrant population, and, consequently, on their demographic characteristics and service needs.[34]

It goes without saying that the age composition and sex ratio of a group has a profound effect on the group's service needs. As an example, the fact that Chinese immigration in the early years of this century was almost entirely male indicates that one will almost certainly find many elderly—and probably unmarried—males among the Chinese American population today. The medical and social needs of this group will surely be quite different from a group such as the Koreans which, from all appearances, consists largely of young married couples with preschool children.

As noted earlier, the 1965 amendments establish a series of priorities for the admission of immigrants, the categories being as follows:[35]

1) Unmarried sons or daughters of U.S. citizens (20% of total)
2) Spouses, unmarried sons or daughters of permanent residents (20%)
3) Persons of exceptional ability in the professions, sciences, or the arts (10%)
4) Married sons and daughters of U.S. citizens (10%)
5) Brothers and sisters of U.S. citizens (24%)
6) Skilled and unskilled labor (10%)
7) Refugees (6%)

Beyond these categories, which apply to the annual quota of 170,000 persons from the Eastern Hemisphere, there is no numerical limit placed on spouses and parents of U.S. citizens who may be admitted, the avowed purpose of the amended act being to preserve family integrity.

In addition to the absolute increase in immigration brought about by the act, the years 1965-1969 saw an 850% increase in the immigration of trained manpower from the Asian countries, while that from Europe and North America actually decreased slightly over the same period.[36] In some areas the influx of highly trained personnel has been particularly great. For instance, in the health care field, fully one-fourth of all interns in the U.S. in 1970 were foreign educated.[37]

It has been observed that this "trained manpower" from the Asian countries is often not fully utilized in the U.S. In 1975, for instance, the California Advisory Committee to the United States Commission on Civil Rights heard testimony that in Southern California alone there were at least 300 experienced Korean pharmacists who were unable to practice their profession because of licensure problems.[38] In other areas of health care it is commonly reported that professionals from Asian countries are routinely employed at low-level technical jobs. In the employment statistics these persons may appear to hold "suitable" employment, but the reality for the individual is harder to assess.

Similar underemployment is experienced by recent Asian-American immigrants in most white-collar and professional areas.[39] Hurh, Kim, and Kim explored this underemployment and its consequent status incongruity and were able to relate it to the immigrant's degree of social, but not cultural, assimilation.[40] In an indirect survey of Korean immigrant service needs conducted by this author, somewhat over a fourth of a sample of 181 households were reported to be suffering problems in the combined areas of underemployment and immigrant status change. Since this survey was conducted by asking ministers of Korean churches to evaluate the needs of their parishioners, there is a possibility that the respondents would know of only the most severe problems experienced by the families.

Overall we may conclude that, although few exact data have been collected, it can be surmised from numerous observations that many Asian Americans who have recently immigrated are underemployed, or have otherwise had to adjust their socioeconomic status as a result of the immigration experience. When combined with the immigrant's obvious need to learn a new—and radically different—language, and adapt to the mechanical aspects of an alien culture, it would seem obvious that an increase in immigration would almost automatically result in an increase in Asian-American service needs.

Health Care

Stereotypic misconceptions also exist in the area of Asian-American health care needs, in part, at least, because of the inadequate demographic base for Asian-American populations. For instance, if the neonatal/infant mortality rate per 1000 live births is computed for Japanese Americans in California on the basis of published figures, one arrives at a low figure of 13.2. This compares to a death rate of 18.8 per 1000 live births for the Caucasian population, and 30.1 for blacks.[41] On the other hand, when a sample population is delineated and followed by the investigators to ascertain that all deaths are reported, and charged against the correct population group, the results may be quite different. Using this method, Norris and Shipley determined the Japanese-American infant mortality rate in California to be 22.0 per 1000 live births, or slightly *higher* than the Caucasian control group rate of 19.3. The black rate determined by this method was 32.3. Thus the mortality rate for all populations was found to be higher when reliable reporting was ensured, but the increase for Japanese Americans was disproportionately large (67%) compared to the increases for the Caucasian and black populations (2.7% and 7.3%, respectively).[42] This result tends to support the allegation often voiced by Asian-American community leaders that the Asian-American population is consistently underreported and undercounted in official statistics.

Using these figures and other collected information on rates of mortality and morbidity, Weaver and Inui[43] have claimed that, although there is a good deal of fluctuation depending on what measure is chosen, there is no consistent evidence that Asian Americans are less disease prone than the rest of the population. The pattern which emerges from the various studies reviewed is that, as Asian Americans become acculturated and adopt the American diet and lifestyle, they fall prey to the same diseases which ravage the general American population. In some instances these environmentally-induced diseases may even strike Asian Americans with greater than normal frequency. For example, adult male Pilipinos in Hawaii are afflicted with hyperuricemia (gouty arthritis) at a rate nearly 20 times that for the general population, apparently because of an inherited inability to handle the high purine level in the American diet.[44]

Weaver and Inui conducted surveys of medical service usage among Japanese, Pilipino, and Anglo-Americans from comparable lower socioeconomic strata in Long Beach, California. They found that, although the Asian Americans (especially the Japanese) made more frequent use of dentists, their rates for visits to a physician and for hospitalization were substantially below those for the Anglo population. When questioned about their opinion of medical costs, larger proportions of the Asian-American groups felt that these costs were "too high." This is of some interest because the Japanese Americans in the sample had a slightly higher income profile than the Anglo Americans.[45]

In interviewing survey respondents, Weaver and Inui determined that some Japanese Americans routinely traveled 30 miles or more to find health care providers of their own nationality group.[46] This may reflect some sort of dissatisfaction with care otherwise available. Furthermore, while a Japanese American living in some areas of California may be able to find a Japanese-American physician or dentist without great difficulty, members of most Asian-American groups in most other areas of the country are not so fortunate. In these instances, underutilization of health care services is almost a foregone conclusion.

A 1976 study of Asian-American access to health care and health careers performed for the Department of Health, Education, and Welfare by JWK International Corporation points to similar problems: mortality/morbidity levels far above those stereotypically ascribed, and limited access to health care providers as a result of a complex of cultural and socioeconomic factors.[47]

Among problems in health care access defined by this report are: lack of transportation to health care facilities, a hostile delivery environment, language and communication problems, the inflexibility of government health services programs, reluctance to apply for Medicaid because of Immigration and Naturalization Service regulations, and institutional racism.[48] All of these factors are believed to reduce service usage, although information in this area is largely anecdotal. Few figures are available on underusage relative to the general population, or on the relative effect of the various factors which may depress usage.

In considering health care service usage in the U.S. we should keep in mind that, as Weaver and Inui point out,[49] health care is underutilized to some extent by all Americans of less than affluent means. In the last decade the American health care system has been under attack from numerous quarters for its failure to meet the needs of various groups which are outside the mainstream of society. To some extent, then, underutilization of health care services by Asian Americans is an expected phenomenon. What is less clear is an exact definition of which factors, besides the general failure of the health care delivery system, may be contributing to this underuse. As in other areas of service need, there are many plausible explanations and few hard facts.

The Aged

Various existing studies indicate that the aged may have more areas of unmet social service needs than any other group of Asian

Americans. Historical factors would tend to suggest that most aged Asian Americans will be of either Chinese or Japanese ancestry, but it must be remembered that many Pilipino field laborers who came to this country before 1934 are now in their 60s and 70s. Also, the provisions of the 1965 immigration law favor immigration of immediate relatives of U.S. citizens. Thus, as the Asian immigrants who have arrived since 1965 are naturalized, we may expect to see an increase in the number of elderly parents who come to the U.S. to join their children.

In a compilation of existing studies, Fujii[50] suggests that, along with very low median income ($1,130 to $2,542 for various groups in 1970), elderly Asian Americans make very little use of the services available to them. Only .3% of all services to the aged administered by fourteen social service agencies in Seattle were found to go to Asian Americans.[51] Among a group of aged Issei in Los Angeles it was found that, while 78% were enrolled for Medicare, only 30% admitted ever having used the benefits.[52] Of elderly Chinese males in New York City, fully a third had never had contact with any sort of agency, public or voluntary.[53]

As Fujii notes, with the exception of survey data on isolated cases of service use, there is little empirical information on elderly Asian Americans and why they do not use services. However, numerous theories have been advanced. It has been pointed out that, because of the social and cultural assimilation of their children, many older Asian Americans are left to make most of their social contacts with their generational cohort group.[54] Combined with language difficulties and poverty, this is likely to lead to enforced isolation; among other things this isolation is likely to mean that the elderly Asian American will be ignorant of many available services, and very reluctant to seek those he does know about. Too, cultural norms which emphasize self-reliance and denial of personal needs are more likely to be strongly in force among elderly Asian Americans, making it hard for them to bring themselves to seek the help they need. As a secondary effect, these factors increase the probability that the elderly Asian American will be found living in a culturally isolated ethnic enclave, where few services are provided by the general community.

Survey Assessment of Service Needs

Relatively few studies which have sought to clarify various aspects of Asian-American service needs have done so by means

of formal survey techniques. There are probably several reasons
which account for this lack. First, it is accepted as a truism by
many investigators that Asian Americans "don't respond to surveys." There is at least some truth to this belief, as evidenced by
Homma-True's experience.[55] Nor is this phenomenon exclusive
with Asian Americans. Sue and Sue have noted that the "record of
past abuse and the continuing discrimination against many minorities have contributed to a climate of mistrust and to feelings of
exploitation."[56] These feelings are likely to be taken out on the
researcher who attempts to penetrate the cultural defenses of an
ethnic minority, since these groups often see research efforts in
the social sciences as "concerned with maintaining the status and
power of the Establishment."

In spite of a high initial refusal rate and many "no response"
answers, Homma-True managed to administer questionnaires to
76 households in the Oakland, California Chinatown area, using
teams of bilingual interviewers. The questionnaire asked questions
relating to adjustment problems of immigrants, types of problems
in the respondent's family, and sources of help to which the respondent would turn. Interestingly, only 2.6% of the respondents
admitted having interpersonal or psychological problems, but
19.6% felt that members of their families had such problems.[58]
For themselves, the respondents viewed language and lifestyle as
the major adjustment problems for immigrants, followed by employment, racism, and an "other" category which included such
items as health, education, and transportation.[59]

In a preliminary attempt to determine service needs of the Korean immigrant population of Chicago, the present author conducted an indirect survey study in 1972. In order to overcome the reluctance of Asian-American respondents to being surveyed about
their problems and service needs, a group of informants (in the anthropologist's usage) were interviewed instead.

Ministers of 18 Korean churches in the Chicago area were contacted and asked to cooperate in obtaining information about
their church members. Eight ministers agreed to cooperate and
they were sent copies of a one-page questionnaire to be filled out
for each church member about whom the minister knew enough
to complete the questionnaire. One hundred eighty-one usable questionnaires were returned.

In addition to basic demographic data, the questionnaire sought
to identify problems which the surveyed households were exper-
iencing, and service needs they were thought to have. As perceived

by the ministers, the most frequently encountered problems of the households were of a financial nature, followed by family relations, the status change and family separation resulting from immigration, underemployment, physical illness, and psychiatric illness. Among the perceived service needs, English improvement was the most frequently cited, by a wide margin, followed by job retraining, and child care. Assistance with marketing, better housing, help in the use of public services, adult education, and tutoring of children were cited consistently, but less frequently.

Several factors limit the usefulness of this survey when it comes to providing "hard" data for the planning of social service delivery. The sample is probably biased, since, in the course of their pastoral care duties, the reporting ministers would be most likely to learn of the existence of those households which have experienced problems and unmet service needs. In all, the ministers judged 56% of the 181 households to have problems of one kind or another, while 85% were judged to have service needs in one or more areas. At first glance these percentages may seem high, but it should be remembered that the population of potential respondents was entirely composed of fairly recent immigrants. Also, the problems and service needs most often cited are somewhat similar to those reported for other Asian American immigrant populations.

A survey of 302 Asian-American families in Sacramento, California was conducted by Lee in 1973.[61] In the families interviewed, members of each generation were studied where possible. The study covered Chinese, Japanese, and Pilipino families and was concerned with demographic information, service needs, adjustment problems, identity, and attitudinal questions.

The results of Lee's survey indicate that, although many of the Asian-American families studied ought to be candidates for social service usage on the basis of educational level, unemployment/underemployment, and income level, actual service usage was relatively low. When presented with a list of 24 of the most common social service organizations in the area, 13% of the Pilipinos, 35% of the Japanese, and 42% of the Chinese respondents stated that they had never used any of the services.

According to the respondents, service usage would be increased if bilingual staff were available at the social service organizations. This was particularly so for the Chinese-American respondents (80%), but a substantial proportion of the Japanese (60%) and Pilipinos (45%) also felt that bilingual services would increase the likelihood of service usage.[62] Likewise, the respondents felt that the presence of a member of their own ethnic group on the organization staff would make them more likely to use the services offered.[63]

The survey also suggests that the method of popularizing social services among Asian Americans is very important: in general, the respondents were far more likely to utilize a service which they had heard about through private sources, such as friends and relatives, than one they had heard about only from public sources, such as publicity from the organization, newspaper articles, or recommendations of social workers. Overall, the most effective means of encouraging service use seemed to be a confluence of information from public and private sources.[64]

Different Asian-American groups named different services as those most needed personally, and for the neighborhood. Police protection and transportation seemed to be the most common concerns, but medical care, bilingual services, employment services, recreation, and services for the elderly were also mentioned. The ranking of priorities varied considerably from one ethnic group to another.[65]

Lee's study indicates that there are substantial service needs among Asian-American populations in Sacramento and that, by and large, these populations do not fully utilize existing services. The sample population collected by Lee may actually be somewhat biased toward those who would be more likely to use services, since some of the names were obtained from the membership lists of Asian-American organizations, and others came from lists compiled for a project on usage of family planning services. Most of the sample population was composed of persons chosen from the telephone directory, a procedure which in itself may tend to eliminate some very poor, socially/culturally unassimilated, or isolated persons. Lee found these techniques of population selection necessary because it was impossible to gain access to government files, a problem often encountered by researchers and social service providers among minority populations.

The study by Hurh, Kim, and Kim, conducted in 1976, is partly devoted to exploring problem areas related to the present study.[66] The respondents in this study were all Korean immigrants residing in the Chicago area and the investigators were chiefly concerned with the cultural and social assimilation of these persons in American life.

When asked to state the most important problem or difficulty they had experienced in their adjustment to American life, the respondents replied as follows:[67]

Problem areas	N	%
Language	106	47.3
Busy routine of urban life	30	13.4
Concern for children's future and welfare	27	12.1
Social isolation	19	8.5
Job–related problems	19	8.5
Inadequate income	14	6.2
Racial discrimination	9	4.0
Total	224	100.0

Not all of the problems experienced by the respondent group would be amenable to easy solutions at the hands of the social service provider—a fact which social service providers ought to bear in mind, no matter what the service population. The language problem, which seems to be the greatest concern of the respondents, could be tackled through appropriate classes and programs in English as a second language. Social isolation may require improvements in the self-help social network within the immigrant group itself; outside agencies can provide guidance, although they cannot actually perform the service. Inadequate income is most likely only a symptom of other problems. Racial discrimination is one problem for which the legal service machinery already exists, although the effectiveness of such machinery is open to question. Such services are often underfunded, understaffed, and essentially unavailable since there are few, if any, bilingual personnel to assist a clientele whose English proficiency is low. The remaining problem areas—the busy routine of urban life, concern for the future and welfare of one's children, and job-related problems—present less clear-cut challenges to the social service provider. Clearly, some sort of education-oriented group counseling is called for, but the pattern for these approaches is not well defined in the repertory of established social services.

It should be noted that the study by Hurh, Kim, and Kim was conducted after the data collection phase of the present study was already completed. Also, their data are concerned only with the Korean immigrant population of Chicago, while the present study covers immigrant and citizen groups of Chinese and Japanese residents as well as Pilipino and Korean immigrants. Despite these differences in population and time frame, the Hurh, Kim, and Kim findings provide a useful perspective in the overall consideration of Asian-American service needs.

Conclusion

Existing research on the problems and service needs of Asian Americans may be said to have established the following points:

Stereotyping. There seems to be little, if any, empirical basis for the existing stereotype of Asian Americans as self-contained, problem-free "model minorities." Although some demographic data appear to suggest a modest level of socioeconomic success for some groups of Asian Americans, there is ample evidence that these data do not reflect the reality of the lives of many Asian Americans.

Existence of needs. Whether it is collected by historical, anecdotal, or survey means, the evidence points to identifiable service needs in several areas. English language improvement, financial counseling, transportation, job counseling, medical and mental health care, help for the aged, and general assistance with adjustment to American life are often mentioned. In their general outlines, the various pictures of Asian-American service needs do not contradict one another, although all of them are at variance with the traditional stereotypes.

Group variability. Despite a fairly uniform spectrum of service needs, particular Asian-American populations have special needs dictated by their unique cultural backgrounds and historical experiences. This is clearly demonstrated by studies such as that of Lee, where several Asian-American populations in the same geographical area are surveyed using the same instrument. Such findings should be a clear warning that various Asian-American groups must not be lumped together indiscriminately when planning social service delivery. The result of such planning is very likely to be a very bad fit between available services and actual needs. This would be an unfortunate situation in serving any population, but the result could be disastrous where Asian Americans are concerned, since one characteristic which most Asian-American populations seem to share is some degree of reluctance to seek social service help in problem solving. However, this area is also unclear, because there has been little comparative study of the problem-solving strategies of different Asian-American groups.

Survey feasibility. The results of several survey studies seem to indicate that, while some care must be utilized in conducting such research, the problems are by no means insurmountable. Both Lee and Homma-True experienced adequate response rates using bilingual interviewers and questionnaires designed to avoid offending the cultural sensibilities of the respondents. To some extent, the problems of data-gathering among Asian-American populations are the same as those experienced by the researcher of any minority which has encountered a history of racial discrimination: the researcher is an automatically-suspect "outsider" and must be able to convince the respondents that the research is being conducted for the benefit of the respondent groups. It seems to be almost a foregone conclusion that in such instances the interviewers must be drawn from the population to be researched.

The major task of the researcher attempting to grasp the primary reality of Asian-American service needs is to introduce the necessary parsimony in order to arrive at a coherent picture of the needs structure, while retaining a keen sense of the great variability of the individual groups involved.

NOTES TO CHAPTER II

1. See, for example, L. Duphiny, *Oriental Americans: An Annotated Bibliography*, New York: Horace Mann-Lincoln Institute, Columbia University, produced for ERIC/IRDC/EDRS, Leasco Information Products, Bethesda, Md., Urban Disadvantaged Series No. 26, 1972. I. Fujimoto, M.Y. Swift, and R. Zucker, *Asians in America: A Selected Annotated Bibliography*, Davis, Cal.: Asian American Research Project, Department of Applied Behavioral Sciences, University of California at Davis, Working Publication 5, 1971.

2. Information from the census, as we have already seen, is of limited value because it tends to undercount Asian Americans severely and fails to disaggregate some of the smaller or more recently arrived groups. The results of the present study suggest that the census may be especially likely to overlook the poor, the aged, and persons living alone—three groups who may have greater unmet service needs than the rest of the ethnic population. In the case of Immigration and Naturalization Service files, the INS has traditionally been reluctant to permit use of this information for research purposes. In addition, it is generally accepted that many aliens fail to register at all.

3. B.B. Berk, and L.C. Hirata, "Mental illness among the Chinese: Myth or reality?" *Journal of Social Issues*, 29(2): 151 (1973).

4. R. Homma-True, "Characteristics of contrasting Chinatowns: 2. Oakland, California," *Social Casework*, 57(3): 155–159 (1976).

5. C.C. Jew, and S.A. Brody, "Mental illness among the Chinese: Hospitalization rates of the past century," *Comprehensive Psychiatry*, 8:129–134. (1967).

6. B.B. Berk, and L.C. Hirata, 1973 151–164.

7. H.H.L. Kitano, *Japanese Americans: The Evolution of a Subculture.* Englewood Cliffs, N.J.: Prentice-Hall, 122–125, Table 10, 161, 1969b. Kitano interviewed a small group of Japanese American professional people to determine their views on problems of deviance in the Japanese-American population.

8. R.T. Brown, K.M. Stein, K. Huang, and D.E. Harris, "Mental illness and the role of mental health facilities in Chinatown," in *Asian-Americans: Psychological Perspectives*, ed. S. Sue and N. Wagner, Palo Alto, Cal.: Science and Behavior Books, 1973, 212–231.

9. There is some disagreement as to the reliability of the diagnoses generally given for mental illness among Chinese Americans. Berk and Hirata (1973, p. 161) find that the diagnoses of Chinese-American patients have tended—historically—to fall within the narrow range of affective reaction and schizophrenic reaction. They suggest that this narrow diagnostic range may result from "stereotypic thinking about Asians" on the part of diagnosing personnel, who are generally not Asians.

Brown, Stein, Huang, and Harris found that Chinese-American patients were frequently labeled as suffering from schizophrenic withdrawal. However, there was no significant difference in the pattern of diagnoses given for the Chinese-American patients and for other, non-Chinese, patients at the same clinics. Thus, the preferred diagnosis of schizophrenic withdrawal may simply reflect current fashions in psychiatry at the clinics studied. In addition, Brown, et al., note that a substantial proportion of the diagnoses of the Chinese-American patients were made by a bilingual/bicultural Asian psychologist. In the other cases, interpreters and bilingual/bycultural professional personnel were on hand when the diagnoses were made, thus minimizing the probability of false diagnosis through the misreading of cultural signals.

Stereotyping and the diagnosis of mental illness among Asian minority groups therefore remains an open question. It is clear, however, that there are certain differences between eastern and western conceptions of what constitutes mental illness. For survey data on Chinese-American attitudes toward various mental conditions, see, P.W.-t. Chen, *Chinese-Americans View Their Mental Health*, Los Angeles: University of Southern California, D.S.W. thesis, 1976, 78–95.

10. S. Sue, and H. McKinney, "Asian Americans in the community mental health care system," *American Journal of Mental Health*, 45(1): 111–118 (1975).

11. J.S. Park, *A Three Generational Study: Traditional Korean Value Systems and Psychosocial Adjustment of Korean Immigrants in Los Angeles*, Los Angeles: University of Southern California, D.S.W. thesis, 1975.

12. H.H.L. Kitano, 1969b, 125.

13. E. Kaneshige, "Cultural factors in group counseling and interaction," *Personnel and Guidance Journal*, 51:407–412 (1973).

14. D.W. Sue, and S. Sue, "Counseling Asian Americans," *Personnel and Guidance Journal*, 50: 637–644 (1973).

15. H.H.L. Kitano, "Japanese-American mental illness," in *Changing Perspectives in Mental Illness*, ed. S.C. Plog and R.B. Edgerton, New York: Holt, Rinehart, and Winston, 1969a, 257–284. Reprinted in *Asian-Americans: Psychological Perspectives*, ed. S. Sue and N. Wagner, Palo Alto, Cal.: Science and Behavior Books, 1973, 181–201.

17. D.F. Duff, and R.J. Arthur, "Between two worlds: Filipinos in the U.S. Navy," *American Journal of Psychiatry*, 123: 836-843 (1967). Reprinted in *Asian Americans: Psychological Perspectives*, ed. S. Sue and N. Wagner, Palo Alto, Cal.: Science and Behavior Books, 1973, 202-211.

18. Typically, Pacific Islanders and Native Americans have been included in this group, at a minimum, although it is often difficult to ascertain just which groups have been included. See J.P. Ryu, *Key Demographic Features of Korean Americans*, Chicago: University of Chicago, working paper, n.d., 2, 28-32.

19. This improvement of the census data base for Asian Americans is also the object of Senator Matsunaga's Senate Joint Resolution No. 47.

20. T. Owan, *Asian Americans: A Case of Benighted Neglect*, Chicago: Asian American Mental Health Research Center, Occasional Paper No. 1, n.d.

21. Ibid., 14.

22. For an account of the dehumanizing effects of the urban environment, see C.H. Meyer, *Social Work Practice: A Response to Urban Crisis*, New York: The Free Press, 1973.

23. T. Owan, n.d., 14.

24. From 1970 census data.

25. T. Owan, n.d., 32-34, Table II.

26. T. Owan, n.d., 39. From, City and County Department of Health, *Reported TB Cases, Deaths, and Rates Per 100,000 Estimated Population by Type of Disease and Ethnic Group, San Francisco Residents, 1973*, San Francisco: Author, 1974.

27. B.B. Berk, and L.C. Hirata, 1973, 165.

28. M. Jung, "Characteristics of contrasting Chinatowns: 1. Philadelphia. Pennsylvania," *Social Casework*, 57: 149-154 (1976).

29. R. Homma-True, 1976.

30. B. Fong-Torres, forward to *"Chink!"*, ed. C.-T. Wu., New York: Meridian, 1972, ix-xiv.

31. Ibid., xi.

32. R. Homma-True, 1976, 156.

33. M. Jung, 1976, 153.

34. For a detailed analysis of the age/sex ratios of Korean immigrants, see H.C. Kim, "Some aspects of social demography of Korean Americans," *International Migration Review*, 8(19): 23-42 (1971).

35. T. Owan, n.d., 6.

36. A.R. Weber, "The role of the U.S. Department of Labor in immigration," *International Migration Review*, 4(3): 4 (1970).

37. Ibid., 45.

38. U.S. Commission on Civil Rights, *A Dream Unfulfilled: Korean and Pilipino Health Professionals in California*, Washington: Author, prepared by the California Advisory Committee to the Commission, 1975.

39. W.H. Hurh, H.C. Kim, and K.C. Kim, *Cultural and Social Adjustment Patterns of Immigrants in the United States: A Case Study of Korean Residents in the Chicago Area*, Washington: Department of Health, Education and Welfare, Grant RO3 MH 27004, Final Report, 1976, 10.

40. Ibid., 88.

41. L. Breslow, and B. Klein, "Health and race in California," *American Journal of Public Health*, 61: 763 (1972).

42. F. Norris, and P.W. Shipley, "A closer look at race differentials in California's infant mortality 1965-67," *NSMHA Health Reports,* 86: 810, (1971).

43. J.L. Weaver, and L.T. Inui, *Social Patterns of Health Care Problems of Asian Americans,* paper presented at the annual meeting of American Public Health Association, Chicago, 1975.

44. Ibid., 14-15.

45. Ibid., 19, Table 4.

46. Ibid., 21-22.

47. JWK International Corporation, *Identification of Problems in Acess to Health Services and Health Careers for Asian Americans: Volume II. Text,* Washington: Office of Health Resources Opportunity, Health Resources Administration, Department of Health, Education and Welfare, 1976.

48. Ibid., III-3-III-18.

49. J.L. Weaver, and L.T. Inui, 1975, 21.

50. S.M. Fujii, "Elderly Asian Americans and use of public services," *Social Casework,* 57: 202-207 (1976).

51. Ibid., 205. Original data from, Training Project for the Asian Elderly, *On the Feasibility of Training Asians to Work With Asian Elderly: A Preliminary Assessment of Needs and Resources Available to Asian Elderly in Seattle,* Seattle: Author, 1973, 63.

52. Ibid., 205. Original data from, Council of Oriental Organizations, *A Study of Issei Pioneers Residing in Little Tokyo,* Los Angeles: Author, 1968, 5.

53. Ibid., 205. Original data from, S.H. Cattell, *Health, Welfare, and Social Organization in Chinatown,* New York: Community Service Society of New York, report prepared for the Chinatown Public Health Nursing Demonstration of the Department of Public Affairs, 1962, 56.

54. J.L. Weaver, and L.T. Inui, 1975, 23.

55. R. Homma-True, 156.

56. D.W. Sue, and S.Sue, "Ethnic minorities: Resistance to being researched," *Professional Psychology,* 3: 11-17 (1972).

57. Ibid., 11.

58. R. Homma-True, 1976, 158, Tables 1 and 2.

59. Ibid., Table 1.

60. B.-L.C. Kim, "An appraisal of Korean service needs," *Social Casework,* 57:139-148 (1976).

61. I. Lee, *A Profile of Asians in Sacramento,* Washington: Department of Health, Education and Welfare, Grant 1RO 1MH 21086-01, Final Report, 1973.

62. Ibid., 34.

63. Ibid., 35.

64. Ibid., 32.

65. Ibid., 43.

66. W.M. Hurh, H.C. Kim, and K.C. Kim, 1976.

67. Ibid., 47, Table 31, adapted.

CHAPTER III

DESIGN OF THE STUDY

The description of study designs ought to be something more than a perfunctory exercise, a recitation of the sequence of procedures which leads, inevitably, from the choice of techniques to the verification of results. In the case of the present study there are no particularly exotic aspects to the design, but the choices made were based on a careful consideration of the problems facing the investigator of sensitive areas among ethnic minorities in America. This chapter, therefore, attempts to explore the development of the study design with respect to these problems. Along the way, I shall take the liberty of making a somewhat discursive presentation of the circumstances surrounding the development and implementation of the design; the problems, solutions, and reception of the study design can shed some important light on the area of Asian-American service needs and the nature of the immigration experience.

The basic data gathering device of the study was a questionnaire survey administered to a systematic sample of the target population. In the sections below, the development and implementation of the survey instrument are described in chronological order; at each stage there is also a description and discussion of the problems encountered. In addition to being of possible use to future investigators, an understanding of these problems provides important insights into the nature of the Asian-American communities which are the subject of the study. In some cases, these insights extend markedly beyond the areas covered by the data, while in other cases they reinforce the quantified findings of the study. For the benefit of the reader who wished to explore and assess the statistical aspects of the study, Appendix A collects and presents this material. Much of the process of data collection for this study was performed by the Survey Research Laboratory (SRL) of the University of Illinois, under the supervision of the researcher.

Sample Selection

The population of this study consisted of four groups of Asian-American community members located in the Chicago metropolitan area: Chinese, Japanese, Pilipino, and Korean. The study objective was to complete 800 interviews from a random sample of this population. On the basis of consultations with Dr. Seymour Sudman of the Survey Research Laboratory of the University of Illinois, it was initially decided to adopt a snowball sampling procedure in order to sample these four groups of Asian-Americans in Chicago. This method was suggested as a means of circumventing a major difficulty facing the researcher of Asian-American groups: the lack of reliable census data on the block level to use as a starting point in the sampling procedure. The snowball sampling procedure called for listing individuals whose names appeared on the membership lists of ethnic organizations and major church groups. The first hundred or so respondents would be asked to furnish names of additional persons whom they knew to be newcomers to the United States and to the neighborhood. ("Newcomers" were to be defined as persons who had been in the United States and the neighborhood for six months or less). This process was to be repeated until 800 interviews had been obtained.

It was recognized that this sampling procedure would inevitably introduce sampling bias. That is, those persons who live isolated lives and do not belong to any ethnic church or organization would not be included in the study. This would have been a serious handicap because the aim of the study was to determine the needs of newcomers and, most importantly, the needs of those who do not use existing social services. On the contrary, there is a strong presumption that persons who are members of church groups and ethnic organizations may be more thoroughly "settled in." Thus, their social services needs and utilization patterns may be quite different from those of persons whose lack of membership in such organizations indicates a higher level of social isolation. Likewise, persons who are known to members of ethnic churches and organizations may be known precisely because they have been helped by the church or organization.

Therefore, in order to obtain a representative sample and to allow population productions to be made, the search for an alternative sample design continued. Fortunately, at this point unexpected access was gained to the Immigration and Naturalization Service files with the assistance of the office of the United States Attorney General. These files provided a basic sample pool for the immigrant groups to be studied.

In the revised sampling procedures there were two major groups of respondents: (1) immigrants, and (2) citizens, both naturalized and American born. To select the immigrant samples of all four groups, the INS files were used exclusively. Thus, the Pilipino and Korean samples for the study were selected entirely from the INS files. Both groups (but especially the Koreans) are relatively recent arrivals in the Chicago area and hence would be unlikely to contain many naturalized citizens. Locating naturalized citizens among the Pilipino group would have been especially difficult because there was no ethnic resident directory for Pilipinos in Chicago and their Spanish surnames preclude using conventional means of identification, such as city telephone directories. Two-thirds of the Japanese and Chinese samples were taken from the INS files and the remainder were from lists compiled from ethnic directories and telephone directories based on geographic delineation. This mixed sampling method provided enough immigrant subjects to compare the Chinese and Japanese groups with the Pilipinos and Koreans, while also tapping the second and third generations of the Chinese and Japanese. The aim in this new sampling design was to achieve a complete sample of 150 Chinese, 150 Japanese, 200 Pilipinos, and 200 Koreans.

The subject pool for the immigrant samples consisted of all names reported on the 1973 alien address report cards for the four nationality groups in the Illinois files of the INS. A respondent was eligible for sample inclusion if he or she met the following criteria: (1) was 18 years of age or older; (2) was classified as a permanent resident; and (3) gave a Chicago address. From the list of eligible persons meeting these criteria, the respondents for the study were selected, using a systematic random sample.

For the U.S. citizen sample of Chinese and Japanese respondents, a subject pool was developed using census information and community informants. From this information, two highly concentrated ethnic areas, one of Chinese and one of Japanese residents, were delineated. Using the *Chicago Japanese American Directory* (Shimpo, Inc.) all persons with Japanese surnames living in the Japanese ethnic area were listed, a total of 839 potential respondents. The Shimpo directory is compiled from numerous sources, including ethnic publication subscription lists, ethnic organization membership lists, gleanings from the telephone directory, and word-of-mouth information. Because of the multiple sources of the Shimpo directory, the Japanese sample is probably quite complete; only a person who is very isolated socially could escape being listed. For the Chinese population of Chicago no such comprehensive directory was available. Therefore, the Chinese list was compiled by listing all persons with Chinese surnames living within the chosen district who could be found in the telephone street address directory, a total of 573 potential respondents. To some extent, both the Shimpo directory and the telephone directory introduce an unavoidable sampling bias, since persons who lead extremely isolated lives may not appear in either of these sorts of compilations. However, aside from conducting a massive (and probably impossible) house-to-house canvass, there seems to be no alternative to the process of spotting ethnic surnames in such directories. Again it should be emphasized that a comprehensive ethnic directory, such as the Shimpo directory, probably introduces less bias than a city telephone directory.

A potential respondent from the lists thus compiled was considered eligible for interviewing only if he or she was, in fact, an American citizen. If the individual was not a U.S. citizen, but another person in the same household was a citizen and of the same ethnic heritage, then this second person was eligible. When more than one person in the household met the citizenship criterion, the order of priority for eligibility was as follows: (1) the person listed; (2) the spouse of the person listed; (3) a child of the person listed (18 years of age or older); (4) any other person related to the listed person who was at least 18 years of age and was a permanent member of the household. A "permanent member" was defined as a relative who had been or planned to be a resident in the household for six months or more.

Because of cost factors, potential respondents who moved out of the designated areas before the questionnaire was administered were considered ineligible and were dropped from the sample. However, two exceptions were made in the immigrant sample (one Japanese and one Korean). In one instance the respondent was so eager to participate that she came to the interviewer's home to be interviewed. In the other, the respondent's new address was only two blocks from where the interviewer lived.

The Questionnaire

The personal interview method for conducting the survey was chosen in preference to mail questionnaires. Because of the problems which other investigators have experienced in achieving adequate response rates among ethnic minorities, it was felt that personal interviews conducted by bilingual/bicultural interviewers might achieve better results. An additional consideration was mentioned earlier in discussing the shortcomings of the decennial census: postal delivery in ethnic neighborhoods is often erratic, and cultural factors may inhibit members of some ethnic groups from responding to mailed queries for information.

The questionnaire was designed to obtain information about the respondent in seven distinct areas: (1) demographic data; (2) perception of the problems and service needs of the ethnic community in Chicago; (3) perception of discrimination in employment and housing; (4) problem-solving strategies, and preferences in the conditions under which help is received; (5) actual experiences of problems with health care, finances, employment, and family relations; (6) reasons for immigration and evaluation of this decision; and (7) sense of ethnic identity.

Based, again, on the experience of previous investigators, it was presumed that some categories of questions would tend to raise a certain amount of resistance on the part of the subjects, while other questions would prove more neutral. Within categories, some areas could also be expected to be more sensitive than others. Therefore, questions belonging to different categories and representing differing levels of sensitivity were mixed and ordered in a sequence ranging from the general and impersonal to the specific and personal. In this way it was hoped that the interviewer would have established a measure of rapport with the respondent before sensitive areas were probed. It would of course be stressed to the respondent that the survey questionnaires would be tabulated anonymously, that data would be used only in aggregate form, and that strict confidentiality would be maintained.

There was no specific model for the questionnaire, either with respect to question items or the exact format used, although there are some general antecedents in both areas. The survey of Ameri-

can views of mental health made by Gurin, Veroff, and Feld[2] provided examples of progressive question patterns leading from less
sensitive to more sensitive areas. Another technique used by
Gurin, Veroff, and Feld is to ask hypothetical, rather than personal, questions about highly personal matters. Thus, instead of
asking, "Have you and your spouse ever consulted a counselor for
marital problems?" the questionnaire might be phrased: "*If* you
and your spouse were having marital problems, where would you
go for help?" In the present study, where the aim was to elicit
attitudes toward and knowledge about sources of help, the hypothetical question is capable of obtaining as much information as
the personal one, and it is far less likely to offend the respondent.
According to reports from the interviewers, their hypothetical
questions elicited much interest on the part of the respondents.

Mr. Ronald Czaja of the University of Illinois Survey Research
Laboratory in Chicago assisted in developing the wording for the
questions and arranged the order of the questions as described
above. During the months of September and October 1973 the
questionnaire was revised and rewritten three times to achieve the
final wording and question order desired. As completed and used,
the questionnaire contains 77 questions, 37 having multiple parts,
and six being open-ended. The resulting questionnaire was translated into Chinese, Japanese, and Korean. The Chinese translation
was made by a Chinese-American graduate student at the University of Illinois, the Korean version was produced by an assistant
to the researcher who later supervised the Korean interviewers,
and the Japanese translation was made by a staff member of the
Japanese-American Service Committee in Chicago and was revised
by Japanese graduate students at the University of Illinois. The
translations were crosschecked for accuracy by other native
speakers associated with the research project. Because of the diversity of dialects among Pilipinos, and the widespread use of English
by this group, no attempt was made to translate the questionnaire
for the Pilipino respondents.

Community Contact

It was considered essential to the success of the study to secure
the support and cooperation of the ethnic communities which
were to be studied. Educators, heads of ethnic organizations, ministers and priests of ethnic religious institutions, community work-

ers, and persons respected in the ethnic communities were contacted personally. The purpose and nature of the study were explained to them and the possible benefits of the study for their communities were described. These persons were also asked to provide suggestions for types of information which they thought would be useful to gather through the study. The response from these community contact persons was very positive and helped to give the study a good prior "press" among the target populations. Articles were also placed in major national and Chicago-based ethnic newspapers explaining the nature, purpose, and importance of the study. Similar articles were published in the newsletters of several ethnic organizations.

In addition to increasing the likelihood of community acceptance of the study survey, this period of community contact helped to enlist possible interviewers for the survey. It was considered essential to make use of bilingual/bicultural interviewers, and it was thought that this period of community contact would help in the recruiting of suitable persons for this work. Over 60% of the interviewers for the survey were recruited in this manner.

Pretesting of the Questionnaire

From the prospective workers recruited during this period of community contact, four interviewers—one from each ethnic group in the study—were chosen to conduct a pretest. This pretest was intended to pinpoint any remaining problems in the wording or structure of the questionnaire, to test ethnic group relevance, and to yield an estimate of the average time that would be required to administer the questionnaire. On the basis of the pretest, the final decisions on the wording and sequence of questions were made. The check on wording was particularly important in achieving uniform meaning for those words and phrases in the questionnaire which did not directly or easily translate into Chinese, Japanese, or Korean.

The sample for the pretest consisted of six respondents from each of the four ethnic groups, selected on a probability basis from the same sources as the actual study sample. Thus, the Pilipino and Korean pretest respondents were selected entirely from the immigration records, while for the Chinese and Japanese groups half of the respondents were selected from the immigration records and half from the citizen lists prepared for the study sample. If the individual chosen no longer resided at the address listed, attempts were made to obtain the correct address. If the new address was not in the city of Chicago, the person was dropped from the sample and another name was selected.

As a means of determining the best method for contacting members of the sample for the main study, two different procedures were utilized in contacting the pretest sample: (1) sample persons were contacted by telephone prior to interviewing to arrange an appointment, or (2) sample persons were contacted in person without prior telephone contact. One half of the sample was contacted using each procedure and interviewers were instructed not to substitute procedures but to use only the procedure which had been selected for their half of the sample. The results showed that telephone contact could be used with all groups to arrange appointments prior to interviewing. Only among the Chinese group were there any reservations about the use of the telephone method, and these stemmed solely from comments made by the interviewer during debriefing; the data did not indicate the existence of any significant problem in this area.

The four pretest interviewers attended the six-hour training sessions during which general interviewing procedures, as well as techniques specific to this study, were explained. Then the interviewers were requested to complete two interviews; one with an ethnic friend or neighbor to gain familiarity with the questionnaire and its skip patterns, and then one with the interviewer's first assigned respondent. When completed, these two interviews were evaluated to determine whether the interviewer was ready to proceed with the rest of his or her pretest interview assignments.

After the collection of the pretest data, a debriefing session was held during which the interviewers evaluated the questionnaire and related any problems they had encountered in the field. Constructive suggestions by the interviewers were incorporated into the interview procedure, although the questionnaire remained essentially as it had been in its original form.

Of the 23 interviews completed for the pretest, 15 used prior contact by telephone, and eight used no prior contact. This indicated that the method of establishing prior telephone contact was a good one, and this procedure was adopted for the study. A summary of the pretest results is given in Table 3, below. As can be seen from the table, failure to contact the respondent was sometimes more of a problem than refusal to be interviewed.

Table 3
Pretest interview results

	Chinese	Japanese	Pilipino	Korean	Total
Response rate	24.5%	20.0%	61.5%	35.7%	39.6%
Refusal rate	27.3	30.0	7.1	35.7	25.9
No-contact rate	18.2	50.0	30.7	28.6	34.5

The average length of the interviews was 59 minutes, with the following averages for the various groups: Korean, 96 minutes; Japanese, 57 minutes, Chinese, 48 minutes; and Pilipino, 44 minutes. At the two extremes, the language in which the interview was conducted seemed to be the determining factor in interview length: all the Korean interviews were conducted in Korean, while all the Pilipino interviews were in English. The interviewers also reported that the length of an interview was in part determined by the time required to couch the interview questions in the polite formulas dictated by the conversational customs in the various ethnic languages.

Interviewer Selection, Training, and Supervision

Prospective interviewers fell into two general categories. One group was composed of persons who knew of the study and had expressed an interest in participating as interviewers. Of these, some were acquaintances and associates of the researcher, and others were members of the ethnic communities who had been contacted during the community contact phase of the development of the study. The second group was composed of persons who answered advertisements for interviewers or responded to articles describing the study in neighborhood ethnic-language news bulletins. Classified advertisements were placed in both community and university-based newspapers: *Hang Kook Ilbo* (Korean), *The Chicago Shimpo, Inc.* (Japanese), and *The Maroon* (University of Chicago). The prospective interviewers were about evenly divided between the two groups.

In addition to meeting the bilingual/bicultural requirement, prospective interviewers had to be willing to devote evenings and weekends for a total of up to 20 hours per week, conducting four interviews per week for an eight week period, and would be required to attend two training sessions. In all, 55 prospective interviewers applied and with one exception (a person who had previously done this sort of interviewing for the Survey Research Laboratory and was hired on the basis of their recommendation) all were interviewed and screened personally by the investigator. Other criteria used in selection were: (1) satisfactory fluency in both the native language and in English; (2) ability to participate in the study without any strong biases (particularly, without negative attitudes toward the study); and (3) ability to put a respondent at ease while obtaining critical information on a variety of personal subjects. Thirty-six interviewers were finally selected.

Because of the large number of interviewers, it was necessary to divide them into two groups for training purposes. Each group attended both a general training session and a specific training session. Each training session was six hours long, and the format was similar to that of the pretest training sessions. The training sessions covered two days. In addition to presentations on the general principles of survey research and interviewing technique, the training included practice interviewing and role-playing sessions. The training was conducted in accordance with a training manual developed for this study by Mr. Michael Cox of the Survey Research Laboratory.

Of the 36 interviewers selected and trained, two dropped out at the beginning of the study, and four of the Japanese interviewers left later in the study. Of the 30 remaining interviewers five had only limited language ability in Japanese or Cantonese and were therefore assigned to conduct English language interviews of American-born or naturalized citizens. Demographically, the survey interviewers proved to be relatively young (most were between the ages of 20 and 40), and quite well educated (22 of the 34 held graduate degrees, including two Ph.D.s). Most (27 out of 34) had had some sort of previous interviewing experience.

From each ethnic group, one individual was designed as the supervisor of the interviewers for that group. Three of the four supervisors were persons who had been pretest interviewers and who, therefore, had some additional field experience to guide them. The supervisors were to maintain regular contact with their interviewers; assign (or reassign) cases; collect, edit, and keep records of case dispositions; and discuss field progress and problems with the field coordinator from the Survey Research Laboratory. Finally, the supervisors were responsible for checking each completed questionnaire for detail and thoroughness, and for verifying interviews by telephoning respondents on a random basis.

Interview Procedure

The Survey Research Laboratory made an effort to verify the addresses of the sample respondents by using a reverse telephone directory. In view of the rate of noncontact in the pretest interviews, this process was considered essential in order to insure that the interviewers would be able to spend their time on interviewing, not on locating respondents. One week prior to the interviewers' approach, a letter was sent to the respondents informing them about the study and requesting their cooperation. The Postal Service was asked to provide address corrections where necessary, and to return letters for addresses not located. Of the 1,392 letters sent out, address corrections were returned for 52 (3.7%), while 144 letters (10.3%) were returned as not forwardable. Those persons whose letters were returned as not forwardable were removed from the sample pool.

Once a respondent was located, the following prcedure was standard. If the respondent had a telephone, the interviewer called first; if there was no telephone, the interviewer went directly to the respondent's residence. The interviewer introduced himself/herself to the respondent by saying, "Hello, I'm _____ from the University of Illinois. I'd like to ask you a few questions on your opinion of the adjustment of [R's ethnic group] people to the United States." (This form of introduction was adopted in order to avoid raising the respondent's expectations by mentioning social services at the outset.) The interviewer would then ask permission to conduct the interview either immediately, or by setting up an appointment at a later date. Interviewers were issued identification cards from the University of Illinois Survey Research Laboratory.

As noted earlier, bilingual/bicultural interviewers were used and were in all cases assigned to conduct interviews with members of their own ethnic groups. In the case of the Chinese sample, this procedure was complicated by the presence of speakers of several different dialects among the respondents. This problem was handled by studying demographic data from the Chinese neighborhoods and then matching the language abilities of the interviewers to the predominant dialect of each area. One interviewer spoke all three dialects common among the Chinese population of Chicago (Mandarin, Cantonese, and Toisanese) and he was often assigned to handle ambiguous cases.

Results of Interviews

Although the data collection phase of the study was originally scheduled for completion within eight weeks, several factors made it necessary to extend this period somewhat. The principal delay arose from the Japanese interviewers. Five of the nine in this group proved relatively unproductive. Two were students who could not devote sufficient time to the interviewing because of their educational commitments, while the other three became discouraged by interview refusals. Although refusals are an expected occurrence in any interview procedure, these interviewers could not overcome the feeling of personal rejection which was caused by refusal. Four of these five interviewers eventually dropped out of the study, and as a result the completion of the Japanese interviews was relatively slow since additional time was required to distribute the unworked cases to the remaining interviewers.

A second difficulty encountered was that, unlike the Chinese, Japanese, and Korean samples, the Pilipino sample was scattered throughout the city of Chicago: in all, 26.9% of the Pilipino sample could not be located. Also, five of the Pilipino interviewers did not have cars and therefore had to depend on public transportation to reach their respondents; this limited the number of contacts they could make on any given interviewing night.

Somewhat surprisingly, the practice of making telephone contact prior to the interview proved to have certain disadvantages, from the aspect of expediting the study. Interviews were quickly arranged for respondents who had phone numbers, while those who did not were left until last. Some interviewers were reluctant to work on cases which did not have phone numbers because of the probability of having to make more than one trip to complete the interview. These cases had to be reassigned to other interviewers.

Finally, there was some difficulty in locating households with American citizens present among the American-born or naturalized Chinese group. Thirty-one percent of the households sampled in this group proved ineligible due to noncitizenship.

Interview Verification

Two-hundred interviews were verified by telephone on a random basis by the supervisors of the ethnic groups and by the Chicago office of the Survey Research Laboratory. The quality of all interviewers' work for the study was found to be good and all cases were verified. In two instances the wrong person had been interviewed. In one of these cases the right person was located and interviewed, while in the other the case was terminated as a noncontact. Thirty cases could not be verified because the respondent did not have a telephone or could not be contacted.

Summary Description of the Interviewing

A summary of the disposition of the cases in the sample is given in Table 4, below. Of particular interest is the fact that the

Table 4
Summary of case dispositions

| | Chinese | | Japanese | | Pilipino | Korean | Total |
	C*	I**	C*	I**			I**
Total eligibles	86	178	85	169	361	324	1,203
Interviews	49	100	50	100	199	228	730
Refusals	16	21	16	14	19	12	98
Noncontact	8	15	4	18	31	10	86
Could not locate	11	36	9	22	97	54	229
Other	2	6	6	15	11	20	64
Total ineligibles	61	20	14	26	32	36	189
Out of area	14	18	7	21	32	36	128
Not American citizen	46	N/A	6	N/A	N/A	N/A	52
Deceased	1	2	1	5	0	0	9
Total cases	147	198	99	195	393	360	1,392
Response rate	57%	56%	59%	59%	56%	70%	61%
Refusal rate	25%	17%	24%	12%	9%	5%	12%
Contact rate	90%	71%	85%	76%	65%	80%	74%
Eligibility rate	59%	90%	86%	87%	92%	90%	86%

*Denotes American citizens.
**Denotes immigrants.

refusal rate was quite low, amounting to only 12% of all cases contacted. This result would seem to discredit the common stereotype that "Asian Americans won't respond to surveys." Quite clearly, in this instance at least, refusal to be interviewed was not a major problem. The bulk of the difference between sample and interviews is the result of failure to locate or failure to contact the prospective respondents. These problems presumably arise from the mobility of the population, together with a relatively low level of cultural assimilation: the persons in the sample simply leave fewer "traces" than one would expect.

When the disposition of cases was analyzed according to interviewers, it was found that only two interviewers had large numbers of refusals. These instances of large numbers of refusals occurred among immigrant members of the Japanese community (nine refusals for one interviewer) and the Chinese community (eight refusals for one interviewer). No attempt was made to analyze the actual probabilities of these occurences, but one suspects that these isolated instances of high refusal rate might indicate that the problem was an idiosyncratic one, involving the interaction of particular interviewers and respondents.

Although the interviewers reported a wide range of general responses to the study on the part of the respondents, there seemed to be little overt hostility, and many indications that the respondents were both eager to participate and genuinely interested in the study. Reactions of respondents varied from one ethnic group to another, reflecting cultural values. The Korean interviewers reported that many of their respondents, who knew that the interviewer was coming, opened their doors at the first knock without ascertaining the identity of the caller. This is not a wise thing to do in many areas where the interviews took place, and it can only be interpreted as an indication of how eager the respondents were to meet the interviewer and cooperate with him or her as a fellow ethnic group member. The Korean interviewers also found that they frequently fell behind schedule because the respondents insisted on serving a meal after the interview. The Pilipino interviewers faced a somewhat different display of hospitality: the respondents frequently insisted on serving hard liquor to male interviewers during the interview. Needless to say, this sometimes made it difficult to complete several interviews in a single evening. Interviewers from the Chinese and Japanese groups in particular reported that it was often difficult to escape from elderly respondents after the interview. The respondents were evidently very lonely and clung to anyone who came to visit them.

There were a few incidents of overt hostility, but they were infrequent and a specific explanation could usually be found. In one case, for instance, an unmarried male interviewer arrived at a home and proceeded to interview the respondent, who was a married woman. While the interview was in progress, the respondent's husband arrived on the scene and insisted that he, rather than his wife, be interviewed. A violent quarrel ensued between husband and wife and the interviewer was forced to abandon the interview. In this instance, the cultural norms of the respondent's ethnic group dictated that all communication between the family and outsiders should be made by the (male) head of the household. The interview with the wife was perceived by the husband as an attempt to bypass his authority. Other interviewers also reported hostility, although of a less pronounced sort, when an unmarried interviewer contacted a married respondent of the opposite sex. Overall, however, these sorts of cultural misunderstandings were rare occurrences.

The interviewers saw the interviewing experience as a positive one, with the exception of a few individuals who became discouraged by respondent refusals. Most interviewers reported that their understanding of problems faced by members of their ethnic group was increased, and that they felt more inclined to become actively involved in solving community problems.

All the interviewers were debriefed after the completion of the interviewing phase of the study. Reactions to the form of the questionnaire were mixed. Some interviewers strongly favored the progressive form of questionnaire used, while others expressed a preference for a form which began by collecting all of the factual information first, and then moved to personal and attitudinal items. Since the latter form is much more commonly used in survey work, the interviewers may simply have been reacting to the unfamiliar design of the progressive questionnaire used in this study.

A debriefing questionnaire, which was returned by 23 of the 34 interviewers who participated actively, showed a wide range of responses to the study. Most interviewers said that they initially wanted to participate in the study in order to learn about their ethnic communities, and in order to participate in a worthy project. In a similar vein, most reported that the contact with respondents and the knowledge subsequently gained about their communities were the most enjoyable aspects of participation in the study. On the other hand, what the interviewers found most frustrating and unpleasant were the difficulties in making contact with respondents: refusals, respondents who were not at home, ineligible respondents, wrong addresses, etc.

Interestingly, once contact had been made, the interviewers reported that a large proportion of the respondents were very cooperative (51–74%, depending on group), while most of the rest (15–30%) were at least neutral. Only among the Chinese respondents was there an appreciable incidence of subject resistance (19%). Thus, the respondents appear to have been generally well disposed toward the study—and toward the interviewers. By the same token, 20 of the 23 interviewers who returned questionnaires expressed a desire to participate in a future study of this sort, thus indicating a high level of interest and satisfaction with their work in the study.

Data Reduction and Data Processing

Shortly after the field work of the survey was completed, the process of converting the questionnaire results into an IBM data file began. The original design of the questionnaire included pre-coding of most of the questions following a system compatible with the IBM card format. However, a large amount of revision was required in order to code the specific answers to those questions which had an "other" category, and for coding the six questions which were open ended.

The process of data reduction involved five discrete steps.

1) Quality control. Each completed questionnaire was inspected by the group supervisor to make certain that it was completely filled out, that the response categories were unambiguously indicated, and that written information was both legible and coherent. Any problems encountered were referred back to the interviewers for clarification.

2) Editing. Response patterns were checked by an editor at the Survey Research Laboratory who examined the questionnaires for inconsistent or impossible entries, and for evidence of unclear or ambiguous responses. Errors which could not be corrected on the basis of information within the questionnaire were referred back to the group supervisors, who resolved the discrepancies either by consultation with the original interviewer or by contacting the respondent.

3) Coding. As noted above, much of the original coding of the questionnaire was revised in order to accomodate the 37 "other" categories, and for the six open-ended questions. All data were then transferred from the questionnaire to the IBM Fortran format by two graduate students in the Jane Addams School of Social Work at the University of Illinois. The coders were trained and supervised in the use of the coding manual by the researcher.

4) Checking. Concurrently with the coding operation, the researcher recoded approximately 15% of each coder's work to ensure accuracy.

5) Key Punching. Both punching and card verification were performed by Georgia State University.

Data Analysis

The study data were analyzed using the Statistical Package for the Social Sciences (SPSS) program. The transformation of the data so that they could be statistically analyzed by the SPSS program was performed by a graduate student under the supervision of Dr. Kee Whan Choi of the Mathematics Department of Georgia State University.

As in all cases of statistical analysis of survey data, the reliability and validity of the results of the present study are limited by sampling and nonsampling error. Nonsampling error includes all of the various kinds of mechanical, typographical, and conceptual errors which affect the accurate recording, storage, analysis, and retrieval of the data. The procedures outlined above in designing the instrument and gathering, coding, and analyzing the data, were all specifically aimed at minimizing nonsampling error effects. The sampling procedures employed in this study preclude the calculation of the exact sampling error on the assumption of a simple, random sample. As detailed earlier, sample selection was performed within certain constraints as to the identity of the total, potential sample population. However, the consensus of the researcher and the survey consultants involved was that the resulting sampling error was not great enough to diminish the usefulness of the results of the study. In a sense, all survey research is a compromise between the ideals of statistics and the exigencies of dealing with real-world populations.

Study Design and Study Response: Conclusions

Many factors enter into the success or failure of survey research, and the researcher is often left with the disquieting suspicion that a study may have succeeded or failed because of environmental factors lying entirely outside the range of contingencies which were so carefully accounted for in the design. Nevertheless, some conclusions about survey studies among Asian–American populations can be drawn on the basis of the experience with the design and execution of the present research project.

First, it seems to be possible to overcome this (supposed) reluctance of Asian–American respondents to participate in studies which probe (supposedly) sensitive areas. There is of course no way to determine whether the design and interview techniques used here were primarily, or even largely, responsible for overcoming this supposed subject reluctance. What can be said is that it is logical to posit, *a priori*, that a design involving a progressive question arrangement and a face-to-face interview technique utilizing bilingual/bicultural interviewers should help to reduce subject reluctance and that, in the event, only a very moderate refusal rate (12%) was encountered.

The second conclusion is that identifying, locating, and contacting the sample population may well be the principal challenge to the investigator of Asian-American groups. The noncontact/failure-to-locate rate in the present study was much higher (26%) than the refusal rate. If one adds the "ineligible" and "other noninterview" groups and calculates on the basis of the entire sample, no less than 40.5% of the total sample failed to be interviewed for reasons other than subject refusal.

All surveys are to some extent plagued by these sorts of information failures, but clearly this is a particularly serious problem where Asian-American groups are concerned. Existing ethnic directories, telephone directories, census information, and even the Immigration and Naturalization Service files do not provide adequate information on the identity and whereabouts of Asian Americans. In part this may be culturally determined: many Asian-American immigrants have come to America from political situations where a measure of anonymity has a high survival value. Likewise, the past history of treatment of Asian Americans in this country has perhaps led older members of these groups to believe that a low profile is a good way to avoid trouble from outsiders. On the other hand, this isolated anonymity is almost certain to work against the development of constructive community identity and community action among Asian Americans. It may be that the Asian-American communities themselves will have to take the initiative in developing comprehensive community directories and otherwise ensuring that ethnic group members do not simply "disappear" from the social and cultural life of the community.

Study Results: Profiles and Composites

The chapters which follow present two different perspectives on the results of the study. In Chapters IV through VII, the results for each group studied—Chinese, Japanese, Pilipino, Korean—are presented as profiles of the individual groups. As elsewhere in this study, the order in which the ethnic groups are studied is historical, based on the order in which the preponderance of the group members arrived in America. It is hoped that this presentation of individual group profiles will emphasize the important inter- and intragroup variation of Asian Americans. At the same time, there are needs and problems which are shared by all Asian Americans, and therefore Chapter VIII seeks to present a composite picture of the study results, covering all four groups of respondents. Finally, Chapter IX attempts to translate the study findings into suggestions for community and government action in the area of providing services and resources to meet the needs delineated by the study data.

NOTES TO CHAPTER III

1. Although the Immigration and Naturalization Service files are the most comprehensive listing of aliens in the United States, there is no way of knowing just how complete these files are. There is speculation that many aliens may fail to register, for a variety of reasons. Some, of course, have entered the country illegally, while others may simply be isolated persons—often aged—who are either unaware of the provisions of the law, or even physically incapable of complying with them. Thus even the INS files may show some inevitable bias.

2. G. Gurin, J. Veroff, and S. Feld, *Americans View Their Mental Health*, New York: Basic Books, 1960.

CHAPTER IV

THE CHINESE SAMPLE

Of the 726 persons interviewed for this study, 100 were Chinese immigrants and 49 were citizens of Chinese descent, either American born or naturalized. In this chapter we shall examine the Chinese respondents with respect to the various areas of concern covered in the study. In this way, a picture of the Chinese-American residents of Chicago should emerge. In most cases, separate data are reported for the immigrant and citizen groups; in some cases the differences are instructive. Where there are no significant differences between the groups, the data are aggregated for the sake of brevity.

Demographic Characteristics

To the casual observer, there might appear to be good reason to aggregate all the data from the Chinese respondents, since fully 39 of the 49 citizens were naturalized. In effect, this means that 139 of the 149 Chinese respondents (93%) are, in one sense, immigrants, a certain number of whom have become naturalized citizens. However, the historical background of the Chicago Chinese community suggests that there will be certain marked differences between the two groups. One would suspect, *a priori,* that many members of the citizen group would tend to be the remnants and descendents of the influx of West Coast Chinese who formed the nucleus of the Chicago Chinese community a half a century ago.[1] This idea is partially supported by the data profiled in Figure 1. While residence lengths over 20.1 years were not broken down further, it is clear that four times as many citizens as immigrants have resided that long in Chicago.

Although it is apparent that the immigrants are relative newcomers compared to the citizens, the difference is not as great as one might expect. In fact, the mean age of the Chinese immigrant respondents was more than three years older than that of the citizens (42.4 versus 39.3 years). This may be partly explained by the provisions of the 1965 amendments to the immigration law, which gives priority to "immediate relatives" of U.S. citizens. One suspects that a certain number of these immediate relatives are parents and siblings who have finally been able to join their families in the United States. While 22.4% of the citizen sample is 51 years of age or older, 33.3% of the immigrants are in this age group.

The sex composition of the various age groups is indicative of the forces which have, historically, affected the ebb and flow of immigration. Although the overall sex ratios of both the immi-

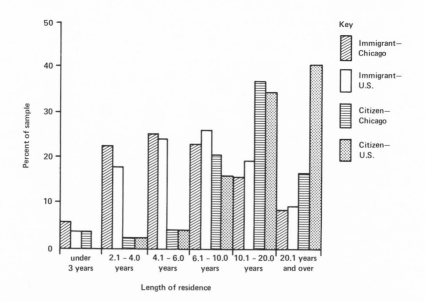

Figure 1. Length of residence in Chicago and the United States by Chinese immigrant and citizen groups

grant and citizen groups are normal (M/F = 48.5/51.5% for immigrants and 51/49% for citizens), few of the individual age groups exhibit anything approaching this normal balance. In part, this fluctuation may be caused by the small size of the sample, but some of the imbalances are both predictable and instructive. For instance, in the "65 and over" age group the immigrant sex ratio (M/F) is 27/71%, probably reflecting the greater life expectancy of females. Conversely, however, the same age group for citizens shows a M/F ratio of 60/40%, which runs contrary to actuarial expectations and probably reflects the fact that the early influx of Chinese immigration to this country was composed almost exclusively of males.[2] (In the 18–30 group for both categories and in the 31–40 citizen group, females are substantially overrepresented, perhaps reflecting an influx of women of marriageable age into the Chinese American community, with its traditional surplus of males.) On the other hand, the 31–40 and 41–50 age groups for immigrants show a strong imbalance in the male direction. One might speculate that we are here seeing a pattern in which the male head of the household immigrates first to pave the way for his family to join him after he establishes himself. As we shall see later, this pattern is evident in the sources of assistance received by Chinese immigrants when they first arrive in the U.S.

Overall, the two Chinese groups are older (39 years) than the Korean (34 years) and Pilipino (32 years) groups, but younger than both of the Japanese respondent groups (47 years). This is of some interest since, historically, the Chicago Chinese community is much older than the Japanese community; the latter has been formed almost entirely since the end of World War II. Compared to the other groups studied, both Chinese groups show a wide dispersion of ages, rather than a unimodal tendency. This may be the result of the large shift in historical trends in Chinese immigration, from heavily male in the early days to heavily female in the more recent past.

As with the other groups studied, a large proportion of the Chinese respondents (70% of the immigrants and 75.5% of the citizens) are married and living with their spouses. This figure is, however, somewhat lower than that shown in the 1970 census for this group (90%). Since the rates for separation and divorce in the study sample are consistent with the census figures, it is apparent that the study sample contains a higher proportion of unmarried adults. This may indicate that the Chicago Chinese population differs slightly from the national population in this respect, or it may simply mean that the study was more effective than the census in locating unmarried respondents.

The Chinese respondents in this study tended to live in households which were larger than those of any other group except the Pilipinos. Unlike the Pilipinos, however, few Chinese households contained persons who were not related to the respondent; the Chinese households seem to be almost exclusively based on the family—extended as well as nuclear. Overall, the average household size for both Chinese groups was about six persons.

Respondents in all groups were asked to list all children living at home. The ages of children living at home ranged from infants to middle-aged adults, with the predominant weighting being somewhat different for each ethnic group. Predictably, the Chinese immigrant group had somewhat more children in the youngest grouping ("under 5") than the citizens (17.5% versus 10%), but both groups had considerably fewer young children at home than did the Pilipino and Korean groups. Overall, the Japanese respondents had slightly fewer children at home than the Chinese, but the Chinese respondents did show a greater percentage of children in the young age groups.

Taken together with the age data given above, these figures indicate that the typical Chinese respondent—whether in the immigrant or citizen group—is likely to be middle-aged, and if he or she has children at home, they are likely to be of elementary or high school age, rather than toddlers. This should be kept in mind when we consider the perceived service needs of this group.

Respondents were also asked to specify the nature of their housing arrangements: did they own or rent, and was the domicile a house or an apartment? Apartment rental was the most common arrangement for all groups, but the Chinese citizen group had the highest percentage of home ownership (30.6%, followed closely by the Japanese citizen group with 30%). The home ownership of the Chinese immigrants was also the highest of any immigrant group at 20%, although the other immigrant groups—with the exception of the Koreans—were all within 2% of this figure. Apartment ownership, at 7% for the Chinese immigrants and 6.1% for the Chinese citizens, fell approximately halfway between the levels for the Pilipino and Korean groups on one hand, and the Japanese groups on the other. House rental accounted for only a small percentage of the accomodations in all of the groups studied; among the Chinese respondents, there were no immigrants renting houses, and only 4.1% of the citizens were doing so. It may be that few rental houses are available in the densely settled urban areas covered by this study.

The religious preferences and frequency of attendance at religious services for the Chinese groups are shown in Table 5. Of all the groups surveyed, the two Chinese groups showed the highest levels of "no preference." Only the Japanese groups were less likely to attend weekly, and the Chinese groups were more likely to attend less than once a month, or never. This general lack of church affiliation and attendance among the Chinese suggests that it may not be feasible to reach this group by means of service and outreach efforts operating through religious institutions.

Along with this trend toward lack of religious affiliation, the Chinese respondents seem, generally, not to be joiners. Fully two-thirds of the Chinese immigrants belong to no clubs or organiza-

Table 5
Religious preference and service attendance among Chinese respondents

	Chinese immigrants		U.S. Citizens of Chinese descent		Totals for all groups in study	
	N	%	N	%	N	%
Religious preference						
Protestant	20	20.0	15	37.7	257	32.6
Catholic	12	12.0	17	34.7	254	35.0
Buddhist	5	5.0	2	4.1	91	12.5
No preference	62	62.0	14	28.6	132	18.2
Other	1	1.0	—	—	12	1.7
Totals	100	100.0	49	100.0	726	100.0
Religious service attendance (Adjusted frequency)						
Once a week	9	24.4	13	33.3	318	52.6
Once a month	3	7.3	—	—	93	15.4
Less than once a month	8	22.0	15	38.5	90	14.9
Never	18	46.3	11	28.2	104	17.2
No answer	62		10		121	
Totals	100	100.0	49	100.0	726	100.0

tions of any kind, and nearly two-thirds of the Chinese citizens are similarly unaffiliated. Twenty-two percent of the Chinese immigrants and 18.4% of the citizens belong to a single organization, and for membership in larger numbers of organizations the percentages fall off very rapidly. Overall, the Chinese were the least likely to join organizations of all groups studied. As in the case of church affiliation, this general nonmembership in organizations suggests that it may be difficult to reach the Chicago Chinese population through this channel. Empirical observation in the Chicago Chinese community suggests that kinship groupings and small, informal groups may be much more important to Chinese residents than formal organizations. Within the confines of the study there is no ready explanation for the paucity of organizational memberships among the Chinese, and this area merits further study.

Interviews in the study were conducted either in English or in the ethnic language of the respondent, according to the respondent's preference. When all or part of the interview was conducted in the ethnic language, the respondent was asked to evaluate his or her own level of English fluency. In those cases where the respondent indicated neither understanding nor speaking ability in English, females outnumber males in all the groups covered in this study. The self-evaluations of the Chinese groups are shown in Table 6. Compared to the other groups, the Chinese groups, both immigrant and citizen, contain a substantially higher percentage of persons with limited or no English skills. When one adds to this the number who understand but do not speak English, more than three-quarters of the Chinese immigrants are included. Only 35% of the interviews of the Chinese citizen group were conducted in English, a fact which may reflect the higher percentage of naturalized citizens in this group. By comparison, 85% of the Japanese citizen group were interviewed in English.

The ability to speak English is a demographic characteristic which may be linked to the economic status of the respondents: a finding which will be noted later is the lower economic status of the Chinese community. The exact nature of the interrelationship between poor English fluency and low economic status is complicated, and may be circular. Nonetheless, this is a connection which should certainly be examined by persons attempting to meet the social service needs of the Chinese-American community.

Because of the high level of urbanization among Asian groups,

Table 6
Self-evaluation of English fluency by Chinese respondents, by sex

Degree of English fluency	Sex	Chinese immigrants N	%	U.S. citizens of Chinese descent N	%	Totals for all groups in study N	%
Fluent	M	4	10.5	5	31.2	59	21.7
	F	2	4.4	1	6.2	58	17.8
Adequate	M	4	10.5	3	18.7	124	45.6
	F	3	6.6	2	12.5	118	36.2
Understand but can't speak	M	16	42.1	5	31.2	69	25.4
	F	15	33.3	9	56.2	95	29.1
No comprehension of English	M	14	36.8	3	18.7	20	7.4
	F	25	55.5	4	25.0	55	16.9
Totals	M	38	99.9	16	99.8	272	100.1
	F	45	99.8	16	99.9	326	100.0

and because this sample was also an urban one, it was considered important to ascertain the community background of the respondents. In part, the adjustment problems of immigrant groups may be compounded by having to adjust to urban life in addition to American life. Therefore, the respondents were asked to give their place of birth and the size of the community in which they had lived prior to the age of eighteen. Table 7 presents the results for the Chinese groups. Of particular interest is the low percentage of American-born citizens. By comparison, 84% of the Japanese citizen group was American born.

With all groups, considerable difficulty was encountered in obtaining information about the size of the communities in which the respondents had grown up. During the pretest it was determined that most respondents did not know the population of their hometowns, although they could give the name of the village or city. Gross categorization, however, enabled the respondents to provide answers to this question. As the figures in Table 7 indicate, both groups of Chinese respondents tended to come from very large cities. This heavily urban background of the majority of the Chinese respondents suggests that, for this group, the usual

Table 7
Birthplace and early community background of
Chinese sample

	Chinese immigrants		U.S. citizens of Chinese descent		Totals for all groups in study	
	N	%	N	%	N	%
Birth place						
U.S.A.	—	—	10	20.4		
Mainland China	87	87.0	36	73.5		
Hong Kong	1	1.0	3	6.1		
Taiwan	8	8.0	—	—		
Japan	—	—	—	—		
Korea	—	—	—	—		
Philippines	1	1.0	—	—		
Others	3	3.0	—	—		
Totals	100	100.0	49	100.0		
Community size						
Farm, village	37	37.0	15	30.6	147	20.7
Under ½ million	7	7.0	3	6.1	185	26.1
½ to 1 million	3	3.0	1	2.0	61	8.6
Over 1 million	53	53.0	30	61.2	317	44.7
Totals	100	100.0	49	100.0	710	100.0

pressures of American city life may be less of a problem than for, say, the Japanese respondents, who tend to come from rural backgrounds.

Demographic summary. In several respects, it is difficult to present a coherent demographic profile of the Chinese respondents in this study: both age and type of hometown, for instance, are quite widely dispersed for this sample. Some generalizations, however, are possible.

The Chinese sample could be described in general terms as middle-aged, with relatively few religious or organizational affiliations, and relatively long residency in both the U.S. and the Chicago area. They are nearly all married, and tend to live in fairly large households which are, however, composed almost exclusively of related persons. If they have children at home, they will probably be of elementary or high school age, rather than toddlers or preschoolers. They generally either own houses or rent apartments for living accomodations, tend to have grown up in urban environments, and are largely foreign born. As a group, their English proficiency tends to be low.

Education, Employment, and Income Characteristics

The two Chinese respondent groups showed the lowest educational levels of any groups included in this study. As Table 8 shows, the general trend is toward somewhat lower educational levels for the citizens than for the immigrants. This pattern is also shown by the Japanese groups, although to a less pronounced degree. As we noted earlier, the 1965 amendments to the immigration law tend to favor skilled and professional immigrants to a slight degree and this fact, combined with a history of educational discrimination against minority groups in this country, probably accounts for the higher educational achievements of the immigrant groups. It has also been hypothesized by some writers[3] that members of the educational elite in some Asian countries may be forced to emigrate because the economic systems of these coun-

Table 8
Highest educational level achieved by Chinese respondents
and spouses, by sex

Educational levels	Sex	Chinese immigrants N	%	U.S. citizens of Chinese descent N	%	Totals for all groups in study N	%
Elementary or	M	13	19.1	8	26.7	25	5.3
under	F	21	42.0	9	42.9	45	11.0
High school graduate	M	32	47.1	15	50.0	82	17.3
or under	F	12	24.0	11	52.4	72	17.5
High school and	M	4	5.9	5	16.7	56	11.8
beyond	F	6	12.0	–	–	45	11.0
College graduate	M	9	13.2	2	6.7	234	49.4
	F	8	16.0	1	4.8	201	48.9
Nursing	M	–	–	–	–	–	–
	F	–	–	–	–	16	3.9
MS and PhD	M	9	13.2	–	–	48	10.1
	F	1	2.0	–	–	13	3.2
MD and dental	M	1	1.5	–	–	12	2.5
	F	–	–	–	–	1	0.2
Post MD and PhD	M	–	–	–	–	17	3.6
	F	2	4.0	–	–	18	4.4
Totals*	M	68	100.0	30	100.0	474	100.0
	F	50	100.0	21	100.0	411	100.0

*The totals include both respondents and their spouses. Therefore, they do not agree with the sample size of the study.

tries cannot absorb the output of the educational systems. Finally, some of the difference in educational level between Chinese citizens and immigrants in this study is accounted for by the fact that this citizen sample shows a lower educational level than that reported for Chinese Americans generally by the 1970 census. The census reports that, nationally, 25% of Chinese Americans have four or more years of college, compared to a combined average of 19.5% for the Chinese groups studied here. In particular, unlike the Korean and Pilipino immigrants, the Chinese groups in this study contain almost no persons holding advanced degrees.

Within the Chinese groups, women are considerably overrepresented at the lowest educational levels. This is perhaps to be expected, since Chinese-American women have shown only minimal gains in higher education, nationally, in recent years. In the decade from 1960 to 1970, for example, the proportion of college-educated Pilipino women in the U.S. more than doubled in the same period.

The Chinese samples showed a relatively low incidence of unemployment, a characteristic which they share with the other groups in this study. Thus, if the respondents have employment problems, one would expect them to be in the area of underemployment rather than unemployment. As will be noted in Table 9, very few respondents reported holding more than one job. This finding runs contrary to expectations based on casual observations of ethnic community members. It should also be noted that the difference between the male and female employment rates is not large, indicating that both spouses are probably employed in many households.

In most employment categories the Chinese respondents do not depart noticeably from the averages for all of the groups studied. As might be expected, given their greater median age, the Chinese groups, like the Japanese groups, contained larger proportions of disabled and retired persons than did the more youthful Pilipino and Korean groups.

Table 10 shows the job categories of the employed residents. While the Chinese respondents are somewhat underrepresented at the professional level, they are probably not as severely underrepresented as some of the other groups in the study (e.g., the Pilipinos and Koreans), because of their generally lower educational level. What is significant, however, is the extremely small proportion of managerial workers among the Chinese respondents (and, indeed, among the other ethnic groups as well). This is a fairly good

Table 9
Employment status of Chinese respondents and spouses, by sex

Employment status	Sex	Chinese immigrants		U.S. citizens of Chinese descent		Totals for all groups in study	
		N	%	N	%	N	%
Full-time	M	63	76.8	31	75.6	505	82.1
	F	45	52.3	19	44.2	393	59.1
Part-time	M	3	3.7	3	7.3	19	3.1
	F	2	2.3	7	16.3	36	5.4
More than one	M	3	3.7	1	2.4	38	6.2
job	F	2	2.3	—	—	17	2.6
Unemployed,	M	2	2.4	2	4.9	5	0.8
sick, disabled	F	3	3.5	—	—	6	0.9
Retired	M	7	8.5	3	7.3	26	4.2
	F	5	5.8	3	7.0	16	2.4
Unemployed,	M	1	1.2	—	—	8	1.3
seeking job	F	2	2.3	—	—	17	2.6
Unemployed, not	M	3	3.7	—	—	9	1.5
seeking job	F	1	1.2	3	7.0	14	2.1
Homemaker	M	—	—	—	—	3	0.5
	F	17	19.8	8	18.6	120	18.1
Never employed	M	—	—	1	2.4	2	0.3
	F	9	10.5	3	7.0	46	6.9
Totals*	M	82	100.0	41	100.0	615	100.0
	F	86	100.0	43	100.0	665	100.0

*The totals include both respondents and their spouses. Therefore they do not agree with the sample size of the study.

indicator of the level of social assimilation of the groups studied: quite clearly, they have not been accepted in society at large to the point of becoming managers of other, probably nonethnic, workers.

The relatively large population of proprietors among the Chinese group lends some support to the stereotype of Chinese Americans as owners of restaurants and hand laundries. Indeed, an examination of individual responses shows a certain number of proprietors of such businesses, but also reveals respondents operating such diverse enterprises as consulting engineering firms and import-export houses. What is important to remember is that being a proprietor in an ethnic enclave does not guarantee even minimal prosperity. This seemed to be particularly true of laundry proprietors, many of whom were elderly and were engaged in a

Changing Patterns, Changing Needs

Table 10
Occupational categories of respondents and spouses in
Chinese groups, by sex

	Sex	Chinese immigrants N	Chinese immigrants %	U.S. citizens of Chinese descent N	U.S. citizens of Chinese descent %	Totals for all groups in study N	Totals for all groups in study %
Professional	M	15	21.4	4	10.9	159	27.7
	F	7	13.5	2	7.7	143	31.5
Managerial	M	—	—	2	5.4	23	4.0
	F	—	—	—	—	9	2.0
Proprietor	M	5	7.2	10	27.0	61	10.6
	F	—	—	4	15.4	11	2.4
Skilled and	M	40	57.1	15	40.5	232	40.4
white collar	F	12	23.1	6	23.1	164	36.1
Semi– and un–	M	10	14.3	6	16.2	99	17.3
skilled	F	33	63.4	14	53.8	127	28.0
Totals*	M	70	100.0	37	100.0	574	100.0
	F	52	100.0	26	100.0	454	100.0

*The totals include both respondents and their spouses. Therefore they do not agree with the sample size of the study.

losing battle against the technology of permanent press clothing and the automatic washing machine.

In all groups studied, there tended to be a greater concentration of females at the low end of the job spectrum. For the Chinese groups, however, this trend was particularly dramatic, with over half of the citizen females engaged in semi- or unskilled occupations. An examination of individual responses shows that a large proportion of these women are employed in the garment industry.

There are several measures that can be used to determine whether or not the jobs currently held by respondents constitute underemployment. In the case of the Chinese sample, a comparison of the categories of jobs held by respondents before and after immigration indicated only a slight degree of downward mobility at the upper end of the job scale, but also a certain amount of upward mobility at the lower end. Thus, the professional and managerial group had decreased by 13.8% and 1.6% upon immigration, while the unskilled/semiskilled group had decreased by 10.9%. In turn, the middle groups showed an increase in frequency (20.5% for white collar/skilled/clerical, and 6.0% for proprietors).

When the job categories of the respondents are compared to

those of their parents in the home country, the main effect observed is a certain amount of shuffling among the categories in the middle of the scale. From parent to respondent the proportion of managers declined by 3.1% and the proprietors group declined by 23.3%. On the other hand, the white collar/skilled/clerical group grew by 20.9% between the parent and respondent generations. At the ends of the scale, the respondents showed an increase of 5.5% in the professional category compared to their parents, while there was no change in the proportion in the unskilled/semiskilled group. Thus, on the basis of the comparison between job levels of Chinese respondents and their parents there seems to be little evidence of pronounced downward—or upward—mobility.

A final measure of underemployment is the comparison of the individual's actual educational level with the educational level required for the respondent's job. In this questionnaire, the respondent was asked to tell what educational level was necessary for his or her job. Therefore the educational level required is a subjective assessment. It should be pointed out, however, that if the respondent assesses the job as one which requires less education than the respondent has attained, this judgment in itself is prima facie evidence of underemployment.

Table 11 compares the respondents' judgments of the educational requirements of their jobs with their actual educational attainments. Of particular interest is that, while over half the re-

Table 11

Educational levels of Chinese respondents and respondent's
perception of education required for jobs

	Education needed for job	Education obtained	
		U.S.	Foreign
Elementary school	51.2	8.5	34.4
Some high school	1.2	10.6	20.0
Trade-commercial	3.5	10.6	3.2
High school graduate	16.3	10.6	20.8
Trade-commercial graduate	1.2	2.1	2.4
Some college	4.7	25.5	0.8
College degree	19.8	10.6	12.8
Master's	—	6.4	2.4
Ph.D.	2.3	4.3	0.8
Nursing	—	—	0.8

spondents stated that their jobs required no more than an elementary school education, only 37.3% reported having this low a level of education. In general there was no very close agreement between educational levels and the respondents' perceptions of the educational requirements of their jobs. In some instances, this discrepancy probably indicates underemployment; at the Ph.D. level, for instance, 3.9% of the respondents held the degree, but only 2.3% reported holding jobs which required this educational attainment. However, in the absence of comparable data for the general population it is not possible to determine whether these discrepancies reflect the visible-minority status of the respondents, or if they simply point to larger problems in the socio-economic system of the United States as a whole.

Job stability and job satisfaction may also indicate how well a person's employment is matched to his or her abilities, education, and experience. The Chinese groups revealed a wide variation in length of time on present job but, generally, showed fewer instances of very long employment in the present position than did the Japanese groups. As might be expected, the Chinese, like the Japanese, showed generally longer employment on current jobs than the more recently arrived Pilipinos and Koreans.

Respondents were also asked whether or not they planned to stay on their present jobs, and to indicate their reasons for either staying or leaving. The Chinese citizen group showed a high percentage of "plan to stay" responses. Good pay, good benefits, and good working conditions were given as the primary reasons for remaining on the job. However, a sizeable proportion (23.6%) of the Chinese immigrants replied that they would keep the job because it was "the best job I could get under the circumstances." This response may indicate a degree of underemployment and job dissatisfaction. The Japanese and Korean immigrants also tended toward this response, but the other groups expressed more positive reasons for keeping current jobs. The reasons given for leaving a job have very low frequencies, no meaningful interpretation can be made.

In almost any sort of survey study, income is one of the most sensitive areas which a researcher can attempt to probe. In view of this fact, it is perhaps surprising that only 5.7% of the respondents in the present study refused to divulge their family income. Another 2.6% claimed not to know the family income. In some cases this may be a polite way of refusing to disclose income, but in many cases respondents who replied in this manner were elderly persons who were supported by their children and who thus might be ignorant of the family income. One additional caution is that respondents who do not wish to divulge their true income may simply name a higher or lower figure, rather than openly refusing to answer the question.[4] In most survey situations—including the present one—there is no means available to check on the accuracy of respondents' replies concerning income.

As shown in Table 12, the Chinese respondents had a much higher than average rate of refusal to state family income. They also had the highest proportion of respondents reporting in the four lowest ranges, and the lowest overall average incomes.

In considering all of these figures, it should be remembered that we are here dealing with *family* income, an amount which may be (and, for the respondents, often is) composed of the earnings of several persons in the family.

Both the Chinese immigrant and citizen groups have median incomes below those for the other groups in the study. Likewise, fewer Chinese (and Japanese) respondents are represented in the higher income categories than is the case for the Pilipino and Korean groups. This finding is at variance with data from the 1970 census, in which higher incomes are reported for the Japanese and Chinese than for the Pilipino and Korean groups. It is quite likely

Table 12
Combined annual family income for the Chinese sample

Family annual income	Chinese immigrants		U.S. citizens of Chinese descent		Totals for all groups in study	
	N	%	N	%	N	%
Under 3,000	5	5.0	3	6.1	18	2.5
3,001–6,999	22	22.0	6	12.2	60	8.3
7,000–8,999	18	18.0	5	10.2	57	7.9
9,000–11,999	11	11.0	9	18.3	93	12.8
12,000–14,999	7	7.0	4	8.2	114	12.8
15,000–19,999	7	7.0	4	8.2	140	19.3
20,000–24,999	8	8.0	2	4.1	108	14.9
25,000–49,999	8	8.0	4	8.2	65	9.0
50,000 and over	2	2.0	2	4.1	11	1.5
Would not state income	12	12.0	10	20.4	41	5.7
Don't know	—	—	—	—	19	2.6
Total	100	100.0	49	100.0	726	100.0
Median	10,286		13,170			
Mean	13,369		14,996			

that this discrepancy represents a difference in the regional populations sampled. We have already noted that the Chicago Chinese sample shows a lower level of educational achievement than that reported for Chinese Americans nationally by the 1970 census. While the 1970 census also indicates that 55% of all Chinese in the state of Illinois had incomes of $10,000 or over, only 44% of the Chicago sample in this study fell into this category. By the same token, the Chicago Pilipino and Korean samples appear to contain far higher proportions of professional persons than is the case nationally.

The lower income among the Chinese and the large income disparity between the Chinese and the other groups in the study may be due to the lower educational attainment level, lower job level, and lower level of English proficiency among the Chinese. As has been suggested earlier, the lower level of English proficiency among the Chinese respondents may have an influence on both educational attainments and job level. Conversely, lack of formal education and employment in a low-level job may provide little precedent or incentive to improve one's level of English proficiency. No attempt has been made here to determine the exact direction of the causality, but the coincident lower levels of income, job category, and English proficiency among the Chicago Chinese respondents is a subject which is worthy of further study. It would be of some interest to pursue the question of family history in this respect. The present study did not go beyond the point of collecting data on the occupational status of the respondents' male parents or guardians, but even these results are enlightening. The parents of the Chinese sample contained a much larger proportion of unskilled and semiskilled laborers than was the case with the Korean and Pilipino samples. The Chinese parents resembled the Japanese parents, but had fewer proprietors, more white collar workers, and more unskilled/semiskilled workers.

In order to clarify the distribution of family income within ethnic groups, the relationship between the age of the respondent and the total family income was analyzed. The Chinese immigrant and citizen groups contain more persons in the under $5,000 category at all age levels than do any of the other groups, as well as fewer persons in the higher income levels. The highest income levels achieved by the Chinese immigrants are in the $5,000 to $9,000 range for most age groups, with only the 51 to 65 year age group showing incomes in the $9,000 to $12,000 range. Few Chinese respondents show a pattern of sharply increasing prosperity in their middle years. This may result from the fact that few of the Chinese are members of the professional, managerial, or skilled labor classes that are amply rewarded by American society. They seem, rather, to be largely employed in jobs without much "future." Their incomes do not show an increase in the middle-aged years because they do not follow a pattern of moving into positions of greater responsibility commensurate with their tenure of employment. This lack of advancement is probably tied to the fact that unskilled and semiskilled Chinese immigrants tend to settle within the city while more highly educated and economically successful immigrants live in suburban areas.

Since income adequacy is largely a subjective quality, the respondents were also asked to indicate what income they would consider "adequate" for their families. In Table 13 the results of this question are compared with the real income reported by the respondents. Interestingly, while the Chinese citizens are the least

Table 13
Relationship of real income to adequate income of Chinese respondents

	Chinese immigrants		U.S. citizens of Chinese descent		Totals for all groups in study	
	N	%	N	%	N	%
Real income greater than						
By 3 or more*	3	3.6	—	—	9	1.3
By 2	8	9.5	3	8.6	28	4.2
By 1	18	21.4	5	13.4	110	16.8
Real income equal to adequate income	41	48.8	11	32.5	303	46.4
Real income less than						
By 1	14	16.7	12	34.3	170	26.0
By 2	—	—	4	11.4	25	3.8
By 3 or more	—	—	—	—	7	1.0
Total of equal or better	70	83.3	19	54.5	450	69.0
Size of responses**	84		35		652	

*Figures in this column express the degree to which real income exceeds or falls short of the income perceived as adequate by the respondent, expressed in income levels. See Table 12 for income levels.

**Since not all respondents answered the two questions about their total annual income ("real") and "adequate" income, the numbers in this row do not correspond to the total sample sizes in the study. The percentages given are based on responses to this item, not on the total number of respondents.

likely of all groups to consider their actual income to be adequate, the Chinese immigrant group contains the highest percentage of persons who consider that their income is adequate or more than adequate. Since the median income of the Chinese citizen group is considerably higher than that of the Chinese immigrants, it can only be assumed that the two groups have different levels of expectation with regard to income. The Chinese immigrants, being on the whole more recently arrived both in the United States and in Chicago, may be more willing to accept their actual level of income, since they have not yet "made it." On the other hand, the Chinese citizen group has apparently not achieved a measure of economic success which is perceived as commensurate with its longer residence and greater personal investment in American society. In historical terms, the Japanese citizen group has made nearly the same sort of investment as the Chinese citizens, but has reaped much greater economic benefits. Thus, it comes as no surprise that over two-thirds of the Japanese citizens feel that their income is adequate or more than adequate.

It should be remembered here, as elsewhere, that a family income may represent two equal incomes, a single income, a large and a small income, or almost any other permutation or combination of earnings. This makes it impossible to compare individual income with any other relevant personal variables. However, comparison of the "adequate income" and "real income" data serves to indicate the level of satisfaction that respondents feel toward their economic status. Quite clearly, the Chinese citizens are less satisfied with their actual earnings than are the other groups in the study. On the other hand, even though the Chinese immigrants reported median family incomes of almost $3,000 less than the citizens, their level of satisfaction more nearly parallels that of the other, more affluent, ethnic groups. The fact is, however, that the Chinese citizens reported median family incomes some $4,500 below the average for the other ethnic groups. A discrepancy of this magnitude may be an indication that the Chinese citizens are in need of social services aimed at helping them to improve their economic condition.

Educational and economic summary. While relatively few of the Chinese respondents in this study appeared to be living in abject poverty or suffering from chronic unemployment, there are other aspects to their educational and economic situation which are far from ideal. The educational attainments of the Chinese are lower than those of the other groups studied, and their job levels are somewhat lower.[5] (In particular, the Chinese groups contain few professional persons). However, it is in the area of reported income that the Chinese are separated most drastically from the other ethnic groups. Even if there were found to be a substantial amount of underreporting of income among the Chinese groups, this is a very large difference indeed. In addition, the Chinese citizen group tended to find their actual incomes to be inadequate to their needs. In short, one may expect that the Chinese groups have problems and unmet service needs in the areas of education, employment, and income.

The Immigration Experience

Foreign born respondents, both recent immigrants and naturalized U.S. citizens, were asked a series of questions relating to their immigration experience. These questions sought information concerning their reasons for coming to this country, the presence of a family network in the United States, their experiences upon arrival, difficulties in adjusting to life in the United States, and the respondents' overall evaluation of their decision to emigrate to the United States. In the case of the Chinese groups, it should be remembered that 39 of the 49 citizens were foreign born, and thus the immigration experience may be an important one for nearly all of the Chinese respondents in the study.

Table 14 shows the reasons given by the respondents for immigrating to the United States. The three categories in which the Chinese respondents were more likely to respond than the other groups studied were "to join family," "better work opportunity," and "to avoid adverse political situation in the home country." The last category may reflect refugees who have arrived since the Communist takeover. The relatively high frequency of "to join family" is to be expected, given the long history of discriminatory immigration policy which previously barred immediate relatives of Chinese immigrants from entering the United States; the Japanese immigrants also show a high proportion of responses in this category.

It is interesting to note that, while the Chinese immigrants had a fairly high proportion of responses to "higher standard of living" and "better work opportunity," their responses to "educational opportunity" are lower than for any other group, and only the Korean immigrants show a lower response to "job training opportunity." The lower level of importance assigned by the Chinese immigrant group to educational and job training opportunities

Table 14
Reasons given for immigration to the United States, by sex
by Chinese immigrants

	Sex	Chinese immigrants*		Totals for all groups in study	
		N	%	N	%
Join family	M	39	23.2	107	14.0
	F	54	25.0	197	26.7
Educational opportunity	M	18	10.7	158	20.7
	F	14	8.8	94	12.8
Job training opportunity	M	11	6.5	104	13.6
	F	14	8.8	95	12.9
Higher standard of living	M	40	17.3	146	19.1
	F	30	19.2	117	15.9
Better work opportunity	M	47	28.0	176	23.1
	F	28	18.0	129	17.5
Education of children	M	1	0.5	10	1.3
	F	1	0.6	14	3.4
Adventure/make fortune	M	–	–	20	2.6
	F	–	–	23	3.1
To get married	M	–	–	2	0.2
	F	4	2.5	42	5.7
To avoid adverse political	M	12	7.1	39	5.1
situation in home country	F	11	7.0	25	3.8
Total of responses**	M	168	100.0	762	100.0
	F	156	100.0	736	100.0

*Includes naturalized citizens.

**Respondents could give as many responses as they wished. Thus the total responses do not correspond to sample size.

may in some way coincide with the relatively low job, educational, and income levels reported by this group. This response tendency may also be related to the family backgrounds of the respondents, few of whom had fathers or male guardians from the upper level job categories. A final possibility is that the Chicago Chinese community simply does not attract educated Chinese immigrants. No definite hypotheses can be advanced on this point. However, since the Pilipino and Korean communities in Chicago seem to attract inordinate numbers of highly educated immigrants, this attraction—or lack of it—is apparently a definite characteristic of at least some ethnic communities.

Overall, the reasons given by the Chinese for immigrating are practical and matter-of-fact: to join family members, get a better job, to achieve a higher standard of living, and, perhaps to escape from adverse political conditions. Conversely, not a single Chinese respondent answered in the "adventure/make fortune" category. (Lest the reader dismiss this as an unlikely reason for immigration, it should be noted that all the other ethnic groups showed some responses of this sort, ranging up to a high of 10.7% for Japanese males, followed by 5.1% for Pilipino females.)

The frequency with which the Chinese immigrants cited "to join the family" as a reason for immigration is probably related to the fact that 92% have relatives in the United States, while 65.1% have relatives living in Chicago. These percentages are higher than for any other group studied. A Chinese respondent was about 8% more likely than a member of the other respondent groups to have relatives in the U.S. and Chicago.

These figures indicate that the Chinese immigrants are especially likely to have an extensive family network in the United States, and in Chicago in particular, where over 65% of these relatives reside. Such figures alone, however, are not sufficient indicators of an effective support system, since additional factors, such as the frequency and quality of interaction within the family, must be taken into account. Furthermore, since, as was also the case with the Pilipinos and Koreans, the relatives of the Chinese are themselves likely to be immigrants, they may not be in a position to offer extensive help to newcomers. These factors were not explored in depth in this study.

Respondents were also asked to tell the relationship to themselves of the relatives living in Chicago. For all groups, parents formed the smallest percentage of those with Chicago relatives (14.9% in the case of the Chinese, and 12.9% overall). Siblings accounted for 19.1% of the Chinese with relatives in Chicago (compared to 21.2% for all groups), and 31.1% of the Chinese reported having "other relatives" in Chicago, considerably higher than the 22.8% average for all groups. As noted earlier, the Chinese households in the study, although large, tended to be composed almost entirely of related persons. Apparently these related persons are part of the extended family, since they are relatively unlikely to be parents or siblings.

In order to ascertain the need for the use of assistance by immigrants upon arrival, respondents were asked what types of assistance they had received as newcomers, and from whom. Interestingly, as indicated by Table 15, respondents were much more

Table 15
Sources of help received by Chinese immigrants upon arrival

Number and source of help	Chinese immigrants*		Totals for all groups in study	
	N	%	N	%
Help received upon arrival in Chicago	119	85.6	571	
Sources of help				
Spouses	73	59.8	229	36.8
Siblings or parents	16	13.1	111	17.8
Non family members	33	27.1	283	45.4
Totals	122	100.0	623	100.0

*Includes naturalized citizens who immigrated earlier.

likely to have received help from spouses and nonfamily members than from siblings and parents. In particular, a very large percentage of the Chinese respondents indicated the spouse as a source of help. This points to a pattern in which the spouse of the respondent immigrates first, and then sends for the respondent once a home is established, a job secured, etc. Conversely, compared to the other groups in the study, the Chinese were the least likely to receive help from non-family members. In this respect, it is possible that the respondents' spouses may have acted as channels for assistance from the family network.

Table 16 details the various kinds of assistance which the respondents received from non-family members upon immigrating. In most respects, the aid received by the Chinese respondents did not differ markedly from that received by members of other groups. There are, however, some differences. Chinese immigrants were much less likely to mention "emotional support and encouragement" as a form of help which they had received. It is possible that this may reflect cultural norms which militate against mentioning such matters. Alternatively, since the person giving such support in the case of a Chinese respondent is quite likely to be the person's spouse, from whom one would generally expect to receive emotional help, this type of assistance may not show up in an enumeration of assistance received from nonrelatives. Two categories which Chinese respondents were more likely than other groups to mention are "loan" and "helped me find a job." Given the relatively long average length of Chicago residence of the Chinese respondents, it may be that these sorts of assistance are ones which can be more readily provided by non-related persons who have become relatively well established in the community.

Overall, the Chinese, together with the Japanese, tended to have received fewer types of assistance, and from fewer sources, than had the Pilipinos and Koreans. This is probably due to the fact that the Japanese and, particularly, the Chinese, received most of their assistance from within the family (from spouses, parents, and siblings) rather than from outsiders. This might tend to narrow the range of types of assistance, as well as reducing the number of persons giving it.

The general types of problems associated with immigration which were encountered by the Chinese respondents are shown in Table 17. There are few differences between the problems perceived by the Chinese, and by the other groups studied. All (with the exception of the Pilipinos) found the language barrier to be quite severe. Conversely, none of the groups found any great problems in the area of food. In the Chicago area this is not likely to be a problem because the presence of sizeable ethnic enclaves tends to mean that ethnic food items are readily available. (Whether the immigrant pays a premium for "eating ethnic" rather than adapting to the American supermarket diet is another question

Table 16
Types of assistance received by immigrants from nonrelatives
upon arrival in Chicago

Types of assistance	Chinese immigrants*		Totals for all groups in study	
	N	%	N	%
Lodging (stayed with them)	22	21.8	229	26.4
Found a place to stay	16	15.8	122	14.1
Loan	12	11.9	54	6.2
Helped to find a job	23	22.8	113	13.0
Introduced me to others who could help	5	5.0	43	5.0
Emotional support, encouragement	5	5.0	125	14.4
Others	18	17.8	182	21.0
Total responses**	101	100.0	868	100.0

*Includes naturalized citizens.
**Respondents could give as many responses as they wished, but only the first two choices were counted for this table. Thus, total responses do not correspond with total respondents.

Changing Patterns, Changing Needs

Table 17
Problem areas associated with immigration by Chinese respondents,
by sex

Problem areas	Sex	Chinese immigrants		Totals for all groups in study	
		N	%	N	%
Language	M	55	82.1	228	74.3
	F	62	88.6	274	75.7
Homesickness	M	28	41.8	136	44.3
	F	33	47.1	231	63.8
Lack of ethnic person contacts	M	25	37.3	93	30.3
	F	28	40.0	115	31.8
Food differences	M	15	22.4	71	23.1
	F	16	22.9	83	22.9
Weather differences	M	30	45.5	139	45.3
	F	40	57.1	181	50.0
Life style/cultural	M	36	53.7	156	50.8
differences	F	45	65.2	174	48.1
Total of responses*	M	189			
	F	224			
Total eligible respondents		139			

*Includes naturalized citizens.

**Respondents could give more than one response to these questions. Therefore, the response total does not agree with the number of respondents.

entirely.) Likewise, lack of contact with fellow ethnic group members was not seen as a major problem, presumably because of the existence of sizeable ethnic populations in Chicago. However, it is important to note that a large population of the elderly respondents complained of loneliness and isolation. Life style and cultural differences were seen as somewhat problematical by all groups. About half of the Chinese respondents were bothered by the Chicago weather. In all problem categories, females reported more problems than males; in some instances this may indicate that the females have had greater difficulty in adjustment. This may result from their lower levels of education and English fluency, lower job levels, or a combination of these factors. It may also be considered more culturally acceptable for women to express their complaints, while tradition requires men to display a "stiff upper lip."

Because of the predominance of English communication difficulties, the respondents were asked if they had taken English conversation classes or lessons. Only 41.7% of the Chinese respondents had taken such classes or lessons; only the Pilipino group had a lower incidence in this respect and, as noted earlier, nearly all the Pilipino residents were claimed to be quite proficient in English already. The Chinese respondents combine a low rate of use of English classes with a low degree of self-evaluated fluency in English. While this study did not probe the availability of English classes for the Chinese relative to the other groups, lack of such classes as a factor in the low Chinese rate of usage can be inferred from the fact that such classes were listed by the Chinese respondents as a top service priority.

Very few respondents from any of the groups studied expressed regrets over their decision to immigrate or expressed an intention of returning to their home countries. As Table 18 shows, the two Chinese groups were slightly more contented in this respect than the other groups studied, although they showed a slightly greater bipolar tendency in this area. That is, while more Chinese expressed satisfaction or reserved satisfaction, their numbers at the other end of the scale were also slightly above average.

For all groups studied, however, a high overall level of expressed

Table 18
Evaluation of decision to emigrate in Chinese sample, by sex

	Sex	Chinese immigrants		U.S. citizens of Chinese descent*		Totals for all groups in study	
		N	%	N	%	N	%
Yes, definitely	M	29	60.4	14	73.7	176	57.5
	F	30	58.8	14	73.7	182	50.4
Yes, with	M	9	18.8	3	15.8	73	23.9
reservation	F	9	17.7	3	15.8	94	26.0
Uncertain	M	6	12.5	1	5.3	36	11.8
	F	6	11.8	2	10.5	63	17.5
Regrets	M	1	2.1	1	5.3	9	2.9
	F	4	7.8	—	—	12	3.3
Plan to	M	3	6.3	—	—	12	3.9
return	F	2	3.9	—	—	10	2.8
Totals	M	48	100.0	19	100.0	306	100.0
	F	51	100.0	19	100.0	361	100.0

*These are naturalized citizens who were asked immigration–related questions.

satisfaction with the decision to immigrate was the general rule. This finding should help to lay to rest the stereotype of Asian immigrants as "sojourners and adventurers," or as "unassimilable." Very few of the respondents have any intention of returning to their countries of origin. Among the more recently arrived groups (the Pilipinos, Koreans, and Chinese and Japanese immigrants) there seems to be some uncertainty, although in all cases strong majorities are to some degree satisfied with the decision to immigrate. Among the Chinese and Japanese citizen groups, there are a few uncertainties and some regrets, but no plans to return to the home country. Perhaps some aspects of assimilation and adjustment simply come about through time.

The immigration experience: Summary. The Chinese immigrant respondents in the study sample tended to have come to the United States for practical reasons; they sought better job opportunities and a better standard of living, or they came to join family members who had already immigrated. Upon arrival, these Chinese immigrants were quite likely to find relatives in the United States, and quite often these relatives were living in the Chicago area.

Compared to the other ethnic groups studied, the Chinese were much more likely to receive aid from spouses who were already residing in the United States, and much less likely to receive help from non family members. Where aid received from non family members is concerned, the Chinese were more likely than other groups to receive material aid such as loans or help in finding employment; they were less likely to perceive that they had received emotional support and encouragement. It is possible that moral support from non family members would be less important to the Chinese immigrants since a relatively large proportion are arriving to join a spouse who may already have made a partial adjustment to American life and thus may be the major source of such support and encouragement.

The problems encountered by the Chinese immigrants do not seem to be very different from those met by members of the other groups studied. It is of interest, however, that, while the Chinese immigrants reported somewhat greater difficulties with the language barrier, they were found to have made relatively little use of English classes or lessons, perhaps because this instruction is not readily available to them.

As was the case with the other groups studied, the Chinese immigrants were generally quite satisfied with their decision to emigrate to the United States. Like the Japanese respondents, the

Chinese were somewhat more positive and less ambivalent in this respect than were the more recently arrived immigrants in the other groups.

Problems and Problem-Solving Activities

Thus far in this chapter we have considered some of the factors which might be expected to contribute to the development of problems and, hence, of service needs among Chinese-Americans—demographic characteristics, education and employment, and the immigration experience. In this section we shall exame the survey results from those items which probed the respondents' perceptions of the problems they had actually encountered, and which explore their problem-solving activities and strategies.

Indirect approaches were used in this portion of the questionnaire since it was expected, on the basis of both informal observations and previous studies, that a certain amount of subject resistance might be encountered in response to direct questions about problems experienced by the respondent. Thus, each problem area was presented first in a hypothetical and then in an experiential context. That is, the respondents were asked to deal with problems in a "what if" situation before they were asked whether they had ever actually experienced the problem or engaged in the particular problem-solving activity. This also served to tap the problem-solving propensities of respondents who might not have encountered a particular problem personally. It should be noted that some tables in this section do not divide the Chinese sample into citizen and immigrant subgroups; in these instances the differences between the two were small.

At both the beginning and end of the interview, the respondents were asked to list those problem areas which they considered to be the most difficult for "a person of [the respondent's ethnic group] background living in Chicago." The answers to these open-ended questions from the whole study sample yielded 83 different problems which were then grouped into seven categories, as shown in Table 19.

All groups indicated a number of problems and concerns related to living in Chicago as Asian persons. Of the Chinese respondents, 19.1% either claimed to have no problems or declined to answer. This is a somewhat higher percentage than for the Korean (6.1%) or Pilipino (13.6%) groups, but less than that for the Japanese

Table 19
Problems related to living in Chicago cited by Chinese respondents

Problem areas	Chinese immigrants and citizens		Totals for all groups in study	
	N	%	N	%
Interpersonal and psychological adjustment	10	6.8	35	4.9
Language and cultural difference adjustment	73	69.7	305	42.3
Discrimination	9	6.1	111	15.4
Employment	4	2.7	40	5.6
City living stress	20	13.6	79	11.0
Ethnic community conflicts	3	2.0	35	4.9
No problems	28	19.1	116	16.1
Total	147	100.0	721	100.0

groups (32%). What is significant here is that in no case is the percentage particularly high: considering all groups together, less than one respondent in five failed to express some problem or other. This appears to be yet another area in which prevailing stereotypes of Asian Americans are not borne out by systematic observation.

In order to analyze problem perceptions on another dimension, socioeconomic indicators such as education, occupational levels, and income were crosstabulated with categories of perceived problems for all the groups in the study. None of the differences in problem perception reached the level of statistical significance. However, the general trends within each ethnic group support the assumption that persons with better jobs, higher educational levels, and more income perceive fewer personal and community problems than do persons at the other end of these socioeconomic scales. The types of problems perceived by the persons at the socioeconomic extremes also differ. It is only at the top end of the scale, for instance, that respondents cited such problems as identity conflicts, interpersonal problems, and concern over broad social issues; the lower socioeconomic groups were largely concerned with survival-related problems of finances and employment. In this respect, the Chinese respondents did not differ noticeably from the other groups studied. For that matter, one would expect that almost any population surveyed would show similar differences in problem perceptions from one socioeconomic level to another.

Table 20 shows the problems reported by the Chinese respondents as having been personally experienced. Of the seven problem categories, the Chinese respondents were somewhat more likely than other groups to indicate that they had actually experienced problems in the areas of language and cultural adjustment, and in obtaining medical services. These problem areas tally well with findings discussed previously. As we have noted, English proficiency among the Chinese seems to be lower than for the other groups studied; in addition to the direct problems caused by this deficiency, it might also contribute to the difficulty experienced in getting medical services. Since the Chinese sample is somewhat older than some of the other groups, they may also require more medical services. In part, the Chinese respondents may have difficulty obtaining medical services because of the general exodus of physicians to the suburbs; the sample group was from a definitely "inner city" area where medical facilities are scarce or inadequate. This shortage is reflected by the fact that, although 75.8% of the Chinese respondents reported that they had health insurance, only 29.5% had a personal physician. The respondents are trying to prepare for medical contingencies but the medical system is not cooperating. Finally, Chinese immigrants often express an aversion to western medical practices and a preference for types of medical treatment, such as herbalism, that are generally unavailable in the United States.

Table 20
Problems actually experienced by Chinese respondents*

Actual problems experienced	Chinese immigrants and Citizens		Totals for all groups in study	
	N	%	N	%
Insufficient income	44	29.5	255	22.5
Locating job	30	20.1	178	15.6
Problems on job	29	19.5	162	14.2
Getting medical service	34	22.8	94	8.2
Locating housing	27	18.1	122	10.7
Adjustment problems due to language and life style differences	70	47.0	254	22.3
Family conflict	15	10.1	71	6.2
Total responses	167		1136	

*Percentage in each cell was derived by dividing positive responses by the total respondents in each ethnic group on each question. Therefore the percentages in each column do not total 100%.

The frequency with which problems were reported indicates that Asian Americans do indeed encounter certain difficulties in coping with life in America. They may not advertise their problems, but this reticence should not—and obviously cannot— be interpreted to mean that they have no problems. The sample surveyed here may even underrepresent the true extent of problems within the Asian American community. The respondents are not necessarily heads of households; those who are not may be unaware of certain problem areas, both in the family and in the community. Among the Chinese respondents this was evidenced by the frequency with which elderly respondents answered "I don't know" to the questions concerning problem areas. As in the case of reporting family income, some of the answers may simply represent reticence, but in most cases do mean that the respondents are ignorant of the matter at hand because of their dependent position in the family.

Experiences of discrimination were disaggregated in the questionnaire in the interest of attempting to introduce some useful distinctions in an area where blanket terms are all too often used. Thus, discrimination in housing was separated from discrimination in employment. The latter category, in turn, was divided into two subareas: (1) losing a job, and (2) being passed over for promotion. Within each subarea, the respondent was asked to judge whether he or she "definitely," "probably," or "was not" discriminated against. The results are shown in Table 21. Of those who said they had not encountered job discrimination, 13.6% felt they had not had this problem because they were self-employed, while 40% felt it was because they worked for an employer from their own ethnic group.

With respect to discrimination, the figures for the Chinese groups do not differ dramatically from those for the other groups. As with all groups, few Chinese reported having actually lost a job through discrimination, but a fifth reported feeling that they had been passed over for promotion because of discrimination. In the area of housing, the Chinese citizen group reported a higher level of perceived discrimination than any other group except the Japanese citizens. The high rate for the Japanese citizens may result from difficulties in resettlement after the World War II period of internment.

When length of residence in the United States is crosstabulated with discrimination experience of all sorts, recent Chinese immigrants are found to have encountered more experiences of discri-

Table 21
Discrimination experienced by Chinese groups*

Discrimination areas	Chinese immigrants N	%	U.S. citizens of Chinese descent N	%	Totals for all groups in study N	%
Housing						
Yes, definitely	2	2.0	4	8.5	59	8.2
Yes, probably	6	6.0	4	8.5	29	4.0
Total	8	8.0	8	17.0	88	12.3
Lost job						
Yes, definitely	—	—	1	2.1	9	1.3
Yes probably	2	2.0	—	—	10	1.4
Total	2	2.0	1	2.1	19	2.7
Passed over for promotion						
Yes, definitely	12	12.0	6	12.8	81	11.3
Yes, probably	9	9.0	3	6.4	61	8.5
Total	21	21.0	9	19.1	142	19.8

*Percentage in each cell was derived by dividing responses with the total respondents in each ethnic group on each question. Thus percentage must be considered relative to total number of respondents in each ethnic group.

mination than have those who have been U.S. residents for longer periods of time. This pattern is the exact opposite of that found for the Japanese sample. Apparently, long-term Chinese residents have tended to take a fatalistic approach to discrimination, while the newcomers are more aware of the problem, or respond more strongly to it.

Knowing what problems people perceive to affect them is only part of the picture; it is also important to know how much information the respondents possess about the availability of resources which could help them with their problems, and the extent to which they use these resources. As in the case of problem perceptions and experiences, the survey questionnaire approached the problem situations first in a hypothetical and then in an experiential context. Respondents were asked how they would handle several hypothetical, "what if" problems. For example, they were asked, "where would you go if a physical accident occurred to you or a member of your family?" The answers to such questions indicate both knowledge of appropriate resources and preferences in choosing these resources.

For both medical emergencies and situations of mental illness, the responses of the Chinese groups followed the pattern for the other groups studied. Respondents showed a strong tendency to cite public rather than private sources of help in both of these types of hypothetical situations. That is, respondents either named a specific physician or hospital, or said they would go to "a doctor" or "the hospital" for help. Much higher proportions of the Chinese respondents failed to name a specific physician or hospital than was the case for the other groups. This may indicate a degree of uncertainty about the details of handling these situations. Also, the Chinese respondents were much more likely than other groups to reply that they did not know where to go: 9.4% did not know where to seek medical help (compared to an average of 2.9% for all groups studied), and 26.2% did not know where to go for help with mental illness (compared to 11.5% for all groups studied). The other alternatives chosen by the respondents (such as relatives, friends, ethnic religious organizations, and fire and police departments) all drew a low frequency of scattered responses.

When asked where they would turn for help in seeking a job, the majority of Chinese respondents (54.7%) said they would rely on friends who were members of their own ethnic group. This is far above the average of 19.1% for all groups studied. Classified ads and employment agencies were chosen less often by the Chinese respondents than by other groups, while relatives and self-reliance were just slightly less popular than with other groups. No Chinese respondent named an ethnic religious organization as a source of help in finding a job. This is not surprising, considering that few of the Chinese respondents were active church members. Here as elsewhere, somewhat more Chinese reported not knowing where to go for help (8.8% vs. 7.3% for all groups studied).

A third hypothetical problem presented to the respondents was, "where would you go for help if you were discriminated against, when applying for a job?" Here there were some differences between the Chinese immigrant and citizen groups. For instance, 18.4% of the citizen group, but only 3.0% of the immigrants, would seek help from a civil rights organization, a distinctly American institution which might well be unfamiliar to the immigrant respondents. Both of these figures are below the 25.0% of all groups studied who would seek help from this source. Only the Korean immigrant group showed a greater tendency to "give up" in the face of discrimination than the Chinese. Nearly half of the Chinese immigrants (48.0%) and citizens (48.9%) said they would give up in this case. As with all groups, a few Chinese respondents would turn to family, friends, ethnic organizations, or self-reliance, or denied that they would ever be discriminated against. All of these responses show low frequencies. However, 31.0% of the Chinese immigrants and 22.4% of the Chinese citizens said they would not know where to go for help. This is somewhat above the average of 18.5% for all groups in the study.

When the responses of the Chinese groups are crosstabulated with length of U.S. residency, it is clear that the longer the period of residence, the greater the tendency either to give up, or to not know where to seek help for job discrimination. This is of some interest since, again, the Japanese groups showed the opposite tendency, with longer residency leading to greater activism. It may be that the internment camp experience of World War II has impressed upon the older Japanese residents the need for taking quick and positive action when faced with discrimination. The resignation of the older Chinese residents may be the result of prolonged life under conditions of reduced expectations in the ethnic enclave. The idea of moving out of the enclave and engaging the American social system on equal terms is a relatively new one for most Chinese Americans.

Hypothetical questions dealing with discrimination in housing evoked response patterns very similar to those for job discrimination. Even larger percentages of Chinese immigrants (54%) and citizens (50%) said they would give up in the face of housing discrimination, while slightly fewer did not know where to go, compared to the case for job discrimination. However, these trends were observed in all groups in the study.

When confronted with financial problems, the Chinese groups would be more likely to depend on self-reliance, or seek help from ethnic friends or organizations, than would respondents in the other groups studied. On the other hand, they would be less likely than the other groups to rely on relatives, banks, or public aid. As in the case of the other hypothetical situations presented, more Chinese respondents (16.1%) did not know where to go for financial problems, than was the case for all groups studied (8.3%).

Another type of personal problem which may require problem-solving resources is marital difficulties. Again, the Chinese groups tended strongly toward self-reliance ("working it out by oneself"); only the Korean group was slightly more likely to choose this option. The Chinese respondents were less likely than other groups to turn to friends, marriage counselors or lawyers, or ministers or priests, or to resort to separation or divorce. They were slightly less likely to turn to family or relatives, but more likely to say that they would do nothing about marital problems, or had never thought about it, or would not know where to go. With the exception of self-reliance, the Chinese respondents seemed to present few active responses to the problem; however, the other groups studied all share this characteristic to some degree where marital difficulties are concerned.

Overall, the responses of the Chinese group to hypothetical problem situations show that, in a substantial number of instances, the respondents simply do not know where to turn. Whether this ignorance of potential resources arises from the inaccessibility of such resources, or from the lower educational and English proficiency level of the Chinese sample is moot. As in other areas, the relationship may be circular. In any case the important point is that the Chinese respondents do not know where to turn for help. Coupled with a tendency to give up or do nothing in the face of certain types of problems, this suggests that there may be a strong need for accessible, relevant, and bilingual services among the Chinese-American population.

While the respondents in the study reported a total of 1,136 problems actually experienced, they had sought help in solving these problems in only 357 instances (31.4%). These figures raise several questions which should be of interest to social service providers: why was help sought in so few instances, and, in those instances where help was sought, how do outside sources of help fit into the problem-solving strategies of the Asian-American respondents?

The numbers of problems encountered and the instances in which help was sought, are shown for the Chinese respondents in Table 22. There are few major differences between the respondents for the Chinese and for the other groups studied. One area where differences are apparent is that of family conflicts. While the Chinese reported having experienced such conflicts with about the same frequency as the other groups, no Chinese respondent reported having sought help for this problem. At the other extreme, over 30% of the Pilipino residents reported that they had sought help in dealing with family conflicts. It is possible that cultural factors account for the apparent reticence of the Chinese respondents in seeking help for problems within the family.

The only other areas in which the Chinese sought help with a frequency noticeably different from that of the other groups was

Table 22
Percentage of Chinese respondents seeking help in
each problem area experienced*

Problems experienced Help sought	Chinese immigrants and citizens		Totals for all groups in study	
	N	%	N	%
Insufficient income	44		255	
Help sought	15	31.0	88	34.3
Job location	30		178	
Help sought	9	30.0	84	47.8
On the job problems	29		162	
Help sought	11	38.0	50	30.8
Medical service	34		94	
Help sought	18	53.0	50	53.0
Locating housing	27		122	
Help sought	8	29.6	30	24.6
Adjustment to U.S.	70		254	
Help sought	15	21.4	46	19.0
Family conflicts	15		71	
Help sought	0	0.0	9	12.6
Total number of problems experienced	249		1136	
Total number in which help was sought	76	29.0	357	31.4

*Percentages in each cell are derived by dividing help sought responses by problems experienced in each problem area. Thus, percentages in each column do not sum to 100%.

in relation to finding a job, or in the event of on-the-job problems. The Chinese respondents were much less likely to have sought outside help in finding a job, but somewhat more likely than the Korean or Japanese to have sought help in dealing with on-the-job problems. Overall, the Chinese were slightly more inclined to seek outside help than were the Koreans, but less so than the Japanese or Pilipino group.

Two specific areas of problem-solving were analyzed; the first of these was the means by which the immigrant respondent obtained his or her first job in the United States. Table 23 shows the results for the Chinese immigrant respondents (including naturalized citizens). The Chinese immigrants show a strong tendency to rely on ethnic friends and organizations, and on family members and relatives. In this respect they are quite similar to the Japanese immigrants, and differ somewhat from the Pilipinos and Koreans, who,

Table 23
Resources cited for obtaining the first job in the
U.S. by Chinese immigrant respondents*

Sources of help	Chinese immigrants		Totals for all groups in study	
	N	%	N	%
Employment agencies, private and public	4	3.5	72	11.6
Classified ads	9	7.8	135	21.7
Professional organizations	3	2.6	10	1.6
Ethnic friends/organizations	53	45.7	216	34.7
Non ethnic friends	6	5.2	32	5.1
Family/relatives	33	28.4	85	13.7
Employment pre-arranged	8	6.9	72	11.6
Total responses**	116	100.0	622	100.0

*Includes naturalized citizens.
**Totals do not agree with total respondents because a respondent could give more than one response.

while still relying heavily on ethnic friends and organizations, tended to make more use of employment agencies and classified ads than of family and relatives. This difference is probably explained by the greater number of relatives and family members that the Chinese and Japanese immigrants find when they arrive in the United States. It is less easy to explain the low percentage of Chinese immigrants whose employment was pre-arranged, compared to the other groups. Because of their long experience, as a group, with U.S. immigration authorities, the Chinese respondents may have been more reluctant to reveal pre-arranged employment since this may, in fact, border on illegal contract labor.

In general, the Chinese immigrant newly arrived in the United States depends upon the informal network of family members, relatives, ethnic friends, and ethnic organizations to obtain a job. These are, of course, the resources which would be least likely to require either proficiency in English or the ability to deal with an alien sociocultural system. The lower job entry skills of the Chinese immigrants would tend to preclude reliance on professional organizations and would also make employment agencies less useful to the immigrants. Finally, many of the older Chinese immigrants came to the United States at a time when public resources were unwilling to serve members of conspicuous ethnic minorities; this may lower the overall figures for the Chinese groups in the area of usage of public resources.

The other problem area which was analyzed in detail was child care for children under the age of five when mothers are working. As Table 24 shows, there are some differences between the problem-solving activities of the Chinese immigrant and citizen groups and, in turn, between the Chinese groups and the other groups studied. Both Chinese groups proved to rely much more heavily on relatives than did any of the other groups. This probably results from the large, extended-family households which are characteristic of the Chinese sample. Curiously, the Chinese immigrants are much more likely to rely on neighbors than are the citizens, perhaps out of necessity. On the other hand, the citizens are more likely to rely on the other spouse. This apparently indicates that more citizen than immigrant families have mothers who work outside the home and fathers who are available to care for a young child. Perhaps this situation arises because of the large number of proprietors among the Chinese citizen group. In common with the other groups in the study, the Chinese respondents seem little inclined to rely on day care centers.

Since one of the major reasons for conducting this study was to discover what factors prevent Asian Americans from using available resources, those respondents who did not seek help when they had problems were examined separately (see Table 25). In all groups, the major reasons given for not seeking help were: (1) problems can be solved individually, or within the family; (2)

Table 24
Child care for children under five in Chinese groups
when mothers work

Type of care	Chinese immigrants N	Chinese immigrants %	U.S. citizens of Chinese descent N	U.S. citizens of Chinese descent %	Totals for all groups in study N	Totals for all groups in study %
Relatives	6	40.0	5	53.6	57	29.2
Neighbors	6	40.0	—	—	47	24.1
Day care centers	—	—	—	—	14	7.2
Spouse	2	13.3	4	44.4	70	35.9
Other	1	6.7	—	—	7	3.6
Totals	15	100.0	9	100.0	195	100.0

Changing Patterns, Changing Needs

Table 25
Reasons cited by Chinese groups for not seeking help, by sex*

Reasons for not seeking help	Sex	Chinese immigrants N	%	U.S. citizens of Chinese descent N	%	Totals for all groups in study N	%
No problems or not	M	14	21.9	11	42.3	104	30.1
serios enough	F	12	18.5	8	28.6	136	34.3
Solve by self	M	18	28.1	7	26.9	134	38.7
or with family	F	11	16.9	6	21.4	123	31.0
Organization	M	5	7.8	3	11.5	33	9.5
can't help	F	4	6.2	1	3.6	18	4.5
Didn't want	M	—	—	1	3.9	12	3.5
others to know	F	1	1.5	1	3.6	11	2.8
Language	M	8	12.5	—	—	11	3.2
barrier	F	11	16.9	5	17.9	34	8.6
Did not know	M	19	29.7	4	15.4	51	14.7
where to go	F	26	40.0	7	25.0	75	18.9
Total responses	M	64	100.0	26	100.0	345	
	F	65	100.0	28	100.0	397	

*This question was asked only of those respondents who did not seek help. Also, these respondents could give more than one response to this question. Thus the totals in the two bottom lines do not represent totals of respondents responding to this question.

problems are not serious enough to require outside help; and (3) respondents are ignorant of available resources. For the Chinese groups, lack of communication skills in English was a particularly important factor in preventing use of resources. Also, as noted earlier, the Chinese respondents are particularly likely not to know where to go for help; only the Korean immigrants approached the level of "did not know where to go" responses shown by the Chinese groups.

Compared to the other groups, the Chinese did not show a particularly high incidence of "no problem" responses. However, when the categories of "did not know where to go" and language barrier" are combined, they account for very nearly half (49.6%) of the instances in which Chinese immigrants did not seek help, and for 30.1% of such instances among the Chinese citizens. These levels are much higher than for the other groups studied; only the Korean immigrants (23.7%) approached it. This finding is consistent with the level of English fluency and the stance toward problem-solving previously noted for the Chinese groups.

All respondents in both the "no problem" and "did not know where to go" categories were examined in terms of demographic variables such as sex, age, marital status, length of U.S. residence, and job level. The only general trend which developed from this analysis is that persons at the upper end of the job scale (professional persons) tend more often to fall in the "no problem" category, while those at the lower end (clerical, unskilled labor) tend to be more likely not to know where to go.

Problem-solving activities: Summary. In brief, those Chinese respondents who do tend to seek help when they have problems tend to rely heavily on personal, intrafamily and intraethnic resources. Those who do not seek assistance tend not to do so because they either do not know where to go, or do not have the English proficiency necessary to seek help from the public, English-speaking resources in the community. This is a strong indication that bilingual services may be essential to increasing the utilization of resources by the Chinese-American community, and that such services, when provided, must be publicized to the service population through media which reach the ethnic community.

Service Characteristics and Priorities

The most direct way to determine what services respondents consider important is simply to ask them to rate a list of services on a rating scale. An indirect benefit of this sort of item is that it may reveal what problems have been experienced by the respondents. In this study, survey respondents were shown a list of eight different services and asked to rate them on a three point scale: Very Important, Somewhat Important, or Not Important.

As Table 26 shows, there are some discrepancies between service priorities as determined by this item, and as revealed by the other items on problems and problem-solving activities. The largest discrepancy was on the item "legal aid service," which was rated important by 60.8% of the Chinese respondents (and by 58.8% of all respondents). This certainly indicates a clear *desire* for such service, but no such need for legal aid services was revealed in the other items on the questionnaire; the respondents simply did not indicate that they had any problems of a legal nature. Perhaps the desire for legal aid services reflects the respondents' sense of powerlessness in the face of the American socio-economic system, with its heavily legalistic underpinnings.

The Chinese, alone of all groups studied, more often rated bi-

Table 26
Services considered important by Chinese respondents*

Types of services	Rank Order	N	Chinese immigrants and citizens %
Child care centers	6	62	41.6
English conversation classes	2	94	63.1
Mental health services	7	50	33.8
Employment services	4	83	55.7
Vocational training	5	80	55.7
Public aid	3	90	60.4
Bilingual referral services	1	105	70.5
Legal aid services	3	90	60.8
Total responses		654	

*Percentages in each cell were derived in relation to total respondents in each ethnic group. Therefore, percentages within columns do not sum to 100%.

lingual referral and newcomers' services and English conversation classes ahead of legal aid services. These responses agree with the low level of English proficiency reported by these groups. Bilingual referral and newcomers' services are also important considering the number of Chinese respondents who did not know where to go for services and assistance resources.

Interestingly, over half of the Chinese respondents considered employment services and vocational training to be important. Other items in the survey have indicated that, in reality, relatively few Chinese use (or say they would use) employment services when seeking a job; perhaps they would like to do so, but do not because such services are usually monolingual (English) and may be located outside the ethnic neighborhoods. By the same token, few Chinese immigrants reported that they came to the United States with job training opportunities in mind. Thus the importance which the Chinese assigned to vocational training may reflect their experience with the hard realities faced by members of a visible minority in the U.S. job market, or may show their desire for upward mobility.

The underlying level of service needs among the Chinese respondents may be reflected by the fact that they rated a larger number of services as "important" than other groups did. Given the rather modest educational, social, and economic status of the Chinese groups it seems logical that they would need more social services than other groups. In this connection, it should be noted that the Chinese gave by far the highest rating of importance to "public aid" of any group studied. On the other hand, in the hypothetical problem items on the questionnaire the Chinese almost never indicated public aid as a potential resource for solving financial difficulties. This sharp discrepancy should perhaps be taken as a warning that the relationship between a group's consciously-perceived service needs and its unconscious problem-solving strategies may not always be simple and direct. The fact that a service is available may sometimes be less important to a potential user than the characteristics of the service and the way it is delivered to the user. For instance, the presence of, say, an employment service in a community may not actually make that service available to a potential user whose English proficiency is low, unless the service is delivered by a bilingual staff. Likewise, it is important that the service be delivered in a manner acceptable to the client.

Because of the importance of delivery style in the utilization of services, the respondents were asked to rank five service characteristics in order of importance, numbering them from one to five. As Table 27 shows, the two characteristics which the respondents considered most important are "helpfulness of staff" and "bilingual staff." Again, the lower level of English proficiency among the Chinese groups is reflected by the fact that they, alone of all groups studied, rated "bilingual staff" ahead of "helpfulness of staff." The importance assigned by the Chinese to the other ser-

Table 27
Service characteristics considered important
by the Chinese respondents

Service characteristic	Chinese immigrants		Citizens of Chinese descent		Totals for all groups in study	
	N	%	N	%	N	%
Bilingual staff	54	54.5	22	44.9	201	28.1
Helpfulness of staff	31	31.3	16	32.6	334	46.6
Convenient access to agencies	6	6.0	6	12.2	73	10.2
Confidentiality	6	6.0	3	6.1	60	8.3
Service fee	2	2.0	2	4.1	48	6.7
Totals	99	99.8	49	99.9	716	99.9

vice characteristics did not differ markedly from that assigned by the other groups in the study.

The Chinese Respondent Groups: A Profile Summary

The danger in rendering a profile of a group is that it may stray across the invisible boundary that separates profiles from the realm of stereotype. When a profile is presented it is important to remember that, with respect to any particular feature of the profile, a large portion of the sample may differ in some degree on that feature. With this caution in mind, the following general profile of the Chinese respondent groups in this study may prove useful. For the purposes of the profile, the immigrant and citizen groups are combined, except where noted.

The typical Chinese respondent in this study is middle-aged (early forties), was born outside the United States (most likely in a large city), and has lived in the United States longer than six years, with almost the whole time of residence being spent in Chicago. He came to the United States for practical reasons: to get a better job, enjoy a higher standard of living, join other family members who had already immigrated, or to escape the political situation of his home country. When he arrived in the United States he found an existing network of family members and relatives, but probably received most of the initial help he needed from a spouse who had immigrated first. He probably got his first job in America with the aid of ethnic friends or organizations, or through family members or relatives.

Our hypothetical respondent probably did not bring a background of higher education or advanced degrees with him from his home country, nor has he pursued additional formal education since coming to the United States. If he is foreign-born, he is twice as likely to have received his education in his home country, rather than in the U.S. His level of English proficiency is low to moderate: he can probably understand English but not speak it fluently. There is a less than even chance that he has taken a course or lessons in English. In his household he generally speaks Chinese. This household is likely to include about six people, all of whom are related to the respondent. He probably lives in a house which he owns, or an apartment which he rents. He is quite likely to be married and if he has children they are probably in grade school or high school.

This Chinese respondent is not affluent, nor does his employment bring him much social prestige. It is almost certain that he is not a professional person, and he probably works in a job somewhere between the middle and the bottom of the job level scale. On the other hand, he is not likely to be unemployed. This is probably the only job he holds, although it is quite possible that his spouse works as well. The respondent's total family income hovers around $10,000 per year—slightly below if he is an immigrant and slightly above if he is a citizen. There is a chance that he may be self-employed as the owner of a small business, but this will not be a guarantee that his family income will be above average for his group. If he is an immigrant, he probably feels that his salary equals or exceeds his needs. If he is a citizen, however, there is a fair chance that he considers his income to be inadequate.

When this respondent thinks over the problems he has encountered, he probably finds that his biggest problem has been adjustment to life in America, due to the differences in language and lifestyle. Insufficient income has been a moderate problem, as has obtaining medical service and finding a job. In general, he probably does not feel that he has been discriminated against in employment or housing, although this is partly as a result of living and working in an ethnic enclave. If he has suffered discrimination, it was probably in the form of being passed over for promotion in his job.

When faced with new and different problem situations, this Chinese respondent may not know excatly where to turn for help: he may not have a clear idea of *which* hospital or doctor to turn to in case of a medical or psychiatric emergency. When seeking a job he will probably limit his efforts to the circle of relatives and ethnic friends. If he encounters discrimination when seeking housing or a job, he will probably give up and look for another job or another house, or he may want to take action but not know where to turn. If he is in financial difficulties, he will tend to turn to sources of help within the circle of relatives and ethnic friends; he is not likely to seek outside help from banks, unemployment compensation, or public aid. There is also a fair chance that he will not know where to turn. When he must obtain child care for his young children, he will shun day care centers in favor of relatives, neighbors, or a spouse who works at home or is otherwise available. For marital problems he is very unlikely to seek outside help, although, again, he may simply not know where to go.

With the exception of medical problems, there is a good

chance—on the order of two to one—that the Chinese respondent will not seek help when he does encounter problems. He may feel that he can handle the problems without outside help, but it is also quite possible that he either does not know where to seek help, or cannot seek help because his limited English proficiency prevents him from dealing with the service delivery system.

In a very important sense, the Chinese respondent knows what his major service needs are: English converstaion classes, employment and job training services, and bilingual referral and newcomers' services are all important to him. Thus he appears to be aware that he has problems in two general areas: perennially low socioeconomic status as a result of lack of education and marketable skills, coupled with past discrimination; and a low level of English proficiency which compounds his socioeconomic problems and makes it even harder for him to locate and utilize the services he needs.

Whether or not this Chinese respondent would utilize such services if they were made available to him is, of course, an unanswerable question. But he is quite definite about two characteristics that such services must have if they are to appeal to him: they must be staffed with bilingual persons, and the staff must proceed in a spirit of helpfulness. It is about equally clear from the data that he either does not know about or does not utilize existing service resources. And it is quite likely that he does not do so because these resources lack the qualities he feels they should have.

NOTES TO CHAPTER IV

1. T.C. Fan, *Chinese Residents in Chicago*, Chicago: University of Chicago, Thesis, 1976. Reprinted, San Francisco: R and E, 1974, Table 1. The 1920 census enumerated 2,353 Chinese residents in Chicago, the majority of whom appear to have settled there after 1900. Even at this early date, Asian-American researchers suspected that the census undercounted ethnic populations. Fan (pp. 18-24) obtained estimates from several sources in the Chicago Chinese community which placed the total number of Chinese residents at between 4,500 and 6,000 or approximately twice the figure reported by the census. It should be noted that Fan's figures are for 1926, the census for 1920; still the discrepancy is quite large.

2. B.L. Sung. *Mountain of Gold*, New York: MacMillan, 1967. Reissued as

Story of The Chinese in America, New York: Collier Books, 1971, 115-118, Figure 8-13. In 1890, Chinese males in the U.S. outnumbered Chinese females by no less than 27 to 1.

3. C.B. Keely, "Effects of the Immigration Act of 1965 on selected population characteristics of immigrants to the United States," *Demography*, 8 (2) :157-169, (1971).

4. There is some evidence that Chinese respondents may tend to under-report their income. For persons who are proprietors of small businesses, actual income is often a nebulous figure, and it should be remembered that the present Chinese sample contains a large proportion of proprietors. Among older Chinese Americans in particular, underreporting of income may simply be another part of the effort to maintain a "low profile" as a survival tactic.

5. Again, the relatively low job levels of the respondents' parents may be indicative of traditionally lower educational levels among the Chicago Chinese group.

CHAPTER V

THE JAPANESE SAMPLE

The Japanese sample in this study consisted of 100 Japanese immigrants and 50 citizens of Japanese descent, both American-born and naturalized. In this respect the Japanese sample bears a superficial resemblance to the Chinese sample in the study; in most substantive areas, however, there are marked differences in the characteristics, needs, and attitudes of the Japanese respondents, compared to both the Chinese groups and the Pilipino and Korean immigrant groups.

Demographic Characteristics

With a median age of 47 years, the Japanese groups were the oldest in the study, with the citizens averaging about five years older than the immigrants. As can be seen in Table 28, the majority of respondents in both Japanese groups are 41 years of age or older, with the citizens being concentrated in the ages between 41 and 65 and the immigrants showing a strong concentration in the over-65 category. These elderly immigrants may well represent aged Issei, remnants of the earlier period of extensive Japanese immigration. According to the 1970 census figures for the state of Illinois, only 7.4% of the state's Japanese population was over 65 years of age, compared to 21.6% in the study. Thus the present sample appears to overrepresent the aged. This may be a result of the area sampled (urban Chicago), or may simply indicate that the survey

Table 28
Ages of respondents and spouses of Japanese sample, by sex

Age	Sex	Japanese immigrants		Japanese citizens		Totals for all groups studied	
		N	%	N	%	N	%
18–30	M	7	19.4	2	6.3	60	17.8
	F	10	16.1	4	22.2	137	36.0
31–40	M	10	27.8	3	9.4	157	46.5
	F	14	22.6	–	–	119	31.2
41–50	M	5	13.9	8	25.0	57	16.9
	F	18	29.0	5	27.8	50	13.1
51–65	M	3	8.3	14	43.8	40	11.8
	F	6	9.7	7	38.9	44	11.6
65 and over	M	11	30.6	5	15.6	24	7.1
	F	14	22.6	2	11.1	31	8.1
Total	M	36	100	32	100	338	100
	F	62	100	18	100	381	100
Mean		45.88		50.06			
Standard deviation		15.84		12.62			

was more effective than the census in reaching elderly Japanese residents.

The sex distribution of the Japanese groups is quite irregular: almost two-thirds of the immigrants are female, while two-thirds of the citizens are male. These findings agree with historical trends in the Japanese-American population. Until 1960, males outnumbered females in all Asian groups for every census count. In 1960, for the first time, Japanese-American women outnumbered men. This is primarily due to the immigration of Japanese women who married American servicemen during the U.S. occupation of Japan after World War II. The 1970 census reports a 46% to 54% ratio of males to females among Japanese Americans nationally. The greater female immigration among the Japanese in recent years is a trend shared with the other groups in this study.

As with the other groups studied, a large proportion of the Japanese respondents are married and living with their spouses (67% of the immigrants and 76% of the citizens). These figures, are, however, lower than the 86% reported for Japanese Americans nationally in the 1970 census. Since the rates for separation and divorce in the sample are consistent with national norms, the sample must contain a larger proportion of unmarried adults than were included in the census. Such persons, particularly if they are elderly and living alone, may easily be overlooked by the census collection procedures.

Table 29
Number of children living at home, by age, in Japanese sample

Ages	Japanese immigrants		U.S. citizens of Japanese descent		Totals for all groups studied	
	N	%	N	%	N	%
Under 5	19	22.3	8	14.0	265	30.8
5–9	17	20.0	5	8.8	219	25.5
10–14	13	15.3	10	17.5	122	14.2
15–19	10	11.8	22	38.6	108	12.6
20–24	10	11.8	9	15.8	74	8.6
25–34	2	2.3	2	3.5	36	4.2
35 and over	14	16.5	1	1.8	36	4.2
Totals	85	100.0	57	100.0	860	100.0

As might be expected for a group with a median age in the late forties, the Japanese respondents had relatively few young children at home. The preponderance of Japanese children, as shown in Table 29, fall in an age grouping which extends roughly from junior high school to college age. Overall, the immigrants had somewhat more young children than the citizens, but also had fewer children per household, on the average (.85 versus 1.04).

This small average number of children in the Japanese households is also reflected in the overall size of the households, which were the smallest of any group studied. No Japanese household surveyed had more than eight members, and 98% had six or fewer. As Table 30 shows, the bulk of the Japanese households are concentrated around the two to four person range, with the citizen households tending to be slightly larger than those of the immigrant respondents.

Table 30
Household size for Japanese sample

Household size	Japanese immigrants		U.S. citizens of Japanese descent		Totals for all groups studied	
	N	%	N	%	N	%
1	13	13.0	5	10.0	52	7.2
2	33	33.0	13	26.0	111	15.3
3–4	40	40.0	17	34.0	317	43.7
5–6	13	13.0	14	28.0	179	24.7
7–10	1	1.0	1	2.0	58	8.0
11 and over	–	–	–	–	9	1.2
Total	100	100.0	50	100.0	726	100.0

Table 31
Housing accomodations for Japanese sample

	Japanese immigrants		U.S. citizens of Japanese descent		Totals for all groups studied	
	N	%	N	%	N	%
Own house	19	19.0	15	30.0	123	17.0
Rent house	2	2.0	–	–	35	4.8
Own apartment	13	13.0	8	16.0	44	6.1
Rent apartment	63	63.0	24	48.0	489	67.5
Other	3	3.0	3	6.0	33	4.6
Total	100	100.0	50	100.0	724	100.0

The housing accomodations reported for these relatively small Japanese households did not differ greatly from those reported by the other groups in the study. Like the Chinese citizens, the Japanese citizens tend to own houses more often than their immigrant counterparts. Interestingly, both Japanese groups show a relatively high percentage of persons who own their own apartments (see Table 31). This may simply reflect the particular economic level and length of U.S. residence of the Japanese sample, relative to the other groups studied. House rental is even less popular among the Japanese than among the other groups studied, perhaps reflecting the small size of the households.

The predominant religious preference of the Japanese respondents is Buddhist, which accounts for 48% of both groups. Protestant is the second choice (24% of the immigrants and 34% of the citizens), followed by no preference (20% of the immigrants and 12% of the citizens), and Catholic (4% of both groups). Among the Japanese there is a uniform spread in the church attendance pattern, with similar numbers of persons in each category from "once a week" to "never." Thus the Japanese preference and attendance patterns fall somewhere between those of the Pilipino and Korean groups (at the extreme of greater religious involvement), and the Chinese groups, which are more likely to express no religious preference, or to express a preference without accompanying regular attendance.

When it comes to membership in organizations, the Japanese respondents differ only slightly from the other groups. Only half as many Japanese as Chinese respondents belong to no organization at all. Overall, the Japanese respondents are more evenly distributed in the various categories of numbers of memberships. This is particularly true of the Japanese citizens, appreciable numbers of whom belong to anywhere from three to ten organizations. This may be due to the relatively large number of well-established Japanese ethnic organizations in the Chicago area or, conversely, it may be that the organizations thrive because of an enthusiastic membership. The Japanese immigrants belong to fewer organizations, the majority to only one. However, one Japanese immigrant respondent holds the distinction of belonging to more organizations—12—than any other respondent in the study. On the basis of organizational figures, it appears that Japanese Americans might be contacted more readily through ethnic organizations than could other Asian-American groups, at least in the Chicago area. In absolute terms, however, even the Japanese respondents do not seem to be avid joiners.

The English proficiency level of the Japanese respondents was relatively high, particularly in the citizen group. There were no Japanese citizen respondents who did not at least understand spoken English and 80% of the interviews with this group were conducted in English. Among the Japanese immigrants the proficiency level was lower, but not markedly so. (It was still higher than the proficiency level of the Chinese citizen group, for instance.) However, it should be noted that a fourth of the Japanese immigrant females who were interviewed in Japanese said they had no comprehension of English, compared to only 3.4% of the immigrant males. In this respect the fluency pattern of the Japanese immigrants is similar to that of the Korean immigrants and both Chinese groups. Overall, the percentage of Japanese immigrants interviewed in English (16%) is not significantly different from the corresponding figure for the Chinese immigrants (17%).

A large proportion of the Japanese citizen group (84%) were born in the United States. This fact may account for the higher level of English proficiency among this group than among the Chinese citizens, of whom only 29% were U.S. born. As shown in Table 32, fairly large proportions of the Japanese respondents—immigrant and citizen alike—come from farm, village, or small city backgrounds. For the immigrants, this reflects patterns of immigration from Japan: most immigrants have come from the rural areas and small towns. For the Japanese citizens, these origins may reflect the transplantation brought about by the forced internment during World War II. Many Japanese Americans who were interned had previously been engaged in farming in California. While it is not known how many of these persons subse-

Table 32
Birthplace and early community background of Japanese sample

	Japanese immigrants		U.S. citizens of Japanese descent		Totals for all groups studied	
	N	%	N	%	N	%
Birth place						
U.S.A.	—	—	42	84.0	52	7.2
Mainland China	6	6.0	—	—	130	17.9
Hong Kong	—	—	—	—	4	0.6
Taiwan	1	1.0	—	—	9	1.2
Japan	93	93.0	8	16.0	109	15.0
Korea	—	—	—	—	218	30.0
Philippines	—	—	—	—	199	27.4
Other	—	—	—	—	5	
Totals	100	100.0	50	100.0	726	100.0
Community size						
Farm, village	34	34.0	14	28.0	147	20.7
Under ½ million	30	30.0	15	30.0	185	26.1
½ to 1 million	8	8.0	4	8.0	61	8.6
Over 1 million	28	28.0	17	34	317	44.7
Totals	100	100.0	50	100.0	710	100.0

quently settled in the Chicago area, it may be assumed that they account for at least part of the citizen sample under consideration here.

There is some evidence to support the assumption that part of the Japanese citizen sample has resettled in Chicago from other parts of the United States. As Figure 2 shows, there is a resettlement of Japanese citizens at some point more than 20 years ago. No other group studied shows such a pattern. Instead, the other groups show a pattern of immediate settlement in the Chicago area, either from birth or upon arriving in the United States.

Demographic summary. The Japanese respondents in this study are older than the other groups surveyed, have fewer young children—and fewer children generally—and tend to live in relatively small households. They are more likely than the other groups to live in houses or apartments which they own. The Japanese respondents seem to have more religious ties than the Chinese, and somewhat more organizational ties than the other groups studied, although many belong to only one organization. The

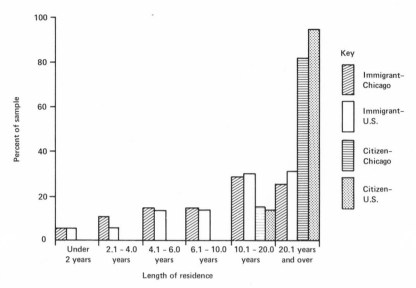

Figure 2. Length of residence in Chicago and the United States by Japanese immigrant and citizen groups

English proficiency level of the Japanese citizen group was quite high, and among the Japanese immigrant groups there are few persons who do not at least understand spoken English. The origins of the Japanese groups are more rural than those of the other groups in the study, and most of the citizens are U.S. born, rather than naturalized as was the case with the Chinese. The migration history of the Japanese citizens points to large-scale resettlement in the Chicago area after the end of World War II.

Education, Employment, and Income Characteristics

The educational level of the Japanese sample fell near the middle of the range for all persons in the study: the Pilipino and Korean group had somewhat higher medians, and the Chinese groups were somewhat lower. These intergroup differences may reflect the particular nature of the study sample. For example, the 1970 census indicates that more Chinese than Japanese Americans have four or more years of college (25% versus 19%). In the present study, these figures are more than reversed, indicating that, in terms of educational level, the Chicago Japanese and Chinese communities may be somewhat atypical of the general U.S. population of these groups. This may be a result of migration from the city to the suburbs. It should be remembered that the citizen sample of the study was selected entirely from the ethnic neighborhoods within the city of Chicago. As in the case of any group, the most successful members have a tendency to move to the suburbs. Hence, a sample from an inner city ethnic neighborhood may tend to contain a disproportionate number of the less successful members of the group. In turn, it is quite likely that these persons will have lower educational levels than those who have moved to the suburbs.

As in the case of the female Chinese respondents, the Japanese females (particularly in the immigrant group) showed markedly lower educational levels than the males. As Table 33 shows, there is a sharp cutoff for females approximately at the level of high

Table 33
Highest educational levels achieved by respondents
and spouses in Japanese sample, by sex

Educational levels	Sex	Japanese immigrants N	%	U.S. citizens of Japanese descent N	%	Totals for all groups studied N	%
Elementary	M	—	—	—	—	25	5.3
or under	F	6	17.7	—	—	45	11.0
High school graduate	M	13	32.5	1	20.0	82	17.3
or under	F	18	52.9	2	66.7	72	17.5
High school and beyond	M	10	25.0	2	40.0	56	11.8
	F	2	5.9	1	33.3	45	11.0
College graduate	M	10	25.0	1	20.0	234	49.4
	F	6	17.7	—	—	201	48.9
Nursing	M	—	—	—	—	—	—
	F	—	—	—	—	16	3.9
MS and PhD	M	4	10.0	—	—	48	10.1
	F	1	2.9	—	—	13	3.2
MD and dental	M	2	5.0	—	—	12	2.5
	F	—	—	—	—	1	0.2
Post MD and	M	1	2.5	1	20.0	17	3.6
PhD	F	1	2.9	—	—	18	4.4
Totals*	M	40	100.0	5	100.0	474	100.0
	F	34	100.0	3	100.0	411	100.0

*These totals include respondents and their spouses. Therefore, they do not correspond to sample size.

Table 34
Employment status of Japanese respondents and spouses, by sex

Employment status	Sex	Japanese immigrants N	%	Japanese citizens N	%	Totals for all groups studied N	%
Full–time	M	61	76.3	31	70.5	505	82.1
	F	29	34.1	22	50.0	393	59.1
Part–time	M	4	5.0	1	2.3	19	3.1
	F	10	11.8	4	9.1	36	5.4
More than	M	4	5.0	5	11.4	38	6.2
one job	F	2	2.4	—	—	17	2.6
Unemployed,	M	—	—	1	2.3	5	0.8
sick, disabled	F	1	1.2	—	—	6	0.9
Retired	M	10	12.5	4	9.1	26	4.2
	F	8	9.4	—	—	16	2.4
Unemployed,	M	—	—	2	4.6	8	1.3
seeking job	F	1	1.2	—	—	17	2.6
Unemployed,	M	1	1.3	—	—	9	1.5
not seeking	F	—	—	—	—	14	2.1
jobs							
Homemaker	M	—	—	—	—	3	0.5
	F	31	36.5	16	36.4	120	18.1
Never	M	—	—	—	—	2	0.3
employed	F	3	3.5	2	4.6	46	6.9
Totals*	M	80	100.0	44	100.0	615	100.0
	F	85	100.0	44	100.0	665	100.0

*Totals include respondents and their spouses. Therefore, they do not correspond to sample size.

school graduation. This finding agrees with national trends: between 1960 and 1970, the proportion of Japanese-American women with college educations increased only 4%.

The Japanese respondents indicated levels of full-time employment comparable to those of other groups (see Table 34), although there are a few notable differences. Japanese immigrant females showed the lowest rate of full-time employment of any group surveyed, while Japanese citizen females were the third lowest in this respect. Instead, the Japanese women are more likely to be homemakers, part-time workers, or retired. Both sexes of Japanese immigrants, together with Japanese citizen males, showed large percentages of retirees, compared to the other groups studied. This would be expected, in view of the greater median age of the Japanese sample. As with the other groups studied, few Japanese reported that they were unemployed and seeking work, although the Japanese citizen males did show the highest unemployment rate for any of the Asian-American groups (4.6%). For the Japanese, as for the other groups studied, underemployment is more likely to be a problem than unemployment.

As Table 35 shows, the Japanese males tend to be concentrated near the middle of the scale of job categories, with the females somewhat lower down. In particular, over half of the immigrant females are employed at semi- and unskilled jobs. In common with the Chinese, the Japanese show relatively few persons in professional or managerial positions and, also like the Chinese, the immigrants are more likely to be professionals, while the citizens tend to be the managers. This is to be expected, given the conditions which send many Asian professionals to America in search of suitable positions. It is of interest, however, that there are fewer professionals among the Japanese immigrants than among any other immigrant group in the study. This may indicate that the highly industrialized Japanese economy is better able to absorb the professional output of its educational system than is the case for other Asian countries.

Table 35
Occupational categories of Japanese respondents and spouses, by sex

Job categories	Sex	Japanese immigrants N	Japanese immigrants %	U.S. citizens of Japanese descent N	U.S. citizens of Japanese descent %	Totals for all groups studied N	Totals for all groups studied %
Professional	M	14	20.3	5	13.2	159	27.7
	F	3	7.1	1	3.7	143	31.5
Managerial	M	2	2.9	6	15.8	23	4.0
	F	2	4.8	3	11.1	9	2.0
Proprietor	M	6	8.7	6	15.8	61	10.6
	F	1	2.4	1	3.7	11	2.4
Skilled and	M	27	39.1	17	44.7	232	40.4
white collar	F	14	33.3	14	51.9	164	36.1
Semi– and	M	20	29.0	4	10.5	99	17.3
unskilled	F	22	52.4	8	29.6	127	28.0
Totals*	M	69	100.0	38	100.0	574	100.0
	F	42	100.0	27	100.0	454	100.0

*Totals include respondents and their spouses. Therefore, they do not correspond to sample size.

A comparison of job levels before and after immigration indicates that among Japanese immigrants there has been a decrease of 4.3% in the proportion of persons holding professional positions, and a 12.7% increase in the proportion of those in semi- and unskilled jobs. These figures suggest an overall shift in the job spectrum in the direction of moderate downward mobility. The shift is not nearly so severe as in the case of the Korean immigrants, for example, but does indicate that underemployment may be a reality among the Japanese immigrants, as among the other groups in the study.

Overall, the Japanese groups expressed a relatively high level of job interest and job satisfaction compared to the other groups in the study. Although the length of time on present job varied widely within the Japanese and Chinese groups, a larger proportion of Japanese had held their jobs for long periods. (Both the Japanese and Chinese groups had longer job tenures than the more recently arrived Korean and Pilipino groups, for obvious reasons.) Furthermore, when asked why they intended to remain on their present jobs, the Japanese were more likely than the Chinese to give reasons which reflected employment satisfaction rather than expediency. In particular, the Japanese were much more likely than any other group to give "job interest" as a reason (26.3% of immigrants and 35.7% of citizens). On the other hand, it should be noted that a fairly high proportion of the Japanese immigrants (17.1%) stated that the present job was "the best I could get under the circumstances." In this respect the Japanese immigrants resemble their Korean and Chinese counterparts. In all such cases, a measure of job dissatisfaction (and, possibly, underemployment) is indicated.

Japanese immigrant respondents in this study reported median family incomes of $16,111, which is just slightly below the figures reported for the Korean and Pilipino immigrants. The citizen Japanese, on the other hand, reported a median income of $18,636, the highest for any group studied. By way of extreme comparison, it should be remembered that the median incomes reported by the Chinese groups were $10,286 for immigrants and $13,170 for citizens.

Table 36 shows the distribution of reported incomes for the Japanese respondent groups. Although there are quite a few Japanese in the higher income brackets, they are not quite so numerous as in the case of the Pilipino and Korean groups. This finding is at variance with the 1970 census: the Japanese in the study had

Table 36
Combined annual family income for the Japanese sample

Family annual income	Japanese immigrants		U.S. citizens of Japanese descent		Totals for all groups studied	
	N	%	N	%	N	%
Under 3,000	5	5.0	2	4.0	18	2.5
3,001-6,999	9	9.0	1	2.0	60	8.3
7,000-8,999	7	7.0	2	4.0	57	7.9
9,000-11,999	10	10.0	8	16.0	93	12.8
12,000-14,999	15	15.0	4	8.0	114	12.8
15,000-19,999	18	18.0	11	22.0	140	19.3
20,000-24,999	9	9.0	3	6.0	108	14.9
25,000-49,999	5	5.0	11	22.0	65	9.0
50,000 and over	2	2.0	2	4.0	11	1.5
Would not state income	7	7.0	4	8.0	41	5.7
Don't know	13	13.0	2	4.0	19	2.6
Total	100	100.0	50	100.0	726	100.0
Median	16,111		18,636			
Mean	14,841		21,284			

income levels almost exactly the same as reported by the census, but the Pilipinos and Koreans reported much higher income levels in the present study. This presumably results from the fact that the Chicago Korean and Pilipino communities contain larger proportions of professional persons than the national populations of these groups.

In all cases, the income figures reported here are for the combined income of all members of a family. However, for the Japanese respondents, families with more than one wage earner did not show significantly higher incomes than did one-income families. This may reflect the socioeconomic condition of the Japanese community as a whole. On the one hand, a certain number of the Japanese respondents seem to have "made it" economically; in these households it is likely that the husband alone holds a well-paying position. This theory is supported by the relatively high percentage of Japanese wives (over 36% in both groups) who reported being homemakers. On the other hand, those households where both spouses are working are probably those where neither has secured a high-paying position.

Of all groups studied, the Japanese immigrant group had the

highest proportion of persons who did not know the family income. Examination of these respondents shows that they are most often elderly, retired persons who are living in their children's households. These persons may thus in fact be ignorant of this information.

When the reported family incomes of the Japanese respondents were crosstabulated with their ages, it was found that 10 of the Japanese immigrants 66 years of age or older were living on less than $5,000 per year. This finding lends some support to the frequently presented picture of the impoverished Issei in Japanese ethnic communities.[1] Aside from this group, the Japanese immigrants are quite evenly spread over the income scale, while the Japanese citizens are grouped with the highest incomes occurring in the 41–65 age range. Since both groups of Japanese respondents show long job tenures, the greater economic success of the middle-aged citizens may reflect more successful overall assimilation in the job market.

In common with the other groups studied, most Japanese respondents felt their family incomes were equal to or greater than an "adequate income." The satisfaction levels for Japanese immigrants (71.4%) and citizens (75.0%) were exceeded only by the Chinese immigrants (83.3%). As noted earlier, the satisfaction level of the Chinese immigrants must reflect the ample satisfaction of very modest expectations, since their reported income level is, by far, the lowest in the study. On the other hand, the relatively high satisfaction levels of the Japanese groups appear to proceed in some measure from their actual economic success, particularly in the case of the citizens.

The Immigration Experience

Those respondents who were foreign-born—both recent immigrants and naturalized U.S. citizens—were asked a series of questions about their immigration experiences. Table 37 shows the reasons for immigration given by the Japanese respondents in the study. In areas related to educational, vocational, and economic opportunities, the motivations of the male Japanese immigrants do not appear to differ markedly from those of the other groups studied. However, it should be noted that the motivations of the Japanese immigrant females seem to be overwhelmingly domestic: 42.4% reported that they immigrated to "join family," and 37.6%,

Table 37
Reasons given for immigration to the United States
by foreign born Japanese respondents, by sex

Reason for immigration	Sex	Japanese immigrants*		Totals for all groups studied	
		N	%	N	%
Join family	M	24	25.8	107	14.0
	F	36	42.4	197	26.7
Educational opportunity	M	14	15.0	158	20.7
	F	1	1.1	94	12.8
Job training opportunity	M	9	9.7	104	13.6
	F	—	—	95	12.9
Higher standard of	M	18	19.3	146	19.1
living	F	8	9.4	117	15.9
Better work opportunity	M	15	16.1	176	23.1
	F	1	1.1	129	17.5
Education of children	M	—	—	10	1.3
	F	—	—	14	3.4
Adventure/make fortune	M	10	10.7	20	2.6
	F	4	4.7	23	3.1
To get married	M	1	1.1	2	0.2
	F	35	37.6	42	5.7
To avoid adverse	M	2	2.2	39	5.1
political situation in	F	—	—	25	3.8
home country					
Size of responses**	M	93	100.0	762	100.0
	F	85	100.0	736	100.0

*Includes naturalized citizens.

**Respondents could give multiple responses; thus response size does not correspond to sample size.

"to get married." Conversely, only a single Japanese female immigrant replied affirmatively to the categories "better work opportunity" and "educational opportunity," and not one reported immigrating for "job training opportunity." One other interesting response category is that of "adventure/make fortune." Of the other groups studied, besides the Japanese only Pilipino females gave any noticeable frequency of responses (5.1%) in this category. At least in the case of the Japanese, this response may simply indicate that the respondents were not driven to immigrate because of unbearable social or economic conditions in the home country.

Like the other groups in the study, the Japanese immigrants reported the existence of a substantial network of family and relatives, both in the United States generally and in Chicago in particular. Overall, 76.8% reported having relatives in the United

States, and 54.6% in Chicago. These figures are somewhat lower than those for the Chinese respondents (92% in the U.S., 65.1% in Chicago), but are similar to those for the Korean and Pilipino immigrants. As with the other groups, relatively few of the Japanese reported that the Chicago relatives were parents (9.2%); they were more likely to be siblings (21.3%) or other relatives (23.6%). In all cases, it must be stressed that the mere presence of relatives does not guarantee the existence of a viable family support network: both quality and frequency of interaction must be taken into account.

When questioned about the help they had received upon arriving in Chicago, 88.8% of the Japanese immigrants said that they had received help of some sort. Of those who had received help, 47.2% had received it from their spouses, 6.6% from siblings or parents, and 46.2% from non–family members. Of all groups studied, the Japanese had received the least help from parents and siblings, a fact which may suggest that the family network is of limited importance to the newly-arrived Japanese immigrant, at least in the Chicago area. In fact, all groups except the Chinese received about half of their assistance from non-family members.

Table 38 shows the frequencies with which newly-arrived Japanese immigrants received various types of assistance from non-relatives in Chicago. As with the other groups studied, one of the

Table 38
Types of assistance received by Japanese immigrant respondents from nonrelatives upon their arrival in Chicago

Types of assistance	Japanese immigrants*		Totals for all groups studied	
	N	%	N	%
Lodging (stayed with them)	20	20.6	229	26.4
Found a place to stay	9	9.3	122	14.1
Loan	6	6.2	54	6.2
Helped to find a job	6	6.2	113	13.0
Introduced me to others who could help	5	5.2	43	5.0
Emotional support, encouragement	22	22.7	125	14.4
Other	29	29.9	182	21.0
Size of responses**	97	100.0	868	100.0

*Includes naturalized citizens.

**Multiple responses were permitted. Therefore response size does not correspond to sample size. Only the respondent's first two choices were counted.

most important forms of assistance was the provision of temporary lodging upon arrival. For the Japanese, however, the most frequently reported type of assistance from non family members was emotional support and encouragement. In the other categories of assistance, the Japanese show uniformly low frequencies compared to the other groups studied.

When asked to name the areas of adjustment to life in the United States that had been most problematic for them, the Japanese immigrants responded as shown in Table 39. There are few differences between their responses and those of the other groups in the study. One finding to be noted, is that adjustment may be difficult for Japanese immigrant females. They reported almost 70% more problems than the males, although this is partly explained by the large imbalance in the sex ratio in favor of females.

In the previous chapter on the Chinese sample it was noted that relatively few respondents in any of the groups had severe regrets about having decided to emigrate. As Table 40 shows, the Japanese immigrants (including naturalized citizens) are no exception. Most

Table 39
Problem areas associated with immigration by Japanese respondents, by sex

Problem areas	Sex	Japanese immigrants*		Totals for all groups studied	
		N	%	N	%
Language	M	36	83.7	228	74.3
	F	57	89.1	274	75.7
Homesickness	M	21	48.8	136	44.3
	F	36	56.3	231	63.8
Lack of ethnic person	M	11	25.6	93	30.3
contacts	F	22	34.4	115	31.8
Food differences	M	12	27.9	71	23.1
	F	21	32.8	83	22.9
Weather differences	M	12	27.9	139	45.3
	F	26	40.6	181	50.0
Life style/	M	27	62.8	156	50.8
cultural differences	F	39	60.0	174	48.1
Size of responses**	M	119			
	F	201			
Total eligible respondents		150			

*Includes naturalized citizens.

**Multiple responses were permitted to these questions.

Table 40
Evaluation of decision to emigrate by Japanese respondents, by sex

Decisions	Sex	Japanese immigrants N	Japanese immigrants %	U.S. citizens of Japanese descent N	U.S. citizens of Japanese descent %	Totals for all groups studied N	Totals for all groups studied %
Yes, definitely	M	22	59.5	4	66.7	176	57.5
happy	F	31	50.8	1	50.0	182	50.4
Yes, with	M	8	21.6	2	33.3	73	23.9
reservation	F	18	29.5	1	50.0	94	26.0
Uncertain	M	5	13.5	–	–	36	11.8
	F	10	16.4	–	–	63	17.5
Regrets	M	2	5.4	–	–	9	2.9
	F	1	1.6	–	–	12	3.3
Plan to	M	–	–	–	–	12	3.9
return	F	1	1.6	–	–	10	2.8
Totals	M	37	100.0	6	100.0	306	100.0
	F	61	100.0	2	100.0	361	100.0

*Naturalized citizens who were asked immigration-related questions.

are quite clearly satisfied with the decision to emigrate. Among the immigrants, somewhat more Japanese than Chinese had reservations or were uncertain about the decision, but the Chinese group had a larger proportion of persons who definitely regretted the decision or planned to return to the homeland. Given the much greater economic success of the Japanese group, one might have expected them to be substantially more satisfied with the decision to emigrate. It might be speculated that the knowledge— or memory, for some—of the bitter experience of World War II may cause the Japanese immigrants to have more ambivalent feelings about life in America. Furthermore, the Japanese may be more ambivalent because the situation in the home country is not so desperate as in the case of the other groups. Because returning to Japan is a viable alternative, they are under less personal pressure to view the immigrantion experience as successful.

Problems and Problem-Solving Activities

Respondents in the study were asked a series of questions which dealt with actual problems they had experienced as Japanese-American persons living in Chicago and with hypothetical problem situations for which they were asked to tell what they would do to get help. In this way it was hoped to get at the general problem-solving strategies of the respondents in addition to probing their actual experiences with problematic situations.

In response to the general open-ended question about problems faced by members of the respondent's ethnic group, some 83 different problems were voiced. These problems were then grouped into seven categories. The responses of the Japanese groups are shown in Table 41. (Immigrant and citizen responses are grouped together whenever the differences between the groups were insignificant.) As noted earlier, few of the respondents claimed to have "no problems," thus calling into question the stereotype of Asian Americans as "model minorities." However, of the groups studied, the Japanese gave the highest proportion of "no problems" responses (32%) to this item. While these responses may reflect cultural factors, they are probably also related to the relatively high level of economic success achieved by the Japanese groups. This theory receives some indirect support from further analysis which was performed on the data within ethnic groups: generally, persons in higher socioeconomic positions perceived themselves and their communities as having fewer problems than did respondents at lower socioeconomic levels.

Compared to the other groups studied, the Japanese respondents perceived just slightly fewer problems overall, although the relative importance of the various categories of problems seemed to be quite similar to that for the other groups. In addition to the difference in "no problems" response discussed above, the Japanese also reported far fewer employment problems than any other

Table 41
Problems related to living in Chicago cited by Japanese respondents

Problem areas	Japanese immigrants and citizens		Totals for all groups studied	
	N	%	N	%
Interpersonal and psychological adjustment	6	4.1	35	4.9
Language and cultural difference adjustment	38	25.9	305	42.3
Discrimination	30	20.4	111	15.4
Employment	1	0.7	40	5.6
City living stress	16	10.9	79	11.0
Ethnic community conflicts	9	6.1	35	4.9
No problems	47	32.0	116	16.1
Total	147	100.0	721	100.0

Table 42
Actual problems experienced by Japanese respondents*

Actual problems experienced	Japanese immigrants and citizens		Totals for all groups studied	
	N	%	N	%
Insufficient income	54	36.0	255	22.5
Locating job	29	19.3	178	15.6
Problems on job	33	22.1	162	14.2
Getting medical service	12	8.1	94	8.2
Locating housing	32	21.3	122	10.7
Adjustment problems due to language and life style differences	34	22.7	254	22.3
Family conflict	14	9.3	71	6.2
Size of responses	208		1136	

*Percentage in each cell derived by dividing positive responses by total respondents in each ethnic group on each question. Thus percentages in each column do not equal 100%.

group. However, they reported "ethnic community conflicts" slightly more often than the other groups, and perceived "discrimination" as a problem more often than any other group except the Pilipinos.

When respondents were asked what problems they themselves had actually encountered, the weighting of problem areas was somewhat different. This difference probably results because this question series was not open-ended. Instead, the respondent was asked whether or not he had encountered each of a fixed list of problems. For the Japanese, "insufficient income" received the largest number of positive responses (see Table 42). This is of some interest since, as noted earlier, most of the Japanese respondents indicated that their incomes were at least adequate. It may be that the phrasing of the present question ("Have you ever had problems with. . .?") brought out the fact that respondents had at some time in the past suffered from insufficient income, even though they might be well off at present.

It is less easy to explain the fact that about a fifth of the Japanese respondents reported having experienced problems on the job or problems in locating employment: in the preceding question series, only a single Japanese respondent cited "employment" as a Japanese community problem. It is possible that this difference may arise from the phrasing of the two items.

"Locating housing," was reported as a problem more often by

the Japanese than by any other group. Housing may have been a particular problem for this group, many members of which had to resettle during the post-World War II housing shortage, a period when hostility toward Japanese Americans was still prevalent.

Overall, the Japanese groups reported levels of problems actually experienced that were similar to those of the Pilipinos and Chinese, and generally quite a bit lower than the Koreans. In considering all of the reported problems, however, it should be remembered that the respondents were not necessarily heads of households and thus may have been unaware of certain categories of problems relating to finances and the outside community. Among the Japanese groups—as among the Chinese—many elderly respondents replied "I don't know," or gave no reply at all, when asked about many types of problems.

To probe the discrimination process more closely, respondents were also asked specifically whether they had "definitely" or "probably" experienced discrimination in three areas: obtaining housing, losing a job, and being passed over for promotion on the job. As Table 43 shows, the Japanese citizens, particularly, reported fairly high levels of perceived discrimination in all three

Table 43
Discrimination experienced by Japanese respondents*

Discrimination areas	Japanese immigrants		U.S. citizens of Japanese descent		Total	
	N	%	N	%	N	%
Housing						
Yes, definitely	8	8.1	18	36.7	59	8.2
Yes, probably	3	3.0	1	2.0	29	4.0
Total	11	11.1	19	38.7	88	12.3
Lost job						
Yes, definitely	3	3.1	—	—	9	1.3
Yes, probably	—	—	4	8.0	10	1.4
Total	3	3.1	4	8.0	19	2.7
Passed over for promotion						
Yes, definitely	7	7.1	7	14.0	81	11.3
Yes, probably	4	4.0	4	8.0	61	8.5
Total	11	11.1	11	22.0	142	19.8

*Percentage in each cell was derived by dividing responses by total respondents in each ethnic group on each question. Thus percentages should be considered in relation to total number of respondents in each ethnic group.

Table 44
Resources cited by Japanese respondents in hypothetical
medical emergency situation

Help sources	Japanese immigrants and citizens		Totals for all groups studied	
	N	%	N	%
Hospital or doctor, named	46	30.7	294	40.6
Hospital or doctor, unnamed	54	36.0	276	38.1
Family/relatives	31	20.7	65	9.0
Friends (ethnic)	6	4.0	21	2.9
Friends (unspecified)	2	1.3	8	1.1
Ethnic religious organization	5	3.3	12	1.7
Had not thought about it	—	—	1	0.1
Fire and police department	4	2.7	27	3.7
Don't know where to go	2	1.3	21	2.9
Totals	150	100.0	725	100.0

areas. The discrimination reported by the Japanese immigrants was more nearly at the level reported by the other groups in the study. The higher levels of discrimination reported by the Japanese citizens may reflect the difficult period of resettlement after the World War II internment, particularly with respect to housing discrimination. In fact, crosstabulation indicates that, for the Japanese groups, there is a positive correlation between discrimination experienced and length of residence in the United States. This relationship does not exist for any of the other groups in the study.

Respondents in the study were also presented with hypothetical "what if" problems and asked how they would solve them. Answers to such questions may indicate the respondent's problem-solving strategies and propensities, as well as revealing his knowledge (or ignorance) of available services and resources in the community. As with other lines of inquiry in this questionnaire, the hypothetical problems progressed from the general and the impersonal to the specific and personal.

Table 44 presents the responses of the Japanese group with respect to a hypothetical medical emergency, while Table 45 covers a hypothetical situation of mental illness. In both instances, the principal difference between the Japanese and the other groups in the study is that the Japanese tend to cite more private sources of help, such as family, relatives, and friends. The other groups tended to rely more exclusively on public resources (hospitals, doctors,

Table 45
Resources cited by Japanese respondents in hypothetical
situation of mental illness

Help sources	Japanese immigrants and citizens		Totals for all groups studied	
	N	%	N	%
Hospital or doctor, named	25	16.8	130	17.9
Hospital or doctor, unnamed	72	48.3	369	50.9
Family/relatives	27	18.1	66	9.1
Friends (ethnic)	5	3.4	27	3.7
Friends (unspecified)	—	—	4	0.6
Ethnic religious organization	10	6.7	31	4.3
Had not thought about it	1	0.7	5	0.7
Police/fire department	3	2.0	10	1.4
Don't know where to go	6	4.0	83	11.5
Totals	149	100.0	725	100.0

police). Also, in both cases the Japanese showed a very low incidence of "don't know where to go" responses, especially when
compared with the Chinese respondents.

When asked where they would turn for help in getting a job, the
Japanese respondents gave replies which, for the most part, did
not differ sharply from those of the other groups (see Table 46).

Table 46
Resources cited by Japanese respondents
in hypothetical search for a job

Sources of help	Japanese immigrants and citizens		Totals for all groups studied	
	N	%	N	%
Classified ads	37	25.9	198	27.8
Employment agency, public/private	33	23.1	149	20.9
Family/relatives	5	3.5	25	3.5
Ethnic friends	21	14.7	136	19.1
Friends (unspecified)	11	7.7	21	3.0
Ethnic church organization	11	7.7	27	3.8
More than one resource	—	—	1	0.1
Self-reliance	14	9.8	104	14.6
Don't know where to go	11	7.7	52	7.3
Totals	143	100.0	713	100.0

One difference is that the Japanese named ethnic religious organizations more often than did any other group. This probably reflects the greater level of organizational activity of the Japanese, which was reported earlier. The Japanese also reported reliance on friends (ethnic and otherwise) more often than did the Pilipino or Korean groups, but much less often than did the Chinese.

Two questions were asked concerning hypothetical discrimination, on the job and in housing. As shown in Tables 47 and 48, the Japanese citizens are slightly less likely to deny the discrimination than the immigrants are, and are more likely to say that they would turn to civil rights organizations for help. These replies might be taken to indicate a more activist stance on the part of the citizens but, surprisingly, the citizens are also a bit more likely to simply give up in the face of discrimination. However, crosstabulation of the data reveals that, for the Japanese citizen group, there is a positive correlation between age or length of residence in the United States and activist approaches to dealing with discrimination. This may be a reflection of hard lessons learned from the World War II internment, particularly in light of the fact that the Chinese citizen group in the study showed an exactly opposite effect. Finally, as in other areas, relatively few of the Japanese respondents said they did not know where to go for help.

Solutions cited for hypothetical financial problems reveal an interesting difference between the Japanese and the other groups

Table 47
Resources cited by Japanese respondents to deal with
hypothetical employment discrimination

Responses to discrimination	Japanese immigrants N	%	U.S. citizens of Japanese descent N	%	Totals for all groups studied N	%
Civil rights organization	13	13.4	18	36.0	181	25.0
Give up	36	37.2	21	42.0	293	40.4
Family and friends	7	7.2	1	2.0	19	2.6
Ethnic organization	7	7.2	1	2.0	19	2.6
Denial of discrimination	14	14.4	5	10.0	45	6.2
Self reliance	6	6.2	1	2.0	29	4.0
Don't know where to go	14	14.4	3	6.0	134	18.5
Total	97	100.0	50	100.0	724	99.3

Table 48
Resources cited by Japanese respondents to deal with
hypothetical housing discrimination

Responses to discrimination	Japanese immigrants		U.S. citizens of Japanese descent		Totals for all groups studied	
	N	%	N	%	N	%
Civil rights organization	15	15.3	20	40.0	183	26.7
Give up	48	48.9	25	50.0	326	45.2
Family and friends	9	9.2	1	2.0	20	2.7
Ethnic organization	2	2.0	—	—	22	3.0
Denial of discrimination	8	8.2	3	6.0	42	5.8
Self reliance	2	2.0	—	—	7	0.9
Don't know where to go	14	14.3	1	2.0	121	16.8
Total	98	100.0	50	100.0	721	101.1

studied: 42.8% of the Japanese respondents said they would rely on family or relatives for financial help (see Table 49). In nearly every other category, the Japanese had fewer positive responses than did the other groups. Combined with other data in the study,

Table 49
Resources cited by Japanese respondents to deal with
hypothetical financial problems

	Japanese immigrants and citizens		Totals for all groups studied	
	N	%	N	%
Self-reliance	14	9.7	80	11.1
Family/relatives	62	42.8	227	31.5
Ethnic friends/organization	13	9.0	109	15.1
Friends (unspecified)	4	2.8	10	1.4
Unemployment compensation	1	0.7	4	0.6
Bank/credit union	24	16.6	147	20.4
Public aid	12	8.3	56	7.8
Never thought about it	5	3.4	27	3.8
Don't know where to go	10	6.9	60	8.3
Totals	145	100.0	720	100.0

this finding seems to indicate that the family (both nuclear and extended) may play a much more important part in the problem-solving strategies of Japanese Americans than it does for other Asian-American groups.

In the area of hypothetical marital problems, however, the Japanese respondents proved to be much more like the other groups in their approaches and preferences. As with the other groups, the largest single category of response for the Japanese was "work it out oneself." Given the realities of attempted self-counseling, this response may in fact represent pursuit of a non solution to the problem. When combined with three other non solutions ("do nothing," "never thought about it," and "don't know where to go"), it appears that over half of the Japanese respondents have opted for strategies which do not address the problem (see Table 50). The results for the other groups are similar and suggest that the provision of highly personal forms of help, such as marital counseling, may present one of the severest challenges to service providers in the Asian-American community.

Those respondents who reported that they had experienced problems were asked whether or not they had sought help: overall, 1,136 problems were reported, but help was sought on only 357 occasions (31.4%). The Japanese groups sought help for 36.3% of their problems, the second highest percentage for the groups in the study. This better than average record in seeking help may be a

Table 50
Resources cited by Japanese respondents to deal with
hypothetical marital problems

Sources of help	Japanese immigrants and citizens		Totals for all groups studied	
	N	%	N	%
Work it out oneself	38	28.4	187	28.2
Family/relatives	13	9.7	63	9.5
Friends, ethnic and non-ethnic	21	15.7	61	9.2
Marriage counselor/lawyer	15	11.2	80	12.1
Separation or divorce	3	21.2	48	7.2
Minister or priest	9	6.7	43	6.5
Do nothing	9	6.7	43	6.5
Never thought about it	15	11.2	54	8.1
Don't know where to go	11	8.2	85	12.8
Totals	134	100.0	664	100.0

reflection of the presence of well-established Japanese service organizations in the Chicago area. There is a long-standing pattern of use of these resources in the Chicago Japanese community, beginning with the Japanese-American Service Committee during the period of resettlement following World War II.

Table 51 presents the percentages of instances in which the Japanese respondents sought help for various categories of problems. In the areas of "insufficient income," "job location," and "adjustment to the U.S." the Japanese sought help more often than did the other groups. On the other hand, they sought help for family conflicts less often than the overall average. This may indicate that the Japanese respondents differentiate more sharply between problem-solving strategies for personal problems and for relatively impersonal economic or cultural problems.

Two areas of problem-solving activity were analyzed in detail for the various groups in the study. The area of child care for pre-

Table 51
Percentage of Japanese respondents seeking help in each problem area*

Problems experienced Help sought	Japanese immigrants and citizens		Totals	
	N	%	N	%
Insufficient income	54		255	
Help sought	29	53.7	88	34.3
Job location	29		178	
Help sought	19	65.5	84	47.8
On the job	33		162	
Help sought	10	30.3	50	30.8
Medical service	12		94	
Help sought	6	50.0	50	53.0
Locating housing	32		122	
Help sought	6	18.7	30	24.6
Adjustment to U.S.	34		254	
Help sought	10	29.4	46	19.0
Family conflicts	14		71	
Help sought	1	7.1	9	12.6
Total number of problems experienced	208		1136	
Total number help sought	81	36.3	357	31.4

*Percentages in cells are derived by dividing help sought responses by problems experienced in each problem area. Therefore, percentages in columns do not total 100%.

Table 52
Resources cited by Japanese immigrant respondents
for obtaining first job in the United States

Sources of help	Japanese immigrants* N	%	Totals for all groups studied N	%
Employment agency, private and public	6	6.5	72	11.6
Classified ads	9	9.7	135	21.7
Professional organization	1	1.1	10	1.6
Ethnic friends/organization	42	45.2	216	34.7
Non ethnic friends	5	5.4	32	5.1
Family/relatives	19	20.4	85	13.7
Employment pre-arranged	11	11.8	72	11.6
Total responses**	93	100.0	622	100.0

*Includes naturalized citizens.

**Multiple responses were permitted. Therefore totals do not correspond with total respondents.

school children was found to be inapplicable to the Japanese groups: no citizens and only four immigrant respondents reported needing or seeking such services. For the most part, the citizens are too old to have children in this age range, while the Japanese immigrant group had few young children, and fewer working mothers than the other groups studied.

The other problem area analyzed in detail was that of locating a job upon first arriving in America. Naturalized citizens were grouped with immigrants for the purposes of this analysis. Table 52 details the responses of the Japanese group, which closely paralleled those of the Chinese. That is, both the Japanese and Chinese immigrants were likely to have obtained their first jobs with the help of ethnic friends or organizations, and in both cases family and relatives were the next most likely source. This reliance on private rather than public resources probably reflects the lower educational and job-entry skill levels of the Japanese and Chinese immigrants, compared with the Pilipinos and Koreans. These latter groups are more likely to use employment agencies or classified ads to find their initial employment, presumably because they are more likely to possess the education and skills to compete openly in the job market. Also, in the case of long-established groups, such as the Chinese and Japanese, members of the community have more contacts to use in aiding one another in the job market. In such cases there is also more opportunity for employment in ethnic businesses.

Service Characteristics and Priorities

Since one of the major reasons for the study was to discover what factors prevent Asian Americans from using available resources, those who did not seek help when they had problems were examined separately. In general, the reasons cited by the Japanese groups were not markedly different from those of the other groups studied (see Table 53). For all groups, the two reasons most often cited were "no problems or not serious enough," and "solve problems by self or with family." However, the ordering of these two reasons varied from group to group and, often, by sex within groups. The two Japanese groups, along with the Pilipinos, showed

Table 53
Reasons cited by Japanese respondents
for not seeking help, by sex

Reasons for not seeking help	Sex	Japanese immigrants		U.S. citizens of Japanese descent		Totals for all groups studied	
		N	%	N	%	N	%
No problems or not serious enough	M	15	45.5	12	46.2	104	30.1
	F	25	39.7	12	63.2	136	34.3
Solve by self or with family	M	12	36.4	11	42.3	134	38.7
	F	25	39.7	5	26.3	123	31.0
Organization can't help	M	1	3.0	–	–	33	9.5
	F	3	4.8	–	–	18	4.5
Didn't want others to know	M	–	–	–	–	12	3.5
	F	2	3.2	–	–	11	2.8
Language barrier	M	2	6.1	–	–	11	3.2
	F	3	4.8	1	5.3	34	8.6
Didn't know where to go	M	3	9.1	3	11.5	51	14.7
	F	5	7.9	1	5.3	75	18.9
Size of responses*	M	33	100.0	26	100.0	345	
	F	63	100.0	19	100.0	397	

*Asked only of respondents who did not seek help. Respondents could give multiple answers. Thus column totals do not represent number of respondents responding.

a balance strongly in favor of "no problems or not serious enough." With respect to the Japanese this finding is consistent with the fact that a relatively large number of Japanese respondents reported having "no problems" at the outset of the questionnaire. On the other hand, the Japanese groups (again, together with the Pilipinos) showed low proportions of respondents who replied that they did not seek aid either because they did not know where to go, or because of the language barrier. Again, these findings are consistent with others in the study with respect to English fluency and general problem-solving stances.

The respondents in the "no problem" and "did not know where to go" categories were analyzed by sex, age, marital status, length of U.S. residence, and job level. No clear patterns emerged, but more professionals did tend to end up in the "no problems" category, and more un-skilled workers in the "did not know where to go" group. Thus there may be a general education/job-level variable at work behind this distinction. In any case, when the Japanese respondents fail to seek help it is generally because they deny the existence of problems, deny the need for external help in solving them, or choose to solve them alone, or within the family structure.

As an additional way to tap the respondents' perceptions of problems present in the community, they were asked to rate the importance of eight different services on a three-point scale. In the preceding chapter it was noted that all groups gave first precedence to legal services, an anomalous choice since legal aid was nowhere else perceived as a service problem by the respondents. When the results are rank-ordered for importance to the Japanese respondents, the order is as shown in Table 54.

The low ranking of child care centers is to be expected, since few of the Japanese respondents had young children. For the other services, with the exception of legal aid, the main observation is that relatively few Japanese respondents assigned importance to *any* service. In this respect, the Japanese groups differ sharply from the Chinese, who tended to rate *all* services as important. This finding lends further support to the picture of the Japanese respondents as persons who see themselves as having few problems and, hence, needing few services.

Respondents were also asked to rank the importance of several characteristics of service agencies. As Table 55 shows, there were some marked differences between the Japanese immigrants and citizens on this item. In particular, a Japanese immigrant is ten

138   *Changing Patterns, Changing Needs*

Table 54
Services considered important by Japanese sample*

	Rank order	Japanese immigrants and citizens N	%	Totals for all groups studied N
Types of services				
Child care centers	7	28	18.7	302
English conversation classes	3	50	33.3	376
Mental health service	6	39	26.0	228
Employment service	4	45	30.0	284
Vocational training	5	43	28.7	277
Public aid	6	39	26.2	276
Bilingual referral service	2	55	36.7	345
Legal aid service	1	68	45.3	425
Size of responses		367		2513

*Percentages in each cell are derived in relation to total respondents in each ethnic group. Thus percentages do not total 100%.

times as likely to consider bilingual staff to be important. The citizens, on the other hand, strongly want the staff to be helpful, but care little that they be bilingual. Overall, the responses of the Japanese citizens closely paralleled those of the Pilipino immigrants (who are also fluent in English), while the responses of the Japanese immigrants more closely resemble those of the other three groups. This may be yet another indication that English fluency may be one of the most important dimensions to consider in developing and delivering social services to Asian Americans.

Table 55
Service characteristics considered important by Japanese respondents

Service characteristic	Japanese immigrants N	%	U.S. citizens of Japanese descent N	%	Totals for all groups studied N	%
Bilingual staff	39	41.0	2	4.1	201	28.1
Helpfulness of staff	40	42.2	30	61.2	334	46.6
Convenient access to agencies	8	8.4	6	12.2	73	10.2
Confidentiality	5	5.2	6	12.2	60	8.3
Service fee	3	3.1	5	10.2	48	6.7
Totals	95	99.9	49	99.9	716	99.9

The Japanese Sample: Composite and Conclusions

If we were to synthesize, and then scrutinize, a typical Japanese respondent in the study, what would this person be like? To begin with, he is probably middle-aged (fortyish, let us say), is probably married, and has one or two children of high school or college age. He and his spouse and children are probably the only members of the household, and if they do not own the house or condominium in which they live, they rent an apartment.

Our hypothetical Japanese respondent has lived in Chicago for a fairly long time, but he probably was not born there. Whether he is an immigrant or a citizen, he probably comes from a rural or small town background, and moved to Chicago at least twenty years ago. If he is a U.S.-born citizen, then he probably relocated to Chicago following a stay in an internment camp during World War II.

There is about an even chance that this respondent is a Buddhist, but he might be a Protestant, or have no religious preference. If he has a religious preference, there is no way to predict how often he goes to services: he may go every week, or almost never. But there is a very good chance that he belongs to an ethnic organization, and if he is a citizen he probably belongs to more than one.

If our respondent is a citizen, he probably is quite fluent in English, although in some cases he may still speak Japanese in the home. If he is an immigrant, he is almost certain to at least understand spoken English, and he probably speaks it as well; however, there is about a 25% chance that his wife understands no English at all.

While our hypothetical Japanese respondent is unlikely to be a holder of advanced or professional degrees, he is reasonably well educated. He almost certainly graduated from high school and probably has some education beyond that, perhaps technical school or an undergraduate degree. On the other hand, his wife probably did not get beyond high school.

This respondent probably has a full-time job, although he is a little more likely to be retired than a respondent from one of the other groups in the study. His wife probably stays home and keeps house or, if his job does not pay well, she may have a part-time job, probably at the semi- or unskilled level.

A male respondent would be likely to hold a job somewhere around the middle of the employment scale: white-collar, clerical, skilled labor, or managerial, but not professional. If the respondent is an immigrant, there is some chance that he has suffered downward mobility of some sort, although not of a precipitous kind. In fact, whether immigrant or citizen, our respondent is probably fairly well satisfied with his job, has held it for a long time, and intends to keep it. However, if he is an immigrant there is some chance he is putting up with his job because it is the best he could get, under the circumstances.

For his efforts, this respondent is pretty well rewarded economically. He probably has a total family income of about $16,000 to $18,000 per year, and if he is a middle-aged citizen he may even be moderately affluent. On the other hand, if he is a retired immigrant he may be subsisting on very meager resources, or perhaps even living on the charity of his children. Aside from these impoverished retirees, however, the respondent is probably earning a fairly good income and, quite importantly, he himself feels his income is adequate, or even ample.

If our respondent is an immigrant male, then he probably immigrated in order to find a better job and enjoy a better standard of living. He may also have come to join other family members, and there is some possibility that he may have been seeking educational opportunities. He may even have come simply for the adventure of it. A female immigrant respondent, on the other hand, probably came for purely domestic reasons: to join other family members or to get married.

Whatever the sex of our immigrant, he or she probably arrived to find relatives or family members waiting. These relatives probably were not the respondent's parents, but they may have been siblings. In any event, these family members did not provide much help to the newcomer, although the respondent's spouse probably did. The respondent probably also received help from persons who were not related to him. These non-relatives may have given him a place to stay for a while, and they may also have provided him with support and encouragement.

Our hypothetical immigrant respondent encountered several problems and difficulties upon arriving in America. The English language almost certainly gave him trouble, he may well have been homesick, and the general life style and culture of America probably were difficult for him to adjust to. On the other hand, he did not have very much trouble finding other Japanese persons for social contact, and he could get ethnic food when he wanted it—in both cases as a result of the fairly large Japanese community in the Chicago area. If the immigrant respondent was female, she was probably bothered by all of these problems to a slightly greater extent than her male counterpart and, in addition, she may have found the Chicago weather objectionable.

Despite these problems with adjustment to life in America, the respondent probably has few regrets about the decision to emigrate. It is very unlikely that he has any intention of returning to Japan, but he may occasionally have ambivalent feelings about the United States, perhaps because of the past experiences of Japanese Americans.

When he looks at his ethnic community, our hypothetical Japanese respondent does not see overwhelming social problems. Some Japanese Americans, he feels, have had trouble with language and cultural adjustment, and he may feel that they are subject to discrimination. There is also a small possibility that the stress of big city living is hard to get used to, but there is about a one in three chance that he feels Japanese Americans have no problems, or, at least, none worth mentioning.

On the other hand, if he reflects on his own experience our respondent probably remembers certain problems he has actually experienced. Although he is fairly well off now, he recalls that there were times when it was hard to make ends meet, times when it was hard to find a job, or when he had employment problems on the job. Sometimes he has had trouble locating housing, and at times he has found it hard to adjust to the language and life style of the majority culture.

Our respondent may see some of his problems in the area of employment as arising from discrimination. Especially, there is a one in three chance that a landlord or realtor has denied him housing because he is Japanese. He may also have been passed over for promotion, or possibly lost a job, because of his ethnic background. He is particularly likely to have encountered discrimination if he is older and if he relocated to the Chicago area after release from a World War II internment camp.

If our Japanese respondent fails to seek aid from outside sources in dealing with his problems, it is not because he does not know where to turn. For real emergencies, he probably knows where to find the necessary help and, in addition, he may feel that he can rely on help from his family, relatives, and friends. He will even rely on these private resources to some extent in looking for a job, and he is very likely to turn to his family, relatives, and friends in dealing with a financial crisis in his life. On the other hand, encountering discrimination in employment or housing may make him simply give up, unless he is a long-time U.S. resident. If he has lived here long enough to remember the World War II experience, then he will probably take an activist approach to discrimination, possibly by contacting a civil rights organization. On the other hand, if our respondent is having marital problems, there is little chance that he will be inclined to seek outside help. He would rather work the problem out himself, possibly with help from relatives, family members, or friends.

Overall, our Japanese respondent only seeks outside help for his problems about a third of the time, although he is more inclined to seek assistance in some areas than in others. If he is suffering from low income, cannot find a job, or needs medical help, then he will probably seek outside help. At the other extreme, it is most unlikely that he will ever seek help in working out family conflicts. In those cases in which he does not seek help, he would probably not have any elaborate excuses to offer: either he does not feel that he has problems serious enough to require outside help, or he feels that he can work out his problems by himself, or with the help of his family.

Our hypothetical Japanese respondent does not generally think that his community needs to have additional services available. He is mildly interested in seeking English conversation classes, a bilingual referral service, and perhaps an employment service. The one service he would really like to see provided is community legal aid service, although he has probably never had many legal problems himself. If such services were offered, he would be more likely to use them if the staff made an extra effort to be helpful. If he is an immigrant, he would also appreciate having bilingual staff available, but if he is a citizen this is not important, since his English is fluent.

Summary: Japanese Americans in Chicago. If one collects together certain characteristics of the Japanese-American sample, and systematically ignores other aspects, one has quite probably isolated the seed of reality that gives rise to the myth of Asian Americans as "model minorities." Picture a middle-aged group, happily married for the most part and with a few children, steadily employed at jobs they generally like, comfortably well off, perhaps even a bit affluent, usually owning a home or condominium. These are the Japanese Americans (particularly from the citizen group) in the study sample. For much of the American public, this is also the stereotype of the model minorities which is applied to all Asian-American groups.

But also picture elderly retirees, living alone on meager pensions, or on the charity of their children; women who speak no English and have no job skills, isolated in the home; workers who are fired or passed over for promotion because of their ethnic background; families denied housing because "we don't rent to your people"; former supervisors who now work on assembly lines; accountants who now sweep floors. These too, are the Chicago Japanese Americans. This is the contradictory stuff of reality that stereotypes cannot convey.

NOTES TO CHAPTER V

1. See, for example, S.M. Fujii, "Elderly Asian Americans and use of public services," *Social Casework,* 57: 202–207, (1976).

CHAPTER VI

THE PILIPINO SAMPLE

It was noted in an earlier chapter that the nationality groups in this study are considered in historical order, that is, in order of the major influxes of immigration to the U.S. for each group. The Chinese and Japanese groups are composed, to a large extent, of persons who immigrated during the early years of this century, and of the descendents of these persons. Although the 1965 immigration act amendments have facilitated new migration of Chinese and Japanese persons, the population increases from such immigration have been low to moderate: the Chinese-American population increased 19% between 1965 and 1974 as a result of immigration, while the corresponding increase for the Japanese-American population was about 3%. On the other hand, although some Pilipinos originally arrived in this country during the earlier (pre-1934) period of immigration, the Pilipino-American population increased fully 36% between 1965 and 1974 as a result of the new wave of immigration.

Demographic Characteristics

The Pilipino sample in the present study—all immigrants—proved to be the youngest of the four groups considered, with a median age of only 32 years. As Table 56 shows, the Pilipino respondents are heavily concentrated in the two youngest age groups, with the females being predominantly a little younger than

Changing Patterns, Changing Needs

Table 56
Ages of Pilipino respondents and spouses, by sex

Age	Sex	Pilipino immigrants		Totals for all groups studied	
		N	%	N	%
18–30	M	22	23.2	60	17.8
	F	47	46.1	137	36.0
31–41	M	51	53.7	157	46.5
	F	38	37.3	119	31.2
41–50	M	16	16.8	57	16.9
	F	9	8.8	50	13.1
51–65	M	5	5.3	40	11.8
	F	8	7.8	44	11.6
65 and over	M	1	1.1	24	7.1
	F	–	–	31	8.1
Total	M	95	100	338	100
	F	102	100	381	100
Mean		35.1			
Standard deviation		8.87			

the males. Overall the sex ratio of the Pilipinos was nearly balanced (48% male to 52% female).

About 76% of the Pilipino sample were found to be married and living with their spouses, compared with 86% reported for Pilipino Americans by the 1970 census. As in the case of the other groups studied, the lower proportion of married persons in the sample may indicate that the sample is somewhat atypical of the national population, or it may simply mean that the study contacted single persons more efficiently than the census did.

Pilipino households showed the widest size variation of any group in the study, ranging from one to seventeen persons. The average Pilipino household contained four or five persons, with 36.2% of the households containing five or more members. One feature of particular interest is that the Pilipino households contained more unrelated persons than the households of any other group in the study. The 1970 census reported that, nationally, 38% of all Pilipino households contained five or more persons and they are quite likely to contain extended and nonlinear family members. Thus the census data are in general agreement with the findings of the present study. As Table 57 shows, the Pilipino households contained fairly large numbers of young children—over two-thirds of them under the age of nine. One could characterize the children of the Pilipino respondent households as being roughly from preschool to junior high school age.

The housing accomodations of the Pilipino respondents do not differ markedly from those of the other groups in the study: over two-thirds rent apartments, a little less than a fifth own houses, and much smaller numbers rent houses (6.1%), or own apartments (4%). Given the large size of the Pilipino households, it is perhaps surprising that house rentals are so infrequent. However, this may be a function of supply conditions in the housing market.

As might be expected from historical factors, the overwhelming majority of Pilipinos reported their religious preference as Catholic (92.5%). An additional 5% were Protestant, and there was a single Buddhist respondent. The religious involvement of the Pilipinos also appeared to be greater than that of the other groups studied: 78.4% reported that they attended services once a week, and 13.1% once a month. Only 2.5% of the Pilipinos said they never attended services. The figures for weekly attendance are much higher than the average for the other groups studied.

The organizational membership pattern of the Pilipino group bears some resemblance to that of the Chinese groups. A little over half of the Pilipinos belong to no organizations, and another third belong to only one or, possibly, two. Thus, the participation by the Pilipinos is somewhat greater than that of the Chinese groups, but substantially lower than that of the Korean and Japanese groups. Informal observation in Pilipino communities indicates that, although there is a high level of socialization and group-oriented behavior among the Pilipinos, such activities seem to be on a nonstructured, nonlabeled basis. Therefore, these group activities would probably not be reported in response to a question concerning organizational membership. It has also been observed

Table 57
Number of children living at home by age in Pilipino sample

Ages	Pilipino immigrants		Total for all groups in study	
	N	%	N	%
Under 5	82	35.7	265	30.8
5–9	76	33.0	219	25.5
10–14	34	14.8	122	14.2
15–19	17	7.4	108	12.6
20–24	14	6.1	74	8.6
25–34	5	2.2	36	4.2
35 and over	2	0.9	36	4.2
Totals	230	100.0	860	100.0

Table 58
Self-evaluation of English fluency by Pilipino respondents, by sex

English fluency	Sex	Pilipino immigrants		Total for all groups in study	
		N	%	N	%
Fluent	M	31	37.8	59	21.7
	F	45	54.2	58	17.8
Adequate	M	45	54.8	124	45.6
	F	35	42.1	118	36.2
Understand but	M	6	7.3	69	25.4
can't speak*	F	3	3.6	95	29.1
No comprehension	M	–	–	20	7.4
of English	F	–	–	55	16.9
Totals	M	82	99.9	272	100.1
	F	83	99.9	326	100.0

*These respondents were assisted in Tagalog by the interviewers.

that Pilipinos tend to go to meetings which hold specific interest for them, rather than those connected with organizational membership. These facts have implications for service delivery in Pilipino communities since they indicate that appropriate programs may be expected to find active group support in these communities, even though there may be few organizations to provide ready-made community structure.

English proficiency does not appear to be a major problem for the Pilipino immigrants. As noted earlier, all of the Pilipino interviews were to be conducted in English, partly because it was known that English is commonly used and understood by the Chicago Pilipino community, and partly because it would have been impractical to provide questionnaires translated into the numerous dialects that constitute the ethnic languages of this community (or to find interviewers to administer them). Thus all the Pilipino interviews were conducted in English, although the interviewers reported that in a few instances they had to assist the respondent by translating questionnaire items into Tagalog, and translating the responses in English. All the respondents were asked to give a self-rating of English proficiency. The results are shown in Table 58. It is of some interest that the Pilipinos are the only group in the study in which more females than males reported speaking English either fluently or adequately. This fact may be related to the large number of female professionals—primarily nurses—in the Pilipino sample.

With the exception of one person who was born in Korea, all of the Pilipino respondents were born in the Philippines; in this respect the Pilipino sample is somewhat more homogenous than the other groups in the study, although this may be a sampling effect. A little more than half of the Pilipino respondents (53%) were born and raised in cities of under a half million population. Another 25.7% reported that their hometowns were of more than one million population, but only 8.2% said they came from cities of between one-half and one million population. This pattern is similar to that of several other groups and may reflect the difficulty experienced by the respondents in categorizing the populations of their hometowns. Only 13.5% of the Pilipinos reported rural backgrounds—fewer than any other group except the Korean immigrants.

As Figure 3 shows, the Pilipino immigrants are a recently-arrived group. Fully 86.5% have lived in the U.S. for six years or less, and 89.5% have lived in Chicago for this brief time span. In this respect, the data of the study are in accord with the immigration figures detailed in Chapter II. The growth in the Chicago Pilipino-American population due to immigration has indeed been phenomenal since the 1965 amendments to the immigration law. If anything, the study group shows even more rapid recent growth

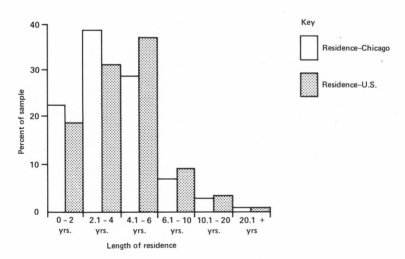

Figure 3. Length of residence in Chicago and U.S. by Pilipino sample

than the Pilipino-American population nationwide. Remembering that the present data were collected in 1974, and then going back nine years to 1965, one finds that fully 95% of the Pilipino study population is composed of persons who have immigrated since the passage of the amended act. It should be remembered that the entire Pilipino sample was drawn from Immigration and Naturalization Service files, and that a true random sample of Pilipino Americans would reveal more persons—now naturalized—who arrived in the early days of Pilipino migration.

Education, Employment, and Income Characteristics

The Pilipino sample proved to be the most highly educated of the four nationality groups in the study. In this respcet, the sample is somewhat atypcial of the general Pilipino American population: the study respondents had attained a median of 16 years of education, while the national median for Pilipino Americans is 11.9 years, according to the 1970 census. This is such a large difference that one suspects Chicago must be acting as some sort of magnet for Pilipino immigrants from the professional classes. It may be that the employment opportunities in the Chicago area are unusually attractive to this group. There is some evidence, however, that Chicago is not unique in this respect and that similar concentrations of Pilipino professionals can be found elsewhere, e.g., Southern California.[1] Overall, the lower educational level reported for Pilipino Americans in the 1970 census must reflect the presence of older persons and rural residents, in contrast to the younger, urban respondents in the present study.

Nationally, the number of college-educated Pilipino-American women more than doubled in the decade between 1960 and 1970. This is a far greater increase than those noted for Chinese-American and Japanese-American women. (Comparable figures are not available for Korean-American women.) In the present study, the Pilipino women show the highest proportion of persons with college degrees of any group surveyed—male or female. Table 59 shows the educational levels achieved by the Pilipino sample. Educational levels for both sexes are high, and women continue to be represented right up to the postdoctoral level. In both respects, the Pilipino sample differs markedly from the Chinese and Japanese samples. The Korean sample showed a somewhat similar trend.

Table 59
Highest educational levels achieved by Pilipino
respondents and spouses, by sex

Educational levels	Sex	Pilipino immigrants		Totals for all groups in study	
		N	%	N	%
Elementary or	M	1	0.7	25	5.3
under	F	—	—	45	11.0
High school graduate or	M	7	4.7	82	17.3
under	F	4	2.6	72	17.5
High School and beyond	M	17	11.3	56	11.8
	F	8	5.1	45	11.0
College	M	103	68.7	234	49.4
graduate	F	112	71.3	201	48.9
Nursing	M	—	—	—	—
	F	14	8.9	16	3.9
MS and PhD	M	8	5.3	48	10.1
	F	7	4.5	13	3.2
MD and dental	M	6	4.0	12	2.5
	F	1	0.6	1	0.2
Post MD and	M	8	5.3	17	3.6
PhD	F	11	7.0	18	4.4
Totals*	M	150	100.0	474	100.0
	F	157	100.0	411	100.0

*Totals include both respondents and their spouses. Therefore, they do not correspond with sample size.

The employment status of the Pilipinos resembles that of the other groups in that most persons hold full-time jobs and few are unemployed, but there are some important differences. First, Pilipino women show a higher full-time employment rate than any other female group in the study—it is higher, in fact, than the full-time employment rate of Chinese or Japanese citizen males. The Pilipino females also show a higher proportion of persons working more than one job than any other group except the Pilipino males and the Japanese citizen males. Likewise the Pilipino females had the lowest proportion of homemakers of any female group in the study, and also the lowest proportion of persons who had never been employed. These findings point to a very high degree of labor force participation on the part of Pilipino women. (See Table 60).

As might be expected from the relative youth of the Pilipino

Table 60
Employment status of Pilipino respondents and spouses, by sex

Employment status	Sex	Pilipino immigrants		Totals for all groups in study	
		N	%	N	%
Full-time	M	141	86.5	505	82.1
	F	142	75.9	393	59.1
Part-time	M	3	1.8	19	3.1
	F	5	2.7	36	5.4
More than	M	13	8.0	38	6.2
one job	F	12	6.4	17	2.6
Unemployed, sick,	M	—	—	5	0.8
disabled	F	2	1.1	6	0.9
Retired	M	2	1.2	26	4.2
	F	—	—	16	2.4
Unemployed, seeking	M	2	1.2	8	1.3
jobs	F	5	2.7	17	2.6
Unemployed, not	M	1	0.6	9	1.5
seeking jobs	F	3	1.6	14	2.1
Homemaker	M	—	—	3	0.5
	F	15	8.0	120	18.1
Never employed	M	1	0.6	2	0.3
	F	3	1.6	46	6.9
Totals*	M	163	100.0	615	100.0
	F	187	100.0	665	100.0

*Totals include both respondents and their spouses. Therefore, totals do not correspond to sample size.

sample, few persons in this group were either disabled or retired.

Table 61 shows the occupational categories reported by the Pilipino respondents. Unlike the Chinese and Japanese groups, the Pilipinos are quite heavily represented at the professional level, and, in addition, the professional group contains slightly more women than men. In part this may reflect the inclusion of nursing in the professional category, but at the very least it indicates that the high educational level of the Pilipino women is reflected in their job levels. Likewise, the Pilipino sample—again, in contrast to the Chinese and Japanese samples—does not show a large concentration of women in the semi- and unskilled categories. On the other hand, the Pilipinos resemble the other groups in the study in having few persons in managerial positions and a fairly large number of persons in the skilled and white collar category. Interestingly, only a single Pilipino respondent reported being a proprietor.

A comparison of respondents' job levels before and after immigration shows a relatively large amount of downward mobility in the Pilipino sample. The professional and managerial categories showed percentage losses of 11.5 and 3.8, respectively. Conversely, the white collar/skilled category—which is likely to absorb those displaced from the higher job categories—showed a gain of 27%.

Underemployment can also be expressed by the incongruity of the individual's educational attainment and job category. In this respect the Pilipinos fared somewhat worse than the other groups in the study, primarily because the Pilipino group contains such a large proportion of highly trained individuals. Such underemployment is often elusive. For instance, few medical professionals were employed in categories totally unrelated to their professional training, but many nurses and physicians reported being employed in the lower strata of their job categories. In many cases, these medical professionals had experienced difficulties in licensure, with the result that they were employed by public institutions in positions which required the full use of their professional expertise,

Table 61
Occupational categories of Pilipino respondents and spouses, by sex

Job categories	Sex	Pilipino immigrants N	%	Totals of all groups in study N	%
Professional	M	71	45.5	159	27.7
	F	75	46.6	143	31.5
Managerial	M	6	3.8	23	4.0
	F	1	0.6	9	2.0
Proprietor	M	1	0.6	61	10.6
	F	–	–	11	2.9
Skilled and	M	66	42.3	232	40.4
white collar	F	78	48.5	164	36.1
Semi- and	M	12	7.7	99	17.3
unskilled	F	7	4.3	127	28.0
Totals*	M	156	100.0	574	100.0
	F	161	100.0	454	100.0

*Totals include both respondents and spouses. Therefore they do not correspond to sample size.

Table 62
Combined annual family income for the Pilipino sample

Family annual income	Pilipino immigrants		Totals for all groups in study	
	N	%	N	%
Under 3,000	—	—	18	2.5
3,001–6,999	12	6.0	60	8.3
7,000–8,999	20	10.1	57	7.9
9,000–11,999	21	10.5	93	12.8
12,000–14,999	37	18.6	114	12.8
15,000–19,999	40	20.1	140	19.3
20,000–24,999	36	18.1	108	14.9
25,000–49,999	22	11.5	65	9.0
50,000 and over	3	1.5	11	1.5
Would not state income	6	3.0	41	5.7
Don't know	2	1.0	19	2.6
Total	199	100.0	726	100.0
Median	16,219			
Mean	18,121			

but where there was no legal requirement for licensure. This "back door" employment of Asian medical professionals probably reflects the acute shortage of medical personnel in the U.S. In academic areas, where there is no such shortage, the Pilipino immigrant usually fares much worse. In the sample for the present study, a fair proportion of the holders of advanced academic degrees were employed in areas completely unrelated to their training and expertise—sometimes at the unskilled or semiskilled level. Overall, however, far fewer Pilipinos than Koreans were in this situation.

Combined family income levels for the Pilipino sample are relatively high, as shown in Table 62. Using both median and mean figures for comparison, the Pilipino incomes are roughly equal to those of the Korean group, and slightly greater than those of the Japanese immigrants. Only the Japanese citizens—a well-established group—have incomes significantly higher than the Pilipinos. In considering these income figures, however, it should be remembered that they represent *family* income for all members of the household. Furthermore, while a little over 50% of all households in this study reported both spouses to be working, fully 84% of the Pilipino households are in this category. Finally, while the other groups—particularly the Chinese and the Japanese, the Koreans to a lesser extent—tended to show a pattern in which the wife holds only an unskilled or semi-skilled job, this is not the case for the Pilipinos. It is quite clear that both spouses in many Pilipino households are employed in professional level jobs. This is a further piece of circumstantial evidence suggesting that, although the job *categories* of Pilipino immigrants appear to be entirely normal, these persons may be largely relegated to the lowest-paying echelons of these categories.

Overall, the Pilipino respondents proved to be quite open about reporting their incomes, although not quite so open as the Koreans in the study. More Pilipinos than Chinese or Japanese are represented in the higher income categories, a finding which is at variance with the 1970 census. Data from the census indicate that 9% of the Japanese, 13% of the Chinese, and 11% of the Pilipinos in the state of Illinois had incomes under $4,000 per year. A smaller percentage of Pilipinos and Japanese in the present study fell into this low income category. Conversely, the 1970 census reported that 68% of the Japanese and 60% of the Pilipinos in Illinois had incomes of $10,000 or more, while in the present study 69% of the Japanese and 78% of the Pilipino respondents fell into this category. This disparity may reflect the high proportion of professional persons in the Chicago Pilipino community, compared with the composition of the group nationally. In common with the Korean group, the Pilipino incomes are distributed almost uniformly over the 18 to 40 age range which encompasses most of the sample. Thus, these groups do not contain a significant number of the "well-to-do middle-aged" such as are found in the Japanese citizen group.

When asked to indicate what they would consider an "adequate" income, the Pilipinos tended to name figures that were closer to their real incomes than was the case for any other group except the Chinese citizens. Still, 63.2% of the Pilipinos gave figures which indicated that they considered their actual incomes to be at least adequate. At the other end of the scale, 36.9% of the Pilipinos considered their incomes to be less than adequate, second only to the 45.7% of the Chinese citizens who felt this way. The very wide spread in actual incomes between the Pilipino immigrant and Chinese citizen groups suggests that "income adequacy" is largely a subjective quality, influenced by expectation levels.

In conclusion, then, it may be said that, although the Pilipino sample is relatively well off economically, it is quite likely that there is a certain amount of status incongruity and downward mo-

Table 63
Reasons given for immigration to the United States by
Pilipino immigrant respondents

Reasons for immigration	Sex	Pilipino immigrants		Totals for all groups in study	
		N	%	N	%
Join family	M	30	9.5	107	14.0
	F	37	11.7	197	26.7
Educational	M	60	19.0	158	20.7
opportunity	F	55	17.4	94	12.8
Job training	M	73	23.1	104	13.6
opportunity	F	70	22.1	95	12.9
Higher standard	M	49	15.6	146	19.1
of living	F	49	15.5	117	15.9
Better work	M	81	25.7	176	23.1
opportunity	F	76	24.0	129	17.5
Education of	M	1	0.3	10	1.3
children	F	1	0.3	14	3.4
Adventure/make	M	7	2.2	20	2.6
fortune	F	16	5.1	23	3.1
To get married	M	1	0.3	2	0.2
	F	2	0.6	42	5.7
To avoid adverse					
political situation	M	13	4.1	39	5.1
in home country	F	10	3.2	25	3.8
Size of responses*	M	315	100.0	762	100.0
	F	316	100.0	736	100.0

*Respondents could give as many responses as they wished. Therefore size of responses does not correspond to sample size.

bility in this group, resulting from underemployment of highly trained individuals. This may be reflected in the level of income satisfaction which, although high, is not as high as one might expect, given the level of reported actual income in this group.

Immigration Experience

The reasons given by the Pilipino respondents for immigration (see Table 63) are largely employment oriented, although they also showed more educational motivation than any other group except the Koreans. The desire for work and for job training opportunities is understandable in view of the high level of education among the Pilipino immigrants. It seems to be a rule of thumb that the educational systems of developing countries begin to produce large numbers of trained persons long before the local economic systems can absorb them into the labor force. The interest in educational opportunities shown by the Pilipino immigrants agrees with the finding that many had obtained one or more of their degrees in the U.S.

More Pilipinos in the study (89.9%) had relatives living in the United States than was the case for any other group except the Chinese. However, only 53.6% of the Pilipinos had relatives living in Chicago, which was the lowest percentage of any group studied. Furthermore, these relatives were less likely to be parents and siblings in the case of the Pilipinos. Thus, the Pilipino family network appears to be not only less extensive, but also less closely related, than those of the other groups, at least in the Chicago area. This accords with the fact that the Pilipino households contained more unrelated persons than those of the other groups. It should also be pointed out that the Pilipino group in the study showed no tendency to form an ethnic neighborhood: to the frustration of interviewing personnel, the Pilipino respondents were found to be scattered throughout the city of Chicago.

The failure of the Chicago Pilipinos to form a geographically concentrated ethnic neighborhood may result from the employment characteristics of this group. Many of the Pilipino respondents were employed in the health professions and their residences tended to cluster around each of the Chicago hospitals. Another factor is that Pilipino ethnic enterprises are virtually nonexistent in Chicago. Only a single respondent reported being employed by a Pilipino employer. In other groups studied, ethnic enterprises seem to provide the nucleus for a concentrated ethnic neighborhood. As a group, the Pilipino respondents do not come from family backgrounds in business ownership—only 23% had fathers who were proprietors, compared to 32-42% for the other groups—and this may be reflected in their occupational choices. In any case, the lack of a concentrated ethnic neighborhood may be expected to have an effect on the extent and quality of the informal self-help network of the ethnic group.

The less extensive family network of the Pilipinos finds reflection in the relatively large percentage who received help from non-family members upon arriving in Chicago; 55.8% received help from this source, compared with 21.0% who received help from spouses, and 23.2% who were aided by siblings or parents. More Pilipinos

Table 64
Types of assistance received by Pilipino immigrant respondents from
nonrelatives upon their arrival in Chicago

Types of assistance	Pilipino immigrants		Totals for all groups in study	
	N	%	N	%
Lodging (stayed with them)	108	32.6	229	26.4
Helped find a place to stay	35	10.6	122	14.1
Loan	26	7.9	54	6.2
Helped to find a job	45	13.6	113	13.0
Introduced me to others who could help	18	5.4	43	5.0
Emotional support, encouragement	35	10.6	125	14.4
Other	64	19.3	182	21.0
Size of responses*	331	100.0	868	100.0

*Respondents could give as many responses as they wished, but for this table only the first two choices were counted. Therefore, the size of responses does not correspond to sample size.

received non family assistance than was the case in any other group, although the overall proportion of Pilipinos receiving aid from all sources (84%) was not markedly different from the figures for the other groups.

The type of assistance received from nonrelatives by the Pilipino immigrants did not differ systematically from that received by other groups (Table 64), except that more Pilipinos reported being given lodging. This is consistent with the finding that the Pilipino households tend to be large, and to contain many unrelated persons. Overall, the Pilipinos, in common with the Koreans in the study, seemed to have received more assistance—and more different kinds of assistance—than the Japanese and Chinese groups from non family members. This would tend to confirm that there are fewer family network resources available to new immigrants in the Pilipino and Korean groups. In part, at least, this may be a result of the fairly recent arrival of these groups in the U.S. compared with the Chinese and the Japanese.

The problem areas perceived by the Pilipino respondents in connection with immigration were somewhat different from those which concerned the other groups in the study. As might be expected from the relatively high level of English fluency among the Pilipino sample, language was seen as a problem far less often by this group than by any other. Still, 45.2% of the Pilipinos considered language a problem, far from a negligible proportion. Homesickness (66.8%) and weather differences (86.3%) were the two areas in which the Pilipinos reported more problems than the other groups. The greater incidence of homesickness may be related to the less extensive—the less closely related—Pilipino family network in the Chicago area. So far as weather differences are concerned, it need only be noted that the tropical climate of the Philippines presents a much greater contrast to that of Chicago than do the climates of the other donor countries in this study.

In other problem areas, the Pilipinos did not differ greatly from the other groups studied. Food differences (22.6%) and lack of contact with ethnic persons (25.1%) were not seen as severe problems. In the area of life style and cultural differences, the Pilipino group perceived the fewest problems (44.2%) of any group studied, although the Korean group is close to this figure. It is possible that the high level of English fluency and a long history of cultural contact with the U.S. contribute to the lower level of life style and cultural problems perceived by the Pilipino respondents. Viewed in absolute terms, however, this problem area is still of substantial concern to the Pilipino respondents.

Because of the predominance of language difficulties in all groups, respondents were asked whether they had ever taken English conversation classes or lessons. Of the Pilipino respondents, 24.2% had done so. This was the lowest percentage—by a wide margin—of any group studied, a finding which agrees well with the relatively high level of English fluency among the Pilipino respondents. Still, the fact that nearly one out of four Pilipinos had taken English classes or lessons indicates that even this group must have certain residual language problems. Since many Pilipinos in the study are members of the professional classes, they may perceive a need to develop their English skills at a higher level.

The Pilipinos in the study were generally satisfied with the decision to emigrate to the United States. As shown in Table 65, nearly two-thirds were definitely happy with the decision, and another fourth evaluated the decision favorably, but with some reservations. Only the naturalized Chinese citizens, of the other groups in the study, showed as high a level of satisfaction. In the case of the Pilipinos, satisfaction with the decision to emigrate may result, in

Table 65
Evaluation of decision to emigrate by Pilipino sample, by sex

Decisions	Sex	Pilipino immigrants		Totals for all groups in study	
		N	%	N	%
Yes, definitely	M	63	66.3	176	57.5
happy	F	61	58.7	182	50.4
Yes, with	M	23	24.2	73	23.9
reservation	F	27	26.0	94	26.0
Uncertain	M	5	5.3	36	11.8
	F	11	10.6	63	17.5
Regrets	M	1	1.1	9	2.9
	F	–	–	12	3.3
Plan to return	M	3	3.2	12	3.9
	F	5	4.8	10	2.8
Totals	M	95	100.0	306	100.0
	F	104	100.0	361	100.0

part, from the respondents' knowledge that the home country offers few suitable employment opportunities for highly-trained professionals.

Problems and Problem-Solving Activities

At both the beginning and the conclusion of the questionnaire interview the respondents were asked to list the major areas of difficulty they perceived for persons of their own ethnic groups. As the results for the Pilipino sample show (Table 66), this group perceived moderate levels of importance for several problems. By contrast, the other groups had a tendency to concentrate their attention on one or two major problems, perceiving the other problem areas as markedly less important.

As might be expected, the Pilipinos named "language and cultural difference adjustment" as a problem less often than the other groups. On the other hand, they reported "discrimination" much more often than the other groups. It may be that the higher level of English fluency among the Pilipinos makes them more aware of verbally-based discriminatory acts. Despite their English fluency, however, the Pilipinos reported "employment" as a problem more often than any other group. It is possible that the high level of education and training among the Pilipino group causes them to have more problems in finding *suitable* employment. Relatively few Pilipinos (13.6%) reported "no problems"—only the Korean group had fewer responses in this category. A low rate of response in the "no problems" category may indicate greater awareness of problems, greater incidence of problems, or a combination of these factors.

When asked what problems they had actually experienced, the Pilipino respondents gave responses which, in many cases, paralleled those of the other groups in the study. Insufficient income was the most frequently reported problem (34.2%), followed by problems on the job and adjustment problems due to differences in language and life style (23.1% each), and difficulties in locating a job (21.2%). The Korean and Chinese groups reported much higher frequencies of adjustment problems (perhaps because of the lower level of English proficiency in these groups), but otherwise the problem frequencies of the Pilipino respondents are not out of the ordinary.

On the other hand, the Pilipinos reported relatively low frequencies for problems in obtaining medical service (5.1%), and locating housing (12.1%), compared to the other groups in the study. These lower frequencies may arise from a higher level of English fluency, although in the case of medical service it may simply mean that the large proportion of medical professionals in this group know where to turn for help. Relative to the number of respondents, the Pilipino group seemed to report somewhat fewer actual problems than the other groups studied.

When the experiences of discrimination were broken down into

Table 66
Problems related to living in Chicago cited by
Pilipino respondents

Problem areas	Pilipino immigrants		Totals for all groups in study	
	N	%	N	%
Interpersonal and psychological adjustment	3	1.5	35	4.9
Language and cultural difference adjustment	57	28.6	305	42.3
Discrimination	55	27.6	111	15.4
Employment	20	10.1	40	5.6
City living stress	27	13.6	79	11.0
Ethnic community conflicts	10	5.0	35	4.9
No problems	27	13.6	116	16.1
Total	199	100.0	721	100.0

housing discrimination and two types of job discrimination, it was found that the most frequent area of discrimination was in being passed over for promotion on the job. Combining those who felt they "definitely" and "probably" had been discriminated against, 14.3% of the Pilipinos reported being passed over for promotion, while 3.0% felt they had lost a job, and 4.6% felt they had had difficulties with housing because of discrimination. Overall, the Pilipino group reported relatively fewer instances of actual discrimination than did the Koreans, the Japanese citizens, or the Chinese citizens. This is of interest because the Pilipinos had a higher frequency than these other groups when it came to naming discrimination as a community problem. This may indicate that the Pilipino group is more sensitive to the discriminatory actions of the majority society. There was no pattern of correlation for the Pilipinos between discrimination experience and length of residence in the United States.

In their responses to hypothetical medical and mental illness emergencies, the Pilipinos did not differ appreciably from the other groups studied. For the medical emergency, 58.1% cited a hospital or physician by name, while 21.2% said they would go to a hospital or physician, but did not give a specific name. These figures are similar to those for the other groups, except that the Pilipinos more often named a specific hospital or physician. This may reflect a higher level of English fluency, the large number of medical professionals in the Pilipino group, or both of these factors. In the hypothetical mental illness emergency, 27.1% of the Pilipinos cited a specific hospital or doctor, while 54.3% cited one of these resources, but without a specific name. Again, more Pilipinos named a specific doctor or hospital than was the case with any other group. For both of these types of emergencies, the other resources cited had low frequencies.

A third hypothetical problem presented was seeking a job. In this case, the responses of the Pilipino group differed from those of the other groups in the study. For the Pilipinos, classified ads (30.8%) and employment agencies (36.9%) were the resources of choice for finding employment. These two resources are ones which place the job seeker in direct competition with the majority society. In such a situation, the minority persons who are most likely to find themselves in a competitive position are those who—like the Pilipinos—are highly trained and possess marketable job skills. The level of English proficiency among the Pilipinos may also contribute to their greater use of public resources in finding jobs.

This tendency to make active use of public resources was also shown in the Pilipinos' responses to a hypothetical problem of employment discrimination: 53.3% said they would seek help from a civil rights organization. This is the highest rate of response in this category for any group studied—by a wide margin. Conversely, only 18.7% of the Pilipino respondents said they would give up in the face of job discrimination, which is by far the lowest response in this area for any group studied. Responses indicating that the respondent would seek help from family and friends, or ethnic organizations, or that the respondent would deny the discrimination or practice self-reliance, showed low frequencies for the Pilipino group. This pattern is similar to that for most of the other groups in the study. Somewhat surprisingly—considering the frequency with which they would seek active remedies—fully 17.8% of the Pilipino respondents said that they would not know where to go for help if they encountered job discrimination. This figure is higher than that for any other group except the Chinese. Thus it seems that even an activist stance and a working command of English cannot guarantee that Asian Americans will know where to turn for assistance in dealing with some types of problems.

The Pilipino respondents showed a similar pattern of responses to a hypothetical problem of housing discrimination. Table 67 compares the sources of help named for situations of job and housing discrimination. The respondents were apparently a little less sure of what to do about housing discrimination, since somewhat fewer of them named the active remedy of a civil rights

Table 67
Resources cited to deal with hypothetical job and housing discrimination by Pilipino sample

Responses to discrimination	Job discrimination				Housing discrimination			
	Pilipino immigrants		Totals		Pilipino immigrants		Totals	
	N	%	N	%	N	%	N	%
Civil rights organization	105	53.3	181	25.0	83	42.1	183	26.7
Give up	37	18.7	293	40.4	42	21.3	326	45.2
Family and friends	3	1.5	19	2.6	6	3.0	20	2.7
Ethnic organization	9	4.6	19	2.6	11	5.6	22	3.0
Denial of discrimination	6	3.0	45	6.2	9	4.6	42	5.8
Self-reliance	2	1.0	29	4.0	1	0.5	7	0.9
Don't know where to go	35	17.8	134	18.5	45	22.8	121	16.8
Total	197	100.0	724	99.3	197	100.0	721	101.1

Table 68
Resources cited for hypothetical financial problems by Pilipino sample

	Pilipino immigrants		Totals for all groups in study	
	N	%	N	%
Self-reliance	6	3.0	80	11.1
Family/relatives	67	33.8	227	31.5
Ethnic friends/ organization	21	10.6	109	15.1
Friends (unspecified)	2	1.0	10	1.4
Unemployment compensation	3	1.5	4	0.6
Bank/credit union	73	36.9	147	20.4
Public aid	17	8.6	56	7.8
Never thought about it	1	0.5	27	3.8
Don't know where to go	8	4.0	60	8.3
Totals	198	100.0	720	100.0

organization, while more would give up, or did not know where to go.

In citing sources of help for a hypothetical financial crisis, the Pilipino respondents again showed a tendency to rely on public resources. As Table 68 shows, 36.9% said they would turn to a bank or credit union, which was the highest rate for this response for any group studied. Public aid was cited by 8.6% (exceeded only by the Korean group), while 1.5% of the Pilipino respondents said they would rely on unemployment compensation. Although this last figure may appear low, it is greater than for the other groups. Together, these public resources account for 47%—nearly half—of the Pilipino responses to a hypothetical financial crisis.

Table 69 shows the responses of the Pilipino group when asked to cite sources of help for hypothetical marital problems. Perhaps the most interesting feature of this set of data is the rather large proportion of Pilipino respondents who said they would turn to a marriage counselor or lawyer. As in other hypothetical problem areas, this may indicate a greater willingness to utilize public resources, even in the case of highly personal problems. While more Pilipinos (9.9%) than any other group indicated that they would seek help from a minister or priest, this proportion does not seem particularly high, considering the high level of reported religious involvement among the Pilipino sample. While the passive response to this problem ("do nothing") showed a fairly low frequency for the Pilipino group, 14.8% said they did not know where to go, which was slightly above the average for all groups in the study.

Respondents in the study were also asked whether they had actually experienced problems in various areas and, if they had, whether they had sought outside help in solving them. As shown in Table 70, the Pilipino respondents reported that they had sought help in 40.7% of the instances in which they had encountered problems. This was the highest proportion reported by any group in the study, although one must still keep in mind that this still means that the Pilipino respondents did *not* seek help for nearly two-thirds of their problems.

The relative frequencies with which a group seeks help for various types of problems are of some interest to the service provider because they may indicate, among other things, the apparent magnitude of the problems to the client, the extent of personal resources available for solving the problems, and, for some cultural groups, the degree of shame attached to the various problems. In the case of the Pilipino respondents, comparison with the other groups in the study is difficult because the Pilipinos sought help with relatively high frequencies in most problem categories. However, in the area of help for insufficient income the Pilipinos sought help less frequently than any other group. Of course, the high overall income level of the Pilipino respondents may account for

Table 69
Resources cited for hypothetical marital
problems by Pilipino sample

Sources of help	Pilipino immigrants		Totals for all groups in study	
	N	%	N	%
Work it out oneself	34	18.7	187	28.2
Family/relatives	24	13.2	63	9.5
Friends, ethnic and non-ethnic	15	8.2	61	9.2
Marriage counselor/ lawyer	42	23.1	80	12.1
Separation or divorce	6	3.3	48	7.2
Minister or priest	18	9.9	43	6.5
Do nothing	9	4.9	43	6.5
Never thought about it	7	3.8	54	8.1
Don't know where to go	27	4.8	85	12.8
Totals	182	100.0	664	100.0

Table 70
Percentage of Pilipino respondents seeking help
in each problem area experienced*

Problems experienced Help sought	Pilipino immigrants		Totals for all groups in study	
	N	%	N	%
Insufficient income	68		255	
Help sought	14	20.5	88	34.3
Job location	42		178	
Help sought	24	57.1	84	47.8
On the job problems	46		162	
Help sought	23	50.0	50	30.8
Medical service	10		94	
Help sought	7	70.0	50	53.0
Locating housing	24		122	
Help sought	9	37.5	30	24.6
Adjustment to U.S.	46		254	
Help sought	9	19.5	46	19.0
Family conflicts	13		71	
Help sought	4	30.7	9	12.6
Total problems experienced	249		1136	
Total help sought	90	40.7	357	31.4

*Percentages in each cell are derived by dividing help-sought responses by number of problems experienced in each problem area. Therefore, the percentage columns do not sum to 100%.

this figure, but it should be noted that the Japanese groups, who enjoy a similar level of income, sought help for insufficient income more than two and a half times as often (53.7%) as did the Pilipinos. One possible explanation is that, while many of the Pilipino respondents possessed professional skills that would assure them of continuous employment, many more of the Japanese respondents were employed in business positions where they would be subject to the forces of the business cycle. Also, the Chicago Japanese community has an effective ethnic credit union, which might encourage Japanese respondents to seek help for financial problems. There is no such resource available in the Pilipino community.

In the areas of "locating a job," "on-the-job problems," "locating housing," and "family conflicts" the Pilipinos sought help more often than the average for all groups in the study. When taken together with data cited earlier which indicate that the Chicago Pilipinos tend to seek help in these areas from public rather than private sources, this pattern of help-seeking may reflect the relative lack of extended family resources and ethnic service providers available to this group. The Pilipino respondents also sought help for medical problems with greater frequency than did the other groups studied. As noted earlier, however, this may be partly due to the large number of medical professionals in the Pilipino sample.

Respondents were also asked to cite the specific resources they had used in two areas: finding their first jobs in the United States and obtaining child care for their young children while the mother was at work. In the case of resources for finding the first job (Table 71), the Pilipino respondents reported using employment agencies and classified ads with greater frequency than was the case for the other groups. This finding agrees with the reported preference of the Pilipino respondents for public resources in this area. Only a single Pilipino respondent, on the other hand, reported having found a first job through a professional organization. While professional organizations showed a very low frequency of response for all groups studied, this finding is perhaps surprising in the case of the Pilipinos, given the large number of professionals in this group. It has been suggested elsewhere[2] that some professional organizations may actually have negative effects on the hiring (or

Table 71
Resources cited for obtaining the first job in the
U.S. by Pilipino immigrant respondents*

Sources of help	Pilipino immigrants		Totals for all groups in study	
	N	%	N	%
Employment agency, private and public	45	18.8	72	11.6
Classified ads	75	31.3	135	21.7
Professional organization	1	0.4	10	1.6
Ethnic friends/organization	63	26.3	216	34.7
Non ethnic friends	11	4.6	32	5.1
Family/relatives	17	7.1	85	13.7
Employment pre-arranged	28	11.7	72	11.6
Total responses*	240	100.0	622	100.0

*Since a respondent could give more than one response, the totals do not correspond with total respondents.

on licensure, which is a prerequisite to hiring) of Asian-born professionals. This charge would seem to be borne out by the results of the present study. At the very least it is clear that professional organizations are not a productive source of help in finding employment among the Asian-American respondents surveyed.

Pilipino respondents were less likely than members of other groups to report that they had found their first jobs with the help of either ethnic friends or organizations, or with the help of family members or relatives. As in other areas, this probably results from the relatively recent arrival of the bulk of the Pilipino immigrants in Chicago, together with the lack of an extensive family network in the Chicago area. In addition, the lack of Pilipino ethnic business enterprises probably contributes to the smaller number of Pilipinos who obtained employment from ethnic sources.

These same demographic conditions are reflected in the sources from which the Pilipinos reported obtaining child care for their young children when the mothers were at work (see Table 72). The Pilipino and Korean groups were the only ones to show a response frequency for day care centers, presumably because these more recently-arrived immigrants have fewer relatives and other persons in the ethnic community upon whom to rely. The relative youth of the Pilipino sample, and the high labor force participation of Pilipino women would also contribute to greater need for child care facilities. Most of the other frequencies of the Pilipino responses are near the average for the whole study, although somewhat fewer Pilipinos said they relied on relatives.

Those respondents who had not sought help were asked why they had not done so. For all groups, the two reasons most often cited were, "no problems, or not serious enough," and "problems

Table 72
Child care for children under five when mothers work in Pilipino sample

Type of care	Pilipino immigrants		Totals for all groups in study	
	N	%	N	%
Relatives	19	23.2	57	29.2
Neighbors	20	24.4	47	24.1
Day care centers	6	7.3	14	7.2
Spouse	33	40.2	70	35.9
Others	4	4.9	7	3.6
Totals	82	100.0	195	100.0

Table 73
Reasons cited by Pilipino respondents for not seeking help, by sex

Reasons for not seeking help	Sex	Pilipino immigrants		Totals for all groups in study	
		N	%	N	%
No problems or not	M	26	37.1	104	30.1
serious enough	F	44	53.0	136	34.3
Solve by self or	M	36	51.4	134	38.7
with family	F	31	37.4	123	31.0
Organizations	M	1	1.4	33	9.5
can't help	F	3	3.6	18	4.5
Didn't want	M	—	—	12	3.5
others to know	F	1	1.2	11	2.8
Language	M	—	—	11	3.2
barrier	F	1	1.2	34	8.6
Didn't know	M	6	8.6	51	14.7
where to go	F	3	3.6	75	18.9
Size of	M	69	100.0	345	
responses*	F	83	100.0	397	

*This question was asked of only those respondents who did not seek help. Also, these respondents could give more than one response. Thus the size of responses does not represent the number of respondents on this question.

can be solved alone or with family help." In the case of the Pilipino group, these two responses were especially predominant, with only a scattering of responses in the other categories (see Table 73). Interestingly, female Pilipino respondents were more likely to choose "no problems or not serious enough," while the males were more likely—by almost exactly the same margin—to indicate that they could solve their problems by themselves, or within the family. The other groups do not show such a clear cut pattern along sex lines. As might be expected, "language barrier" and "did not know where to go" were relatively minor problems for the Pilipinos.

Service Characteristics and Priorities

When they were asked to rate the importance of eight different services, the Pilipino respondents indicated priorities that fall roughly in the middle of the scale for all groups studied: most of their rank orders are near the average, and the general level of im-

Table 74
Services considered important in Pilipino sample*

| Types of services | Rank order | Pilipino immigrants | | Totals for all groups in study |
		N	%	N
Child care centers	2	110	55.8	302
English conversation classes	3	93	46.7	376
Mental health service	8	57	28.6	228
Employment service	6	82	41.2	284
Vocational training	5	83	41.9	277
Public aid	7	63	31.8	276
Bilingual referral service	4	87	44.2	345
Legal aid service	1	116	58.6	425
Size or responses		691		2513

*Percentages in each cell are derived in relation to total respondents in each ethnic group. Thus the column percentage totals do not sum to 100%.

portance they assigned to most services fell between the extremes of the Japanese (low importance) and Chinese (high importance) groups. As Table 74 shows, child care centers are of high importance to the Pilipino respondents, a finding which agrees with the reported use of child care centers by this group. Like all the other groups, the Pilipinos also assigned high priority to legal aid services, in spite of a dearth of actual legal problems.

The relatively high level of importance assigned to English conversation classes by the Pilipinos is harder to explain, since as a group they demonstrate a fairly high level of English fluency. This priority may indicate a need for English conversation classes on more advanced levels. The Pilipino respondents may be sensing a need for sophisticated language and communications skills to aid them in professional advancement. Likewise, the Pilipinos indicated about the same priority level as other groups for bilingual referral service and newcomers' services. In evaluating this data it should be remembered that, although the Pilipino group reported a relatively high level of English proficiency, most are also quite recently arrived in the United States. Thus the respondents appear to feel a need for such services in spite of their generally adequate English skills.

Although the Pilipinos are perhaps the most highly trained group in the study, they placed considerable importance on vocational training. This may reflect the difficulties they have encountered in transferring their skills to the U.S. job market.

The Pilipino group also assigns high priority to employment services. It was noted earlier that the Pilipinos made more use of employment services than any other group, a finding which agrees with the priority assigned here.

The Pilipino respondents assigned almost the same importance to various service characteristics as did the Japanese citizen group. Few of the Pilipinos (3.5%) considered bilingual staffing of agencies to be important but a large number (62.2%) assigned high importance to the helpfulness of the service agency staff. Convenient access and confidentiality were each ranked most important by 12.8% of the Pilipino respondents, while only 8.6% assigned first importance to the cost of the service. These figures are, however, slightly above the average for the other groups, aside from the Japanese citizens. For most of the other groups, a bilingual staff is of such importance that convenient access, cost, and even confidentiality, are of minor consequence by comparison. On the other hand, although the Pilipinos do not give much weight to bilingual staff, they do assign great importance to the helpfulness of the staff. This may indicate that it is not enough that minority clients be able to communicate adequately with agency personnel—as most of the Pilipino respondents could. Rather, it is apparently also quite important that agency personnel be able to provide appropriate help delivered in a form acceptable to the client. The greater English fluency of the Pilipino respondents may in fact make them more keenly aware of the shortcomings of agency personnel with whom they have attempted to deal.

The Pilipino Sample: Composite and Conclusions

As we proceed to construct a profile of a respondent from the Chicago Pilipino community, a few preliminary cautions should be observed. There is some evidence that this Chicago Pilipino American may not be representative of national norms. Both census data and casual observation indicate that this typical respondent is both better educated and better paid than Pilipinos in some other areas of the country. On the other hand, because of the long cultural association of the United States and the Philippines, one would expect that the English fluency and general level of acculturation of our Chicago respondent would be found in most other young, urban Pilipino Americans. Here too, however, the educational level of the individual could be expected to have some effect.

In broad terms, the Chicago Pilipino respondent can be categorized as young, well-educated, and fairly well-off financially: he is in his early thirties, has finished college, and may have a graduate or professional degree. Unlike most of the other groups in the study, it does not matter in this area whether the Pilipino respondent is male or female. In either case, the educational level and job level—skilled, white collar, or professional—will probably be about the same. The Pilipino female respondent will also be just about as likely as her male counterpart to have a full-time job, or to hold more than one job.

This respondent is probably married and living with his or her spouse. There does not seem to be a "typical" size for our respondent's household: it may contain just one or two persons, or a dozen or more, although the average is about four or five persons. It is quite likely, however, that several of the persons in this household are not related to the respondent. If the respondent is married, he will typically have two or three young children (under the age of nine). As in the case of the other groups studied, this household is probably housed in a rented apartment, although there is about a one in five chance that the respondent owns a house. He is not very likely to rent a house, or to own an apartment.

It is nearly a foregone conclusion that our typical Pilipino respondent is Catholic, and he is almost certain to attend church at least once a month, and probably more often than that. On the other hand, aside from church membership he is not much of a joiner of organizations. If he belongs to any organizations at all, he probably limits his membership to one or two. This does not mean, however, that the Pilipino respondent is apathetic about community activities. He may often attend a meeting that is of particular interest to him even though he will probably not become an official member of the organization.

English is not much of a problem for the Pilipino respondent, who can at least understand the spoken language and may be quite fluent. Unlike the respondents from the other groups studied, the female Pilipino respondent is somewhat more likely to be fluent than her male counterpart. This typical respondent was born in the Philippines and was raised in an urban environment. He probably emigrated to the United States less than six years ago.

On the average, the Pilipino respondent from Chicago has had 16 years of schooling; if he is from other areas of the country we would probably find it more likely that he had only finished high school. He is almost certain to hold a full-time job, and he is somewhat more likely than a member of the other study groups to hold more than one job. A female Pilipino respondent is also quite likely to be employed full time; she is very unlikely to be a homemaker, and even if she is, she probably has a history of outside employment as well.

There is a good chance that the Pilipino respondent is employed as a professional, as a skilled worker, or in a white collar/clerical job. Compared to this job level before immigration, however, his present position may represent a step downward on the job scale. If he was a professional or managerial person before immigrating, he may have had to accept a skilled or white collar position. If he was an academic he has probably fared worse—perhaps even being forced into manual labor totally unrelated to his education and experience. Even if he has a job within the same category as before immigration, the Pilipino respondent may feel underemployed. That is, he may feel that he holds a position near the bottom of the job category, where his education is not fully utilized. This is especially likely if he is a member of the health professions, in which case he has probably also experienced difficulties in obtaining a professional license.

Despite these problems, the typical Pilipino respondent is doing fairly well in terms of reported family income. His family income level is near that of the Japanese citizen respondent, but it should be remembered that in many cases both the Pilipino respondent and his spouse are working full-time at fairly high level jobs in order to earn this family income. Thus, although he does not have difficulty with the basic problems of economic survival, the Pilipino respondent may have some sense of being underpaid for his job position, and he may be dissatisfied with his income, although he is somewhat more likely to consider it to be at least adequate.

The Pilipino respondent may also view his job status and economic condition with mixed feelings because he probably came to the U.S. in search of greater employment opportunities. He was also interested in the educational opportunities in the United States, and he may even hold one or more degrees from U.S. schools. He is very likely to have had relatives already residing in the U.S. at the time he immigrated, but he probably did not immigrate to join his family. Instead, these relatives are about as likely as not to reside in another city. Apparently it is more important to the Pilipino respondent to pursue educational and vocational opportunities than to stay close to a concentration of related persons. In addition, there is no concentration of ethnic businesses to attract him to one neighborhood rather than another.

When this typical respondent arrived in Chicago, he probably received help from various persons, most of whom were not related to him. Most often, the type of assistance offered was to provide lodging while the newcomer got settled and found a job.

There were some problems for the respondent as he got settled in Chicago, but they were different from the problems facing members of the other groups studied. He had trouble with English and had to adjust to the new culture and lifestyle, but he experienced these problems less severely than did most other Asian immigrants. If he had trouble with English, he probably worked it out himself, because there is only a one in four chance that he has taken English conversation classes or lessons, perhaps because they are not readily available to him. On the other hand, he was probably homesick at some point because, although he had little trouble making contact with other Pilipinos, they were probably not members of his family. And the Chicago weather was hard to get used to, presumably because it is such a sharp contrast to the tropical Philippine climate. In spite of these problems, however, the Pilipino respondent is generally quite happy with his decision to come to the United States.

If he is asked about the general problems facing Pilipinos in Chicago, this typical respondent will probably name several areas of difficulty, but will not see any of them as highly problematic. One area in which he sees more problems than members of other groups is that of discrimination.

As he thinks back over the problems he has experienced as a Pilipino immigrant to America, our respondent may recall having had economic difficulties, even though he is better off now. He also may recall a few difficulties with the language and culture of the new country, and there is a one in five chance that he had trouble locating a job.

When he encounters problems in his own life, this Pilipino respondent usually has a reasonably good idea of where to turn for help. He also differs from members of some other Asian-American groups in that he is quite willing to utilize public resources of help, both for relatively neutral problems, such as obtaining a job or getting medical assistance, and for more sensitive matters such as financial problems and marital difficulties. This general willingness to use public resources also carries over into practice, for this Pilipino respondent typically makes use of outside assistance in solving his problems somewhat more often than do members of the other groups studied.

Because of his relatively high level of English fluency, this typical Pilipino respondent does not feel it is important that the service agencies he uses have bilingual staff available. He does, however, feel quite strongly that the personnel should be helpful, and it is moderately important to him that the services be confidential, conveniently located, and inexpensive.

In one sense, the Pilipino immigrants are a "best case" example among Asian-American groups. They are relatively well educated, usually have at least adequate fluency in English, often possess marketable job skills, and come from a country which has some history of cultural connections with the United States. The study sample may somewhat exaggerate these advantages, compared to the Pilipino-American population nationwide. What is of greatest importance however is that, in spite of these apparent advantages, the Pilipinos as a group do not meet the stereotypic expectations of the majority society: they are not "problem free," they do not manage fully to "take care of their own," and, if anything, they are more severely underemployed than other groups which bring less education and fewer skills to the labor marketplace.

The solutions to the problems of Pilipino Americans may at times be somewhat more complex and indirect than those for other groups. For example, although many members of the Pilipino sample were professional persons, very few reported that their professional organizations had helped them find jobs when they arrived in the U.S. Solutions to these sorts of problems—here perhaps involving reform of the inner dynamics of some professional organizations—lie outside the usual sphere of activity of social service providers. Another example would be the desire of many Pilipino respondents to gain greater English proficiency, despite the fact that most are already moderately fluent. Most available English conversation classes and lessons concentrate on what might be termed "survival English." Apparently, the Pilipino respondents want something more sophisticated, and, equally apparently, they are not getting it, since relatively few reported that they had ever taken English conversation classes or lessons.

Finally, the delivery of social services to this group may present special problems in some localities. In Chicago, for instance, there is no geographically concentrated Pilipino community. On the other hand, in some cities the Pilipino community may present itself as a "Manilla Town," with its own special set of urban problems. In the present sample, too, it was found that, aside from the Catholic church, there were few formal organizational structures present in the Pilipino community to aid in the delivery of social services. Thus, as in the case of the other groups studied, it will be necessary to tailor both the content and delivery mode of social services to the particular conditions of the local Pilipino community.

NOTES TO CHAPTER VI

1. U.S. Commission on Civil Rights, *Asian Americans and Pacific Peoples: A Case of Mistaken Identity*, Washington: Author, prepared by the California Advisory Committee to the Commission, 1975, 40–41.

2. U.S. Commission on Civil Rights, *A Dream Unfulfilled: Korean and Pilipino Health Professionals in California*, Washington: Author, prepared by the California Advisory Committee to the Commission, 1975, 13–39. All of the licensing bodies of the health professions proved to have some sort of restrictions on licensing foreign-educated health professionals. In most cases it is safe to say that the attitudes of professional licensing bodies represent the sentiment of the mass of professionals who are ostensibly controlled by these bodies.

CHAPTER VII

THE KOREAN SAMPLE

Among major Asian-American groups, probably less is known about Korean Americans than about any other. Although there are presently approximately 175,000 persons of Korean ancestry in the United States, the decennial census only began to disaggregate Korean Americans from the "other Asians" category in 1970. To some extent this is understandable, since the Koreans, unlike the other Asian groups, have very little history of "early" migration to the United States. Some Korean contract laborers were brought to Hawaii and, eventually, to the West Coast in the early 1900s[1], but Korean immigration never reached the proportions of the Chinese, Japanese, or Pilipino influxes during the early period. For all practical purposes of policy and social service program development, Korean immigration begins with the 1965 amendments to the immigration law. Since that time, Korean immigration has been very heavy, and Koreans rose in rank from twenty-eight to fourth among donor nations over the period of 1965 to 1973. From 1970 to 1975 alone, Korean immigration increased by more than 304%.

Demographic Characteristics

All of the persons in the Korean sample for the present study were immigrants, selected from the Immigration and Naturalization

Service files. For the most part, they were relatively young (average age, about 36 years), with the females being a little younger than the males. Only two Korean respondents were 65 or older, and most were under 50. The sex ratio was nearly even, at 45% male to 55% female; this is close to the ratio of 40% to 60% reported by the 1970 Census. The trend toward greater immigration of females is shared with the other groups in the study.

A large proportion of the Korean respondents (88.2%) were married and living with their spouses. This was the largest proportion of any group studied and the Korean group also contained the smallest proportion of persons who had never been married (6.1%).

The Korean households tended to be relatively small, usually containing not more than three or four persons, and very rarely more than six. In this respect, they somewhat resemble the Japanese immigrant households. Like the Pilipino immigrant group households, the Korean households often contained young children (68.7% under the age of nine). Most of these households are housed in rented apartments (80.2%), while only 7.9% own homes, which was the lowest proportion for any group studied. While apartment ownership (2.2%) was less popular among the Koreans than in any other group, house rental was more popular (8.4%). The predominance of renting among the Koreans may be partly a result of their recent arrival in the U.S., although the Pilipino group, which is also recently arrived, shows a level of home and apartment ownership that is about twice as high. Therefore, other cultural and economic factors may be at work here.

The religious preferences and frequencies of the Korean respondents are shown in Table 75. Overall, the religious involvement of this group is greater than that of any other group except the Pilipinos, although it is not so monolithic. It is true that slightly fewer Japanese citizens than Koreans responded in the "no preference" category, but the Koreans who do have a religious preference showed a higher level of attendance at services. Because of this fairly high level of church involvement, the Koreans, like the Pilipinos, might possibly be contacted and served through existing religious institutions.

It may also be possible to reach Korean persons through organizational contact. As Table 76 shows, only 19.3% of the Korean respondents belong to no organization at all; this is the lowest proportion for any group studied. Depending on which criterion one chooses, the Koreans have the highest overall organizational

Table 75
Religious preference and religious service attendance for
Korean immigrants

	Korean immigrants		Totals for all groups in study	
	N	%	N	%
Religious preference				
Protestant	150	65.8	257	32.6
Catholic	35	15.4	254	35.0
Buddhist	11	4.8	91	12.5
No preference	30	13.2	132	18.2
Other	2	0.9	12	1.7
Totals	228	100.0	726	100.0
Religious service attendance				
(Adjusted frequency)				
Once a week	108	54.3	318	52.6
Once a month	41	20.6	93	15.4
Less than once a month	25	12.6	90	14.9
Never	25	12.6	104	17.2
No answer	29		121	
Totals	228	100.0	726	100.0

Table 76
Membership in organizations by
Korean sample

Numbers of organizations	Korean immigrants		Totals for all groups in study	
	N	%	N	%
0	44	19.3	297	40.9
1	98	43.0	229	31.5
2	54	23.7	110	15.2
3	21	9.2	49	6.8
4–5	10	4.4	29	4.0
6–10	1	0.4	11	1.5
10 and over	—	—	1	0.1
Totals	228	100.0	726	100.0

Table 77
Self-evaluation of English fluency by Korean respondents

English fluency	Sex	Korean immigrants		Totals for all groups in study	
		N	%	N	%
Fluently	M	12	11.8	59	21.7
	F	6	4.8	58	17.8
Adequately	M	54	53.4	124	45.6
	F	53	43.0	118	36.2
Understand but	M	33	32.6	69	25.4
can't speak	F	52	42.2	95	29.1
No comprehension	M	2	1.9	20	7.4
of English	F	12	9.7	55	16.9
Totals	M	101	99.7	272	100.1
	F	123	99.7	326	100.0

membership level, or the second highest, after the Japanese citizens. However, the Japanese participation seems to consist of a smaller proportion of persons belonging to a larger number of organizations, while in the Korean group, participation is spread more uniformly over all the members of the group.

An examination of individual responses indicates that, although many of the organizational memberships of the Korean respondents are in unions and professional organizations, nearly a half appear to be ethnic organizations of one sort or other. (An exact figure cannot be given because the item was not structured to collect the exact names of the organizations and hence they are identified only by general types on the questionnaires.) The ethnic organization membership of the Korean group may be expected to be considerably larger at the present time, since at the time these data were collected (1974), the Chicago Korean community was still in its infancy. Since that time there has been a continuing increase of population and progressive emergence of more organizations.

Only 1.8% of the Korean interviews were conducted entirely in English. While this was the lowest proportion for any group studied, it does not necessarily indicate that the Koreans lack English proficiency as a group. As Table 77 indicates, nearly half of the female Korean respondents, and nearly two-thirds of the males, evaluated their own English proficiency as fluent or adequate, despite the fact that they asked to be interviewed in Korean. Informal observation in Korean-American communities indicates that there are strong social pressures among Koreans toward the use of the Korean language when talking with other Korean persons. One speculation is that this social pressure results from a reaction against the enforced use of the Japanese language during the Japanese occupation of Korea (1905-1945). Also, English contains no honorific forms; hence many Asian persons feel socially uncomfortable addressing one another in English. The use of Korean is necessary in order to maintain social propriety. Vertical relationships are very important. In any case, the interviewers were all Korean persons and therefore nearly all of the Korean respondents apparently felt they should be interviewed in Korean, regardless of their level of English fluency.

Overall, the English fluency of the Korean immigrants seems to be similar to that of the Japanese immigrants, and slightly lower than that of the Pilipino immigrants and Japanese citizens. As in the case of all other groups (with the partial exception of the Pilipinos) the Korean males reported higher levels of English fluency than the females. It should be remembered that these are self-ratings of English fluency. Therefore, various cultural factors may affect whether or not a respondent considers his/her English to be "adequate."

Over 95% of the Korean respondents were born in Korea, with most of the remaining number being born in Japan. Most of the Korean respondents (62.3%) reported that they had grown up in cities of over one million population, while only 10.1% came from rural backgrounds. The remaining Korean respondents were from medium-sized cities. These figures indicate that the Korean group has the most definitely urban background of any group studied. Only the Chinese groups approached the Korean proportion of persons from very large cities, but the Chinese groups also contained larger numbers of persons from rural backgrounds. The proportion of Koreans from rural backgrounds was similar to that in the Pilipino group, but the Pilipinos with urban backgrounds tended to be from the group of smallest cities.

Like the Pilipino group, most of the Korean respondents had arrived in the U.S. and Chicago within the last six years. This is to be expected since both groups have begun to immigrate in significant numbers only since the passage of the 1965 amendments to the immigration law. Remembering that these data were collected in 1974, the sharp increase in immigration shown in Figure 4 corre-

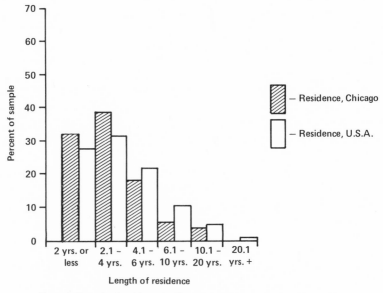

Figure 4. Length of residence in Chicago and U.S. by Korean respondents

sponds to the implementation of the new numerical ceilings for Asian immigration under the amended act.

Education, Employment, and Income Characteristics

As a group, the Korean sample proved to be well educated, in some respects slightly more so than the Pilipinos: while 12.2% of Pilipino females and 14.6% of Pilipino males held advanced degrees (for an aggregate of 13.4%), in the Korean sample 5.4% of the females and 20.5% of the males hold advanced degrees (for an aggregate of 13.8%). Going down the scale to undergraduate degrees, however, the Pilipinos show more persons at this level, and also seven times as many females with nursing degrees.

Table 78 gives a breakdown of the educational attainments of the Korean sample. It is of some concern that the Korean group contains a large number of males with advanced academic degrees (MS and Ph.D.), since the experience of the survey shows that Asian persons holding such degrees may have unusual difficulties in finding suitable employment. By comparison, the Pilipinos were more likely to hold professional degrees, especially in the medical professions. Persons holding such degrees will probably be able to find employment in their fields, although they will often be hired for the lowest position within the profession. Also unlike the Pilipino group, the Korean sample follows the pattern of the other groups in the study in which women become increasingly underrepresented as one ascends the educational scale.

The full-time employment rate of Korean males (86.8%) was the highest of any group in the study, although it only slightly exceeded the rate for Pilipino males (86.5%). The full-time employment rate for Korean females was also high (61.8%), second only to that for Pilipino females (75.9). As might be expected in a relatively young group such as this, there were no retired or disabled persons among the Koreans. Although the unemployment level among the Koreans was low, it was somewhat higher than that for most other groups. As Table 79 shows, there are fair numbers of

Table 78
Highest educational levels achieved
by respondents and spouses in Korean sample, by sex

Educational levels	Sex	Korean immigrants		Totals for all groups in study	
		N	%	N	%
Elementary or under	M	3	1.7	25	5.3
	F	9	6.2	45	11.0
High school graduate or under	M	14	7.7	82	17.3
	F	25	17.1	72	17.5
High school and beyond	M	18	9.9	56	11.8
	F	28	19.2	45	11.0
College graduate	M	109	60.2	234	49.4
	F	74	50.7	201	48.9
Nursing	M	—	—	—	—
	F	2	1.4	16	3.9
MS and PhD	M	27	14.9	48	10.1
	F	4	2.7	13	3.2
MD and dental	M	3	1.7	12	2.5
	F	—	—	1	0.2
Post-MD and PhD	M	7	3.9	17	3.6
	F	4	2.7	18	4.4
Totals*	M	181	100.0	474	100.0
	F	146	100.0	411	100.0

*Totals include both respondents and spouses. Therefore they do not correspond to sample size.

Table 79
Employment status of Korean respondents and spouses,
by sex

Employment status	Sex	Korean immigrants		Totals	
		N	%	N	%
Full-time	M	178	86.8	505	82.1
	F	136	61.8	393	59.1
Part-time	M	5	2.4	19	3.1
	F	8	3.6	36	5.4
More than one	M	12	5.9	38	6.2
job	F	1	0.5	17	2.6
Unemployed,	M	—	—	5	0.8
sick, disabled	F	—	—	6	0.9
Retired	M	—	—	26	4.2
	F	—	—	16	2.4
Unemployed,	M	3	1.5	8	1.3
seeking job	F	9	4.1	17	2.6
Unemployed, not	M	4	2.0	9	1.5
seeking job	F	7	3.2	14	2.1
Homemaker	M	3	1.5	3	0.5
	F	33	15.0	120	18.1
Never employed	M	—	—	2	0.3
	F	26	11.8	46	6.9
Totals*	M	205	100.0	615	100.0
	F	220	100.0	665	100.0

*Totals include respondents and their spouses. Therefore they do not correspond to sample size.

Korean women who reported being "homemakers" or "never employed," in contrast to the Pilipino group. The "never employed" responses among the Koreans may reflect the youth of this group. It should also be noted that, although more Korean than Pilipino women reported being homemakers, still the Korean group contains fewer female homemakers than the Japanese and Chinese groups in the study. Together with the fact that three Korean males reported being homemakers, these data indicate a fairly high level of labor force involvement by Korean females.

Like the Pilipino group, the Koreans also show a pattern of near-equal male and female participation at the higher job levels (see Table 80). As was the case with the Pilipino group the greater number of females than males in the professional category may be due to the inclusion of nursing in the professions. Overall, the

Korean group contains more professional persons than any other group except the Pilipinos, and more proprietors than any other group except the Chinese citizens. Like the other groups, the Korean sample contains few managers, and a fairly large group of skilled and white collar workers. Compared to the Pilipino group, the Korean sample shows a stronger bipolar tendency in job levels. That is, although the Korean sample contains a relatively large number of professionals, there is about an equal proportion of respondents at the other end of the scale, in the semi- and unskilled job categories.

There are several areas of data collected in this survey from which one can determine whether or not respondents are underemployed relative to their training and experience. One item on the questionnaire asked those respondents who had been employed before immigration whether they felt their present jobs entailed more or less responsibility than their jobs in the home country. Of the Korean respondents who had been employed before immigration, 53% felt that their present jobs had less responsibility, while 23.1% felt they now had more responsibility, 18.7% felt there was no change, and 5.2% were uncertain. Thus over half of the Koreans

Table 80
Occupational categories of Korean respondents and spouses,
by sex

Job categories	Sex	Korean immigrants		Totals	
		N	%	N	%
Professional	M	50	24.5	159	27.7
	F	55	37.7	143	31.5
Managerial	M	7	3.4	23	4.0
	F	3	2.1	9	2.0
Proprietor	M	33	16.2	61	10.6
	F	5	3.4	11	2.4
Skilled and white	M	67	32.8	232	40.4
collar	F	40	27.4	164	36.1
Semi- and unskilled	M	47	23.0	99	17.3
	F	43	29.4	127	28.0
Totals*	M	204	100.0	574	100.0
	F	146	100.0	454	100.0

*Totals include respondents and their spouses. Therefore they do not correspond to sample size.

felt they now held less responsible jobs than they had held in Korea.

Those who felt they now held less responsible jobs were asked why they felt this was so. The most frequent answer given was the language barrier, although respondents also often cited their inability to transfer training or experience, and licensing requirements.

Underemployment can also be expressed as the incongruity between the individual's actual educational level and the educational requirements of the job he holds. Therefore, in addition to ascertaining the respondent's educational level, the study questionnaire asked the respondent to evaluate the educational level required for his or her present job. While this sort of evaluation is highly subjective, it may still be quite revealing: if the employee *perceives* the job to require less education than he actually possesses, then this makes it quite likely that the employee will perceive himself as being underemployed. In the case of the Korean sample, 16.5% of the respondents felt that their jobs required only an elementary school education, but only 7.0% of the employed respondents had this low a level of education. At the other end of the scale, 44.5% of the respondents held college degrees, but only 23.3% felt that they held jobs requiring this level of education. These discrepancies may indicate a certain degree of underemployment among the Korean sample group.

It is also possible to compare the reported job levels of the respondents before and after immigration. When this is done, there appears to be a moderate shift from the two highest job categories (professional and managerial) into the middle job categories (skilled/ white collar and proprietors). This is a trend which was also observable in the Pilipino sample and it may reflect the greater effect of the language barrier and licensing problems on persons in the higher job categories.

It is also instructive to compare the job status of the respondent with that of his father or male guardian. Under normal conditions, one expects to see a certain amount of stability from generation to generation, or some degree of upward mobility. Table 81 compares the job categories of the Korean respondents with those of their fathers or male guardians. These data are open to several possible interpretations. For example, the sizeable drop in the proportion of managers across generations may be indicative of problems of social assimilation on the part of the younger (immigrant) generation. On the other hand, the decrease in the number of proprietors may suggest the difficulty of establishing an economic base in a new country. Finally, the increase in the proportions in the highest and lowest job categories across generations may indicate that the old maxim that "the rich get richer and the poor get poorer" holds true in the immigration experience.

As with the other groups studied, most of the Korean respondents (62.8%) said they intended to stay in the jobs they presently held. For the most part, they reported "good pay and benefits (41%)" and "good working conditions (21%)" as reasons for keeping a job. "Job interest" was cited by 13.5% of those Korean respondents who intended to keep their present jobs. This figure is about the same as that for the Pilipino and Chinese groups, but well below that for both Japanese groups. Nearly a fifth of the Korean respondents reported they would keep the job because it was "the best I could get under the circumstances." Only the Chinese immigrants reported this reason with greater frequency. Together with the data cited above, these responses tend to indicate a moderate level of underemployment for at least part of the Korean sample.

Median family income for the Korean sample was $16,622 per year (see Table 82). This is just slightly more than the figure for the Pilipino group, and about $2,000 below the median family income of the Japanese citizen group. Thus the Korean group seems to be reasonably well off, although it is important to remember that these are *family* income figures and may thus represent the earnings of more than one person. About half of the Korean households surveyed did in fact contain two working spouses. Among the respondents, however, the employment levels of Korean women were nearly equal to those of the men. Therefore, as in the case of the Pilipino group, the family income figures may often conceal the somewhat substandard income of two spouses who may

Table 81
Korean respondents' job categories compared to those of
fathers or male guardians

Job category	Fathers or male guardians	Respondents
Professional	19.8	27.9
Managerial	14.1	2.8
Skilled/white collar	11.9	31.8
Proprietor	35.2	6.1
Semi-skilled/unskilled	17.6	31.3

Table 82
Combined annual family income for the Korean sample

Annual family income	Korean immigrants		Totals for all groups in study	
	N	%	N	%
Under 3,000	3	1.3	18	2.5
3,001–6,999	10	4.4	60	8.3
7,000–8,999	5	2.2	57	7.9
9,000–11,999	34	15.0	93	12.8
12,000–14,999	47	20.6	114	12.8
15,000–19,999	60	26.3	140	19.0
20,000–24,999	50	21.9	108	14.9
25,000–49,999	15	6.6	65	9.0
50,000 and over	–	–	11	1.5
Would not state income	2	0.9	41	5.7
Don't know	2	0.9	19	2.6
Total	228	100.0	726	100.0
Median	16,622			
Mean	17,162			

both hold high level jobs for which they are underpaid. This contrasts with the Japanese citizen group, where it is more usual for the husband to hold a fairly high level position, and the wife to hold a more or less menial job.

The Korean respondents showed a fairly high level of satisfaction with their income levels: 68.9% said that their actual income equalled or exceeded what they regarded as an "adequate" income. This figure is right at the average for all groups in the study. By comparison, 63.2% of the Pilipino group (which is demographically most like the Korean group) felt that their incomes were adequate or more than adequate.

The Immigration Experience

The reasons given for immigration by the Korean group (shown in Table 83) are concentrated in the educational and vocational areas, although the female respondents showed a large proportion of "to join family" responses. Interestingly, the Korean respondents showed the lowest frequency of any group in the area of "job training opportunities," despite their high level of interest in educational opportunities, better work opportunities, and a higher standard of living. Thus the Koreans appear to perceive the United States primarily as a place to gain education or utilize existing skills, rather than as a source of job training. The Korean interest in education may also be inferred from the 5.5% of the respondents who indicated that they had immigrated in order to secure greater educational opportunities for their children. While this response rate is not high, the Korean group was the only one in which there was a noticeable frequency in this category (no other group exceeded 0.6%).

Although the Korean sample did not have a particularly large number of relatives present in the U.S., there is some evidence to suggest that the family network may be more closely related than

Table 83
Reasons given for immigration to the United States by
Korean respondents, by sex

Reasons for immigration	Sex	Korean immigrants		Totals for all groups in study	
		N	%	N	%
To join family	M	14	7.2	107	14.0
	F	70	39.1	197	26.7
Educational opportunity	M	66	35.5	158	20.7
	F	24	13.4	94	12.8
Job-training opportunity	M	11	5.9	104	13.6
	F	11	6.1	95	12.9
Higher standard of living	M	39	21.0	146	19.1
	F	30	16.8	117	15.9
Better work opportunity	M	33	17.7	176	23.1
	F	24	13.4	129	17.5
Education of children	M	8	4.3	10	1.3
	F	12	6.7	14	3.4
Adventure/make fortune	M	3	1.6	20	2.6
	F	3	1.7	23	3.1
To get married	M	—	—	2	0.2
	F	1	0.6	42	5.7
To avoid adverse political situation in home country	M	12	6.4	39	5.1
	F	4	2.2	25	3.8
Size of responses*	M	186	100.0	762	100.0
	F	179	100.0	736	100.0

*Respondents could give as many responses as they wished. Thus size of responses does not correspond to sample size.

Table 84
Sources of help received by Korean immigrant respondents
upon their arrival in Chicago

Number and source of help	Korean immigrants		Totals for all groups in study	
	N	%	N	%
Help received upon arrival in Chicago	189	82.8	571	
Sources of help				
Spouses	66	32.2	229	36.8
Siblings and/or parents	44	21.5	111	17.8
Non family members	95	46.3	283	45.4
Totals	205	100.0	623	100.0

that of some of the other groups. A total of 79.8% of the Korean respondents had relatives living in the United States, while 55.6% had relatives in Chicago. These figures are similar to those for the Pilipino and Japanese immigrants, and quite a bit below those for the Chinese immigrants. However, the Korean relatives living in Chicago contained the highest proportion of parents (30.4%) and siblings (48.4%) of any group studied, while only 21.2% were "other relatives." This may indicate somewhat closer ties in the family structure among Koreans than among the other Chicago groups, in which from 43% to 51% of the relatives are "other relatives."

Korean immigrants arriving in Chicago appear to receive a relatively large number of different types of assistance from non relatives—43.3% of those who received help received three or more types of assistance. This figure is similar to that for the Pilipinos, and greater than that for the Chinese and Japanese groups. Despite the large proportion of immediate family members among the Korean group, however, this group still received nearly half of its assistance from nonfamily members (Table 84).

As Table 85 shows, the types of assistance received by the newly arrived Korean immigrants did not differ greatly from those received by the other groups. Two findings are of some interest, however. The Korean newcomers were relatively unlikely to receive assistance in the form of loans. One could ascribe this to the fact that many of the persons giving help in this group are newcomers themselves, although the Pilipino immigrants, who are recently arrived, gave loans much more frequently. As in the other groups, the Korean newcomers often received assistance in the form of lodging. The Korean newcomers was more likely than members of other groups to receive emotional support and encouragement; only the Japanese group gave this sort of assistance somewhat more frequently. These findings suggest that cultural factors within the individual groups may be at work in determining the kinds of aid extended to new-comers. If this is the case, then it may be necessary to adjust the emphasis and content of social services to complement and supple-ment the existing patterns of self-help aid within the different ethnic communities.

Like all of the other groups studied, the Korean immigrants reported various problem areas associated with immigration (Table 86). It is perhaps surprising that 89.5% of the Korean respondents reported difficulties with language in their adjustment to life in the United States, since the self-rated fluency of this group is fairly high. As noted earlier, there seem to be certain social pressures toward the use of the Korean language within the ethnic commun-ity, and these pressures may slow the acquisition and use of English by this group.

In most other problem areas, the responses of the Korean respon-

Table 85
Types of assistance received by Korean immigrant respondents
from nonrelatives upon their arrival in Chicago

Types of assistance	Korean immigrants		Totals for all groups in study	
	N	%	N	%
Lodging (stayed with them)	79	23.3	229	26.4
Found a place to stay	62	18.3	122	14.1
Loan	10	2.9	54	6.2
Helped to find a job	39	11.5	113	13.0
Introduced me to others who could help	15	4.4	43	5.0
Emotional support, encouragement	63	18.6	125	14.4
Other	71	20.9	182	21.0
Size of responses*	339	100.0	868	100.0

*Respondents could give as many responses as they wished, but only the first two are counted for this table. Therefore total responses do not equal total respondents.

Table 86
Problem areas associated with immigration
in Korean sample, by sex

Problem areas	Sex	Korean immigrants		Totals for all groups in study	
		N	%	N	%
Language	M	91	89.2	228	74.3
	F	111	89.5	274	75.7
Homesickness	M	35	34.3	136	44.3
	F	81	65.3	231	63.8
Lack of ethnic	M	31	30.4	93	30.3
person contacts	F	41	33.3	115	31.8
Food differences	M	18	17.6	71	23.1
	F	27	21.8	83	22.9
Weather differences	M	15	14.7	139	45.3
	F	26	21.0	181	50.0
Life style/cultural	M	49	48.0	156	50.8
differences	F	51	41.1	174	48.1
Size of responses*	M	239			
	F	337			
Total eligible respondents		228			

*Respondents could give more than one response to these questions.

dents do not differ markedly from those of the other groups in the study. The one clear exception is in the area of weather differences: in this respect the Korean respondents were troubled less than any other group, perhaps reflecting some similarity in the Korean and Chicago climates.

As in the case of the Pilipino group, the Korean female respondents showed the same frequency of problems as the males (except in the area of homesickness). Since the education level, labor force involvement, and job level of the Korean females are relatively high, they apparently do not lead the isolated life that would tend to exacerbate the problems associated with initial adjustment to immigration.

The English language was apparently the greatest problem for the Korean immigrants, but this group seems to make substantial use of English conversation classes and lessons. Fully 59% of the Korean sample reported taking such classes or lessons. This was the highest proportion of any group studied and probably indicates a high level of interest and motivation to adjust and integrate into American life. This is in sharp contrast to the findings for the Chinese group, which tended to combine low fluency with low usage of classes and lessons. Still, 41% of the Korean sample had *not* taken English conversation classes or lessons, while only 10.5% of the sample said they had not found English to be a problem. While it is difficult to determine the reasons for not taking classes, one can only conclude that, even among the Korean group, this service area is far from saturated.

Like all of the other groups in the study, the Korean respondents are generally satisfied with their decision to emigrate to the United States: 68% reported being either definitely happy, or happy with reservations, in this respect. While this is a fairly high proportion, it is not nearly so high as that for the other groups, which ranged from 80% to 100%. When the other responses shown in Table 87 are compared with those from the other groups, there does not appear to be a particularly large number of Korean respondents in the "regrets" and "plan to return" categories. However, 23.6% of the Korean respondents were uncertain about the decision to emigrate, while this response accounted for 10% or less of the other groups studied. Since the Korean sample also contains the smallest number of persons who are definitely happy with the decision to emigrate, this group may be characterized as being somewhat more ambivalent than the other groups about this decision.

Table 87
Evaluation of the decision to emmigrate by Korean respondents, by sex

Evaluation	Sex	Korean immigrants		Totals for all groups in study	
		N	%	N	%
Yes, definitely	M	44	43.6	176	57.5
happy	F	45	36.3	182	50.4
Yes, with	M	28	27.7	73	23.9
reservation	F	36	29.0	94	26.0
Uncertain	M	19	18.8	36	11.8
	F	34	27.4	63	17.5
Regrets	M	4	4.0	9	2.9
	F	7	5.7	12	3.3
Plan to return	M	6	5.9	12	3.9
	F	2	1.6	10	2.8
Totals	M	101	100.0	306	100.0
	F	124	100.0	361	100.0

Problems and Problem-Solving Activities

All respondents in the study were asked to enumerate the problems they perceived for persons of their ethnic groups living in Chicago. Few respondents failed to name at least one problem, and only 6.1% of the Koreans fell into this category—the lowest proportion for any group in the study. The problem perceptions of the Korean group appear to be strongly concentrated in the area of language and cultural adjustment, which was named by 60% of the respondents as the major problem area facing Korean immigrants in Chicago. No other problem area drew more than scattered responses. The other groups tended to assign more moderate levels of importance to several problem areas. Clearly, language and cultural adjustment is an area of great concern to the Korean respondents; not only did they perceive it as a community problem, but nearly 90% reported having problems personally with English as part of the immigration experience.

When they were asked whether they had actually experienced various problems, the responses of the Korean immigrants were as shown in Table 88. Overall, the Korean group reported a higher incidence of problems than the other groups. In three categories—getting medical service, locating housing, and adjustment problems due to language and life-style differences—the Chinese groups re-

Table 88
Actual problems experienced by Korean respondents*

Actual problems experienced	Korean immigrants		Totals	
	N	%	N	%
Insufficient income	89	39.0	255	22.5
Locating job	77	33.8	178	15.6
Problems on the job	54	23.7	162	14.2
Getting medical service	38	16.7	94	8.2
Locating housing	39	17.2	122	10.7
Adjustment problems due to language and life style differences	104	45.6	254	22.3
Family conflicts	29	12.7	71	6.2
Size of responses	430		1136	

*Percentage in each cell was derived by dividing positive responses by the total respondents in the ethnic group on each question. Thus the percentages do not sum to 100%.

Table 89
Discrimination experienced by Korean respondents
in housing and employment situation*

Discrimination areas	Korean immigrants		Totals	
	N	%	N	%
Housing				
Yes, definitely	20	8.8	59	8.2
Yes, probably	13	5.7	29	4.0
Total	33	14.5	88	12.3
Lost job				
Yes, definitely	2	0.9	9	1.3
Yes, probably	1	0.4	10	1.4
Total	3	1.3	19	2.7
Passed over for promotion				
Yes, definitely	40	17.5	81	11.3
Yes, probably	22	9.6	61	8.5
Total	62	27.3	142	19.8

*Percentage in each cell was derived by dividing responses by the total respondents in the ethnic group on each question. Thus the percentages need to be considered in relation to the total numbers of respondents in the ethnic group.

ported slightly more problems than the Koreans. However, in terms of overall problem incidence, the Korean group is substantially higher than the Chinese groups. There is some evidence—gained from debriefing the survey interviewers—that the Korean group is unusually open about revealing problems. Hence the high reported incidence of problems among the Korean group may not necessarily indicate that the Koreans have more problems, but only that the other groups are underreporting their problems.

The problem area of discrimination was broken down into discrimination in employment and in obtaining housing, with employment discrimination being further subdivided into situations in which the respondent felt he had been passed over for promotion, and cases in which there had been actual loss of a job because of discrimination. As a group, the Korean respondents appear to have encountered more housing discrimination than the other immigrant groups, but less than the Chinese and Japanese citizen groups (see Table 89). The area of job discrimination was less clear cut, since the Korean respondents had the lowest frequency for losing a job, but the highest frequency for being passed over for promotion, of all groups in the study. It is not possible to determine from the data whether these findings indicate actual differences in patterns of discrimination experienced by different groups, or whether the differences may be due to culturally determined perceptions of what is and is not discrimination. This area requires further investigation if social service providers are to be able to deliver appropriate assistance in cases of discrimination.

When asked where they would go for help in a hypothetical medical emergency, the Korean respondents named resources which largely paralleled those cited by the Pilipino respondents: 42.5% named a specific physician or hospital, while 44.3% said they would go to "a doctor" or "the hospital," but did not give a specific name. The total for these two categories of public medical resources (86.8%) was somewhat higher than the total for the Pilipino group (79.3%). However, Pilipino respondents were more likely to name a specific physician or hospital (58.1%) than were the Koreans (42.5%). As noted earlier, the Pilipino group contained a large number of health professionals, who would presumably be more likely to have a specific hospital or physician in mind. Only a few Korean respondents cited other resources for a medical emergency, and only a single respondent did not know where to go for help.

For a hypothetical situation of mental illness, the resources cited by the Korean group nearly paralleled those chosen by the other groups studied. The largest number (52.6%) cited a physician or hospital without naming it, while a much smaller number (18.2%) named a specific physician or hospital. Family or relatives were cited by 7.5% of the Korean sample, which was about average for all groups studied. One interesting finding is that 7.5% of the Korean respondents cited an ethnic religious organization for help in the hypothetical situation of mental illness. Only the Japanese groups approached this figure (6.7%), while the Pilipino group failed to cite religious resources at all, despite their apparently high level of religious involvement. In the Korean group, 7.9% did not know where to go for a mental illness emergency; only the Japanese group had fewer in this category.

Table 90 shows the various resources cited by the Korean respondents in a hypothetical search for a job. Like the Pilipinos, the Koreans cited classified ads with fairly high frequency, although they were much less likely than the Pilipinos to cite employment agencies as a resource. In most of the other response categories the Korean respondents were near the average for all groups in the study. One exception is the category of "self-reliance," which was

Table 90
Resources cited in hypothetical search for a job
by Korean sample

Sources of help	Korean immigrants		Totals	
	N	%	N	%
Classified ads	80	35.7	198	27.8
Employment agency, public/private	30	13.4	149	20.9
Family/relatives	8	3.6	25	3.5
Ethnic friends	17	7.6	136	19.1
Friends (unspecified)	2	0.9	21	3.0
Ethnic church organization	14	6.3	27	3.8
More than one resource	—	—	1	0.1
Self-reliance	60	26.8	104	14.6
Don't know where to go	13	5.8	52	7.3
Totals	224	100.0	713	100.0

much more popular with the Koreans than with any other group. This questionnaire item—like all of the hypothetical problem items—was asked as an open-ended question in the general form of: "What would you do if . . . ?" The respondents' replies were subsequently grouped into the response categories shown in Table 90. Thus, the response of "self-reliance" may simply represent an underlying assertion in the respondents' mind to the effect that: "I would certainly do something, but I'm not sure what." If this is the case, then the "self-reliance" responses in the various groups should perhaps be summed with the "don't know where to go" responses in order to arrive at a realistic picture of the proportion of respondents who have no clear idea of what to do in the problem situation. However, debriefing the survey interviewers gives a strong indication that this may not be appropriate in the case of the Korean sample. It was learned that when the Korean respondents said they would depend on "self-reliance," what they meant was that they would pursue several sources of information in order to locate a job. Apparently the Korean respondents tend to see their own action as central and service resources as peripheral in the problem-solving process.

Job discrimination and housing discrimination appear to be two problem areas that may offer special challenges to social service providers in Korean-American communities. As Table 91 indicates, the responses of the Korean sample to these problems are characterized by an almost total lack of active approaches. When one combines the non active choices—"give up," "denial of discrimination," and "don't know where to go"—one finds 77.1% of the Korean respondents taking these approaches to job discrimination, and 75.1% to housing discrimination. Only the Chinese groups approached or exceeded these figures, and the Korean respondents were more likely in both instances to say that they would give up in the face of discrimination.

This sort of passive response may be attributable to certain factors in Korean cultural history. It should be remembered that Korea has had a long and rather unpleasant colonial experience in the fairly recent past. Together with subsequent political events, this has tended to imbue many Koreans with an attitude of passive pessimism toward governments in general. Also, government action in Korea has traditionally taken the form of preferential treatment for special groups; hence Koreans may have little precedent for seeing government intervention as a means of alleviating discrimination.

When they were asked how they would solve hypothetical financial problems, the Korean respondents cited various resources with frequencies that closely parallel the averages for all groups in the

Table 91

Responses of Korean sample to hypothetical
situations of job and housing discrimination

Responses to discrimination	Housing discrimination				Job discrimination			
	Korean immigrants		Totals		Korean immigrants		Totals	
	N	%	N	%	N	%	N	%
Civil rights organization	44	19.3	183	26.7	33	14.5	181	25.0
Give up	133	58.4	326	45.2	127	55.7	293	40.4
Family and friends	3	1.3	20	2.7	2	0.8	19	2.6
Ethnic organization	6	2.6	22	3.0	1	0.4	19	2.6
Denial of discrimination	15	6.6	42	5.8	9	3.9	45	6.2
Self-reliance	4	1.8	7	0.9	16	7.0	29	4.0
Don't know where to go	23	10.1	121	16.8	40	17.5	134	18.5
Total	228	100.0	721	101.1	228	100.0	724	99.3

Table 92
Resources cited for hypothetical financial problems by
Korean sample

	Korean immigrants		Totals for all groups in study	
	N	%	N	%
Self-reliance	28	12.3	80	11.1
Family/relatives	64	28.1	227	31.5
Ethnic friends/organization	41	18.0	109	15.1
Friends (unspecified)	2	0.9	10	1.4
Unemployment compensation	—	—	4	0.6
Bank/credit union	37	16.2	147	20.4
Public aid	23	10.1	56	7.8
Never thought about it	15	6.6	27	3.8
Don't know where to go	18	7.9	60	8.3
Totals	228	100.0	720	100.0

study (Table 92). It is of some interest that more Koreans said they had "never thought about" financial problems than was the case for any other group, especially since the Korean group had the highest frequency (39%) of reported actual problems from "insufficient income" (see Table 88). Here, as in other cases, the subjective perception of problems may be at variance with actual experience. It is also interesting that the Koreans mentioned "public aid" more often than any other group.

The pattern of problem-solving strategies cited by the Korean respondents for hypothetical marital problems differs in several respects from that for the other groups (see Table 93). First, the Koreans showed an unusually high frequency of responses in the "separation or divorce" category, while they were the least likely to say they would "do nothing." Second, the Korean group cited outside sources of help with relatively low frequency. This includes marriage counselors, lawyers, ministers or priests, friends, and even family members and relatives. Finally, the Koreans had the highest frequency for "work it out oneself." Overall, this pattern suggests that the Korean respondents may be quite reluctant to seek help for marital problems, or perhaps they may simply feel that this is an area in which there is little possibility of meaningful assistance. The Korean sample group exhibited a very low divorce rate (.9%, about the same as the other young groups). However, informal

Table 93
Resources cited in hypothetical marital problems by
Korean sample

Sources of help	Korean immigrants		Totals	
	N	%	N	%
Work it out oneself	71	33.2	187	28.2
Family/relatives	14	6.5	63	9.5
Friends, ethnic and nonethnic	17	7.9	61	9.2
Marriage counselor/lawyer	16	7.5	80	12.1
Separation or divorce	37	17.3	48	7.2
Minister or priest	12	5.6	43	6.5
Do nothing	8	3.7	43	6.5
Never thought about it	18	8.4	54	8.1
Don't know where to go	21	9.8	85	12.8
Totals	214	100.0	664	100.0

sources in various Korean communities suggest that the stress of immigration may be leading to an increased number of divorces and separations. This phenomenon was not yet manifested in the data at the time this survey was conducted (1974), but the tendency of the respondent to choose the alternatives of separation or divorce may be a prelude to actually taking such steps under stressful circumstances.

In many of the hypothetical problem items discussed above, it will be noted that the Korean respondents had a tendency to cite "self-reliance," or "work it out oneself" as their preferred solution. This tendency may be reflected in the low frequency with which the Korean group reported actually seeking help for problems they had experienced. As Table 94 shows, the Korean respondents reported encountering substantial numbers of problems in all categories, but often did not seek outside help. Only in the case of insufficient income, job location, and medical service did the Koreans seek help with frequencies which approached the averages for all groups in the study. In the case of family conflicts, the Koreans exceeded the average, but only because the Japanese and Chinese groups had very low to nonexistent frequencies. Overall, the Koreans sought help for a lower proportion of experienced problems than any other group in the study.

The causes for this low frequency of help seeking may hinge upon the interpretation one chooses to give to the large number of "self-reliance" responses among the Korean sample. If one accepts that these responses indicate that the Korean respondents are choosing a problem-solving stance characterized by an active form of "rugged individualism," then this may explain the low frequency with which this group sought outside help. Conversations with survey respondents and debriefing of interviewers suggest that this is certainly true in a good number of instances: many of the Korean respondents did feel that they could, and should, solve their problems by forthright action.

In other cases, however, the Koreans appeared to see certain problem-solving activities as "self-reliance" even though the strategy obviously required the use of other resources. Thus, a Korean respondent who replied that he would find a job by "self-reliance" might, upon further questioning, admit that he would make use of

Table 94
Percentage of Korean respondents seeking help in each problem area*

Problems experienced Help sought	Korean immigrants		Totals	
	N	%	N	%
Insufficient income	89		255	
Help sought	30	33.7	88	34.3
Job location	77		178	
Help sought	32	41.5	84	47.8
On the job	54		162	
Help sought	6	11.1	50	30.8
Medical service	38		94	
Help sought	19	50.0	50	53.0
Locating housing	39		120	
Help sought	7	18.0	30	24.6
Adjustment to U.S.	104		254	
Help sought	12	12.0	46	19.0
Family conflicts	29		71	
Help sought	4	13.7	9	12.6
Total problems experienced	430		1136	
Total help sought	110	25.7	357	31.4

*Percentages in each cell are derived by dividing help sought responses by problems experienced in each area. Therefore, the percentages in each column do not sum to 100%.

Table 95
Resources cited for obtaining the first job
in the U.S. by Korean immigrant respondents

Sources of help	Korean immigrants		Totals	
	N	%	N	%
Employment agency, private and public	17	9.8	72	11.6
Classified ads	42	24.3	135	21.7
Professional organization	5	2.9	10	1.6
Ethnic friends/organization	58	33.5	216	34.7
Non-ethnic friends	10	5.8	32	5.1
Family/relatives	16	9.3	85	13.7
Employment pre-arranged	25	14.5	72	11.6
Size of responses*	173	100.0	622	100.0

*Respondents could give more than one response. Therefore, total responses do not equal sample size.

want ads, employment agencies, and suggestions from friends in locating employment. This suggests that a social service provider in a Korean community might find greater utilization and better acceptance of services if it were emphasized that the primary purpose of such services was to provide useful background information so that clients could solve their own problems. In this way the cultural predilections of the service population could be utilized in the problem-solving process. Contrary to the usual stereotype, many of the Korean respondents would actually meet the social service provider's definition of an "ideal client": they are self-motivated and appear to have an active interest in solving their own problems.

All respondents in the study were also asked to detail the sources of help they had received in two specific problem situations: locating their first job in America, and obtaining child care for children under five years of age if and when the mother is at work.

The Korean respondents tended to have found their first jobs in America through nonethnic resources, either public or private (see Table 95). Compared with the other groups, the Koreans used these nonethnic resources more than the Chinese or Japanese immigrants, but less than the Pilipinos. Although the Koreans used professional organizations more often than the other groups, this resource still accounts for only a very small portion of the initial jobs. The Korean group also showed the highest proportion of pre-arranged employment; one can assume that such initial employment belongs in the category of nonethnic resources since only 1.3% of the Korean sample reported being employed by Korean employers. This general trend toward the use of nonethnic resources in finding the first job in the U.S. probably reflects the relatively recent arrival of the majority of the members of the Korean-American community. There are not many "old timers" to assist the newcomers.

The resources used by the Korean respondents to obtain child care also reflect the relatively recent arrival of this group. The proportion of Korean respondents (30.6%) who obtained child care from relatives is substantially below that for the longer-established groups—the Chinese immigrants and citizens. So few Japanese respondents had young children that no useful comparison can be made with this group. Only 9.4% of the Korean respondents said they relied on day care centers, but this is the largest proportion in the study. Neighbors were cited in 23.5% of the cases, and the other spouses in 35.3%. These figures are similar to those for the other groups studied. Both the Korean and Pilipino respondent groups have many young children, a high level of female labor force participation, and—presumably—the means to afford the use of day care centers. It remains to be shown whether the low usage rate of day care centers by these groups is caused by a lack of suitable facilities or by preference.

In those instances where respondents had not sought help for their expressed problems, they were asked why they had not done so. The reasons given by the Korean respondents are shown in Table 96. Like the other groups in the study, the Koreans most often said they had not sought help because they had no problems (thus contradicting their expression of problems in other contexts), the problems were not serious enough, or they could solve the problems alone or within the family. The language barrier was only a minor problem. On the other hand, a surprising 18.4% of the Korean respondents said they had not sought help because they had not known where to go. This figure is lower than that for the Chinese groups, but markedly higher than those for the Pilipinos and both Japanese groups. Furthermore, far fewer Korean respondents reported that they did not know where to go for help in the hypothetical problem situations. This may indicate that it is not enough to know where one ought to go in a problem situation. Alternatively, the "did not know where to go" response may indicate that the respondent was ignorant of resources when s/he first immi-

Table 96
Reasons cited for not seeking help by Korean sample, by sex*

Reasons for not seeking help	Sex	Korean immigrants		Totals	
		N	%	N	%
No problems or	M	26	20.5	104	30.1
not serious	F	35	25.2	136	34.3
Solve by self	M	50	39.4	134	38.7
or with family	F	45	32.4	123	31.0
Organization can't help	M	23	18.1	33	9.5
	F	7	5.0	18	4.5
Didn't want	M	11	8.7	12	3.5
others to know	F	6	4.3	11	2.8
Language barrier	M	1	0.8	11	3.2
	F	13	9.4	34	8.6
Don't know where to go	M	16	12.6	51	14.7
	F	33	23.7	75	18.9
Size of responses	M	127	100.0	345	
	F	139	100.0	397	

*Asked only of those who had not sought help. Respondents could give more than one response. Thus, size of responses does not represent total respondents responding.

grated; this ignorance may have been corrected by later experience.

In two areas the responses of the Koreans differ somewhat from the pattern of the other groups. First, there is the large number of Korean respondents (18.1% of males, 5.0% of the females, 11.3% composite) who said they did not seek help because they felt the organization could not help them. This seems to be consistent with the large proportion of Koreans (particularly, males) who named "self-reliance" as their preferred resource in solving some hypothetical problems. Taken together, these findings seem to indicate a faith in personal effort—together with some distrust of the efficacy of institutions. Also prominent among the Korean responses is the number of persons who said they did not seek help because they did not want others to know about their problems. In the popular stereotype, this is supposed to be a major reason for the failure of Asian Americans to seek help. Yet the Korean group was the only one to show what might be called a noticeable frequency in this category. There is always the possibility that this motivation is so submerged that Asian Americans would not report it when questioned directly. This, however, does not seem likely: only 8.3% of the entire study sample gave a high priority to confidentiality in ranking the characteristics of social services. If such concerns as "shame" and "face saving" play a role in the utilization of social services by Asian Americans, it appears to be a relatively minor one.

Service Characteristics and Priorities

The priorities assigned to various social services by the Korean respondents are shown in Table 97. Together with the Pilipinos, the Koreans assign a fairly high priority to child care centers. This is consistent with the large number of young children in these groups, and with their history of use of these centers. The priority assigned by the Koreans to English conversation classes was second only to that given by the Chinese groups—an interesting finding because the Koreans generally gave a higher self-rating of English fluency. As noted earlier, however, there are definite pressures within the Korean community to use the Korean language for communication between ethnic persons. Hence the subjects may recognize that if they are to improve their English it will have to be by means of classes or lessons. In fact, the Koreans reported taking English classes or lessons more often than any other group. By

Table 97
Services considered important by Korean sample*

Types of services	Rank order	Korean immigrants N	%	Totals N	%
Child care centers	3	102	44.7	303	41.9
English conversation class	2	139	61.2	376	52.2
Mental health service	6	82	36.0	228	31.7
Employment service	7	74	32.5	284	39.4
Vocational training	8	71	31.1	277	38.5
Public aid	5	84	36.8	276	38.3
Bilingual referral service	4	98	43.0	345	47.9
Legal aid service	1	151	66.2	425	59.0
Size of responses		801		2513	

*Percentages in each cell were derived in relation to total respondents in the ethnic group. Therefore, the percentage totals in each column do not equal 100%.

comparison, there was a much larger difference between the priorities assigned to bilingual referral services by the Korean and Chinese
group. The Koreans placed much less importance on such services,
perhaps indicating that one may consider one's English adequate
for everyday purposes, but still wish to improve it for other reasons.
Like all the other groups, the Korean respondents assigned high
priority to legal aid service, perhaps reflecting a general feeling of
helplessness in the face of the American legal system.

Employment service and vocational training are of only moderate
importance to the Korean respondents, a finding which may seem
surprising since a fair portion of the Korean sample is composed of
persons who have had difficulty in transferring their professional
training and education to the American labor market. Observation
within the Korean-American community indicates, however, that
these persons usually do not respond by seeking retraining that
would allow them to practice their original professions. Instead,
the tendency is to practice "self-reliance" and move off into entirely
different areas of work. The Chicago Korean community contains
a constantly expanding number of ethnic enterprises which have
been founded by persons holding advanced academic degrees who
were unable to find employment which utilized their existing
training.

The Korean respondents ranked the service characteristics they
desired for service agencies in approximately the same order as
most of the other groups in the study. Perhaps it would be more
accurate to say that their ranks fell about half way between the
extremes of the other groups in most instances. As with most other
groups, the Koreans rated "helpfulness of staff" (41.6%) as most
important, followed by "bilingual staff" (33.7%). The other characteristics showed low frequencies. Of particular interest, the Korean
rating of "confidentiality" was at the low end of the range for all
groups (6.6%).

The Korean Sample: Composite and Conclusions

As we consider the profile of the typical respondent from the
Chicago Korean community we must keep in mind that, like the
typical Chicago Pilipino correspondent, he may be somewhat atypical of Korean Americans nationally. The Chicago respondent is
probably somewhat better educated, more affluent, and probably
holds a job in a somewhat higher occupational category than his

counterpart in, say, Los Angeles or Hawaii. However, although these differences may have some effect on the exact needs of the population, their effect on service utilization patterns and preferences is probably minor.

The typical Korean immigrant respondent whom we will consider in this profile is young—in his early to mid-thirties—is almost certain to be married and living with his spouse, and probably came to the United States less than six years ago. His household is relatively small, usually consisting of the respondent, spouse, and one or two young children (less than nine years old)—a total of only three or four persons, almost never more than six. In most cases, this household is housed in a rented apartment. Our typical Korean respondent is very unlikely to own an apartment, but there is some chance he may be buying or renting a house.

We can be fairly certain that this typical Korean is a church member—usually Protestant—and that he attends church regularly. Chances are quite good that he also belongs to one or two organizations of some sort. Almost half of these organizations are ethnically based, and they may be connected with the ethnic church he attends.

Although this Korean respondent probably speaks English at least adequately, it is still definitely a second language for him. At home, and when conversing with Koreans generally, he feels more socially comfortable speaking Korean. If our respondent is male, he is somewhat more likely to posses adequate English skills than his female counterpart.

Before he came to the United States, the respondent grew up and lived in one of the larger Korean cities. It is not very likely that he grew up in a rural area. There is a pretty good chance that his father was a proprietor or a managerial or professional person, and the respondent has probably followed this pattern by pursuing higher education and striving for employment in the higher job categories. The respondent has been successful in his pursuits in that he has probably obtained a college degree, and may have an advanced degree as well. However, if he does have advanced degrees, they are probably of an academic rather than professional nature. Thus, there is a good chance that he has been unable to find employment in his field of study since he emigrated to the U.S. If our respondent is male, then he is probably somewhat better educated than his female counterpart.

This typical Korean respondent is almost certain to hold a full-time job if he is male, and his female counterpart is quite likely to be employed full-time as well. If the female Korean respondent is not employed full-time, she may be employed part-time. There is also some chance that she may be a homemaker, or that she has never been employed.

Our Korean respondent—whether male or female—probably holds a job somewhere between the middle and the top of the scale of employment. While he is not very likely to be a manager, our respondent may be a professional person, a proprietor, or a skilled or white collar worker. Despite this overall job level, however, our Korean respondent may well be somewhat underemployed. There is about an even chance that he feels his present job entails less responsibility than the last one he held before immigrating, and he may feel that his present job requires somewhat less education than he actually possesses. There is also some chance that he is now employed in a job in a category below that in which he was employed in Korea.

Despite some feelings that he may be underemployed, our Korean respondent intends to remain in this job for the foreseeable future. His reasons for remaining are the usual ones—good pay and benefits, good working conditions, or, perhaps, because of job interest. However, there is a one in five chance that he will keep the job only because he considers that it is the best he can do under the circumstances.

Our typical respondent has a total family income of about $15,000 to $17,000, but in many cases both he and his wife are holding down full-time jobs in order to earn this total. The family income is less likely to result from the respondent alone holding a high-paying job. Most likely, the respondent feels that this family income is adequate, or a little more than adequate.

When he came to the United States, the Korean respondent probably came with the intention of completing his education, or finding a better job. He probably did not immigrate with the idea of getting advanced job training in his field; rather, he was looking for a better-paying position in his present field so that he would be able to enjoy a better standard of living. If he immigrated for the educational opportunities in the U.S., it was probably in order to obtain graduate academic education. This desire for education may have been important to him in another way: he may have been motivated to immigrate for the sake of his children's education.

When this respondent immigrated, he probably had relatives already living in the United States, who may also have been recent arrivals. There is only an even chance that they were residing in Chicago, but if he did have relatives in Chicago, they were probably members of his immediate family—parents or siblings. Upon arriving in Chicago, the respondent probably received several different kinds of assistance from several sources. The members of his immediate family may not have been as helpful as one might expect—perhaps because they had only recently immigrated themselves—and he probably received quite a bit of this assistance from other relatives and from nonfamily members. Since the other persons in the respondent's family were also likely to be recent immigrants, they were not usually able to help the newcomer with loans, but they did provide lodging, support, and encouragement.

Despite the fact that our respondent has at least adequate command of English, he found the language barrier to be a severe problem, and there is a good chance that he has enrolled in English conversation classes or lessons in order to improve his fluency. The other adjustment problems attendant to immigration have been only moderately troubling to him, and one bright spot is that the Chicago weather does not seem to bother him. Overall, our respondent is satisfied with his decision to immigrate, although he is likely to have some reservations or ambivalent feelings.

When asked whether he feels that Korean Americans have problems, our respondent will readily admit that they do, but he tends to see most of the problems as lying in the single area of language and cultural adjustment. If he is asked whether he has personally experienced problems in living in the U.S., this respondent will also admit that he has. On the experiential level, however, he feels that he has had problems in many different areas, not just with language and cultural adjustment. Among other things, he may feel that he has been passed over for promotion on the job because of discrimination.

When he must deal with problem situations such as medical emergencies, this typical Korean respondent generally knows where to seek help, although he may not have a specific, named resource in mind. In facing some problems, such as finding a job, he takes a certain amount of pride in being self-reliant, although this approach may often entail using several outside resources to solve a problem. However, some types of problems seem to be more difficult for the Korean respondent to manage: when faced with discrimination he may simply give up, and he tends to see divorce or separation as a resolution for marital problems. When he considers specific problem-solving situations he has experienced or encountered, this

Korean respondent may find that he has used numerous nonethnic resources. This is true, for instance, in the case of finding his first job in the U.S. and also tends to apply to many hypothetical problem situations.

Our respondent, then, admits to having problems, and usually knows where to go for help—but he probably does not customarily seek outside assistance in handling his problems. If he were asked why he has not sought outside help, our respondent would probably say that, although he has problems, he does not consider them serious enough to require outside assistance in solving them. Along with this, he may not want others to know he has problems and—especially if the respondent is male—he may feel that the available services are unable to help him.

Sometimes this Korean respondent does not utilize services because they are simply not available. For instance, there is only about a one in ten chance that he sends his children to a day care center while his wife is at work, yet he considers day care centers to be an important service. He probably would utilize such services if they were more readily available. Other services that he would particularly like to see are English conversation classes and legal aid service—the latter being of importance not because he has actually experienced legal problems, but because he finds the prospect of American legal dealings to be somewhat disquieting. On the other hand, he does not see job training and employment services as particularly important, preferring to confront the job market more or less on his own terms. Like most other Asian Americans, our Korean respondent would like to have bilingual staff persons available at the various service agencies. This however, is not of pressing importance since he can at least manage to make himself understood in English. It is somewhat more important to him that the agency staff make an effort to be helpful.

At first sight it seems reasonable to characterize the Korean immigrants in the study in much the same way as the Pilipino group: young, urbanized, well-educated, and employed in middle- to upper-level jobs. The Korean respondents do show these basic characteristics, although often in different degrees from the Pilipinos. What is significant, however, is that, despite these similarities, the two groups have very different service needs and problem-solving strategies. These differences have important implications for both the content and delivery style of social services to be provided for these groups.

The contrasting problem-solving styles of the two groups might be called "group-oriented activism" on the part of the Pilipinos, and "individual-centered self-reliance" for the Koreans. Although the Pilipinos are not avid joiners of groups, they seem to look to outside groups and public resources in their problem-solving strategies. By contrast, the Korean respondents tend to see outside groups and public resources as mere adjuncts to their personal efforts at problem solving. Because they tend to see groups and resources as secondary to their own efforts, the Koreans were more likely than other respondents to see the groups and resources as being unable to help them in their problem-solving activities.

The style of problem-solving strategy adopted by the Korean respondents has implications for the development and delivery of services to this group. It appears, for example, that such services will be more acceptable to Korean clients if they are presented as sources of information that the client can use to make his own problem-solving activities more effective. Most social service providers would probably agree that this is a desirable characteristic of service delivery in general, since it seeks to develop the client's own problem-solving abilities, rather than making him dependent on the agency. However, some groups have more tolerance than others when it comes to this agency dependence, and some groups may be quickly overwhelmed by attempts to get them to solve their own problems. In the case of the Koreans, on the other hand, there seems to be an ethic of self-reliance which must be taken into account. It seems reasonable to expect that this self-help ethic could be furthered by providing services which are concerned with conveying factual and procedural information for the use of the Korean-American client in his problem-solving activities. In this way the culturally based respect for self-reliance exhibited by many of the Korean respondents could be used to increase utilization and effectiveness of the social services provided to this group.

CHAPTER VIII

A COMPOSITE VIEW

At the outset of this study, we suggested that the characteristics and needs of the various Asian-American groups might be quite varied, and that this heterogeneity—which runs contrary to stereotypic expectations—might cause problems in service needs assessment and delivery among those groups. The data in the study provide support for this hypothesis in a number of areas of concern. In this chapter we will provide a composite view of the four respondent groups on selected dimensions, and we will discuss the implications of the heterogeneity of these groups for the design of service delivery systems. This will lay the basis for the discussion in the final chapter, in which some guidelines for service delivery to Asian Americans are presented.

Traditionally, American society has been considered to be a "melting pot" in which persons of many cultural backgrounds are blended together to form one culture which is thought to be devoid of idiosyncratic cultural characteristics. When scrutinized, the melting pot model breaks down in two areas. First, the resulting, supposedly "blended," culture tends actually to be heavily patterned on white, Protestant, northern European models. Second, the melting pot process by and large does not take place for visible minorities. Thus, although it has now been over three centuries since the first slave ships arrived in the New World, Black-American culture remains very much a thing apart. Likewise, in the present study there were a number of Chinese respondents who had little or no knowledge of English, despite nearly lifelong residence in the United States.

To the objective observer, cultural pluralism in America has often seemed to be more in evidence than the melting pot image would suggest. Most large cities, in particular, continue to have their ethnic neighborhoods, ethnic churches, ethnic organizations, and ethnic-language newspapers. On the other hand, it is no less true that the most economically successful members of ethnic minorities seem to be those who have discarded their ethnicity, moved to the suburbs, and adopted the values of the white, northern European, Protestant culture.

The issue of cultural pluralism has important implications in the development of social service delivery systems for distinct ethnic groups such as those included in the present studies. These Asian-American groups constitute visible minorities; their members do not have the option of trying to "pass for" members of the majority society. Some members of these ethnic groups have achieved economic success and have subsequently moved to the suburbs. The study respondents, however, are all persons who have remained within the city, often in geographically defined ethnic neighborhoods. For these persons, one must begin with the assumption that their characteristics and needs as ethnic persons will play an important role in how they will respond to social services delivered by persons who are "outsiders."

Demographic Characteristics Compared

The four groups in the study proved to vary on most of the demographic characteristics which were surveyed. In many cases, these differences suggest differing service needs. As Table 98 shows, the ages of the groups varied considerably, a factor which may make certain services much more important to some groups than to others.

As extreme examples, one might speculate that child care facilities would be of much greater interest to the Pilipino and Korean immigrants than to the Japanese citizens, while the reverse might be true with respect to programs designed to encourage use of medical services by the elderly. One note of caution which should be interjected here is that some of the study groups may misrepresent the national populations of their ethnic groups. This is almost certainly the case for the Pilipinos, among whom a sample which included citizens and rural immigrants would almost certainly show a higher mean age, larger standard deviation, and lower educational level than the study sample. However, one must also keep in mind that the data on Asian Americans collected by the decennial census are often demonstrably in error, and that these census data are the only available basis for comparison with the local data of the present study.

The sex ratios of the Chinese, Pilipino, and Korean groups are near normal. The two Japanese groups depart from the norm in that almost two-thirds of the Japanese immigrants are female, while two-thirds of the Japanese citizens are male. When national data are considered, this trend is observable for all Asian-American groups: until 1960, males heavily outnumbered females, reflecting the patterns of the earlier periods of immigration. By 1970, however, this trend had been reversed. In the case of the Japanese and Korean groups, the immigration of large numbers of "war brides" may be a factor. Quite clearly, the gross imbalance of males versus females which was a characteristic of earlier Asian-American immigrant communities (particularly in the case of the Chinese and Pilipinos) is now a thing of the past. If anything, one suspects that the future may bring a surplus of females in some Asian-American communities.

From 67% to 88% of the respondents in the study groups were married and living with their spouses. While these percentages are high, they are not as high as those reported by the 1970 census, although the study figures for divorce and separation do agree with census figures. One possibility is that the study groups are atypical

Table 98
Mean ages of respondents and spouses

Group	Mean	Standard deviation
Chinese immigrants	42.43	16.04
Chinese citizens	39.32	15.80
Japanese immigrants	45.88	15.84
Japanese citizens	50.06	12.62
Pilipino immigrants	35.10	8.87
Korean immigrants	36.35	13.50

of the national populations of their ethnic groups in this respect. However, an alternative explanation that deserves consideration is that the study was more effective than the census in reaching unmarried adults.

Examination of the study data shows that the unmarried respondents varied widely in age, but that most (62%) were 30 years of age or younger. It is possible that the major referent in the lives of these persons would be the job rather than the home. Because of their work schedules, they might be overlooked by census takers. (In the present survey, contacts and interviews took place at various hours to suit the schedules of the respondents.) These young, unmarried persons represent an immigration trend among Asian Americans. They have, presumably, immigrated before marrying in order to meet educational or career objectives. The older groups of unmarried persons present a different sort of problem. These persons are likely to lead isolated lives because of the lack of family contacts. They are the invisible persons in the community who may not only be cut off from extra-community contacts (as evidenced by the failure of the census to enumerate them) but may also receive little assistance from the self-help network within the community. This isolation may either be self-imposed or simply occur by default; in either case it should be taken into account when assessing social service needs within Asian-American communities.

The size and composition of the respondents' households varied from group to group. The Pilipino households were the largest, followed by the Chinese; the Korean households were next in size, and the Japanese were the smallest. However, although the Pilipino and Chinese households were of similar size, the Pilipino households contained large numbers of unrelated persons, while the Chinese households were almost totally composed of related persons. The Japanese and Korean households generally consisted of a relatively small nuclear family. These differences in household composition may have a bearing on the appropriateness of various types of social services. Overall, the households in the sample were not unduly large, averaging about four persons. However, the Chinese and Pilipino groups had appreciable numbers of households consisting of seven or more persons. As might be expected, the oldest groups in the study—the Chinese immigrants and both Japanese groups—had the largest proportions of single persons in the community. The interviewers reported that elderly respondents who lived alone frequently appeared to be starved for social contact, sometimes to the point of detaining the interviewer after the interview was completed.

The 726 respondents in the study reported a total of 860 children living at home; of these children 56.3% were nine years of age or younger. From group to group, however, there was considerable variation in the concentration of children in various age groups, as is shown in Figure 5.

The types of housing accommodations reported by the various groups seem, at least partly, to be related to the length of time that most members of the group have resided in the U.S. Thus, about 30% of the Japanese and Chinese citizen groups own houses, while the Japanese, Chinese, and Pilipino immigrant groups average about 19%, and only 7.9% of the Korean immigrants—the most recently arrived group—are homeowners. In all groups, the most common form of housing was the rented apartment, while few persons rented houses. Both of these findings may simply reflect the conditions of the housing market in urban areas. Interestingly, 13% of the Japanese immigrants and 16% of the Japanese citizens are owners of apartments (i.e., condominiums). These percentages are so much higher than those for the other groups (2.2% to 7.0%) that one suspects cultural factors must be at work here, although the small

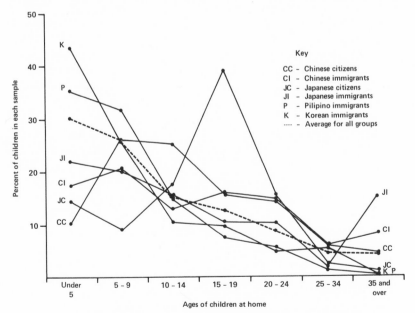

Figure 5. Proportions of children in different age groups reported to be living at home

family size and relative affluence of the Japanese sample may be involved as well.

Both religious preference and degree of apparent religious involvement varied widely from group to group. A majority of the Koreans were Protestant, while nearly all the Pilipinos were Catholic. Buddhism was predominant in both groups of Japanese respondents, while those Chinese who expressed a religious preference were about evenly divided between Protestants and Catholics. In all groups except the Chinese immigrants, most respondents expressed some religious preference or other; among the Chinese immigrants, 62% had no religious preference. Only the Koreans and Pilipinos could be characterized as regular church goers. In the other groups, only about a fourth to a third of those who had a religious preference attended services regularly. These findings suggest that churches may be an effective means of community contact and service delivery for some Asian-American groups, but not for others. In this regard it should be noted that even those groups which showed high levels of church attendance rarely cited religious institutions or organizations as sources of help in problem solving. This finding suggests that the social service potential of Asian-American ethnic churches is now largely unrealized.

The role of organizational membership in service delivery is likewise unclear. The Chinese and Pilipino groups belonged to very few organizations, while the Japanese and Korean respondents showed a moderate level of organizational activity. However, relatively few respondents cited organizations (ethnic or otherwise) as sources of help in either hypothetical or actual problem-solving activities. Thus, although organizations may provide some framework for community contact and service delivery, they are not in themselves an important component of problem-solving strategies among the Asian Americans studied. A partial exception to this generalization must be made for the Japanese groups, since the Chicago Japanese community has a number of viable ethnic service organizations. Interestingly, the Japanese respondents reported fewer perceived problems than did the other groups. This may reflect the efficacy of existing Japanese ethnic service organizations in the Chicago area. However, this connection is largely circumstantial; the lower frequency of perceived problems among the Japanese may be due to cultural factors, such as levels of expectation, or may be related to the economic success of this group.

English proficiency emerged in this study as one of the most crucial elements in the overall picture of the service needs and problem-solving strategies of Asian Americans. Although English proficiency was self-rated, there is adequate secondary evidence to suggest that there is some correlation between English language proficiency and several other dimensions, such as the frequency and nature of problems encountered, overall economic success, and the adoption and avoidance of various problem-solving strategies. The Chinese groups appear to have the greatest trouble with English, and to suffer the greatest consequences for their lack of proficiency. On the other hand, the Korean and Pilipino groups seemed to experience more subtle problems with English proficiency: their self-rated proficiency was high, yet many still felt a strong need for English conversation classes and bilingual referral services. It is possible that the self-rating of English proficiency may reflect an appraisal of one's abilities based on formal criteria—the individual's emotional confidence level may be much lower. Thus the self-rating may reflect the respondent's appraisal of his schoolbook knowledge of English, while in actual conversation he may have many difficulties due to imperfect accent or misreading of culture-specific conversational cues.

What does seem to be clear from the study evidence is that lack of English language proficiency seems to exacerbate almost every problem area, as well as limiting the individual's choice of problem-solving strategies. It is quite possible that there is a circular relationship between poor English proficiency, and a high level of perceived and experienced problems together with a lack of active, effective problem-solving strategies. Whether the relationship is circular or unidirectional, however, it seems clear that appropriate service intervention to help Asian Americans improve their level of English proficiency might help to end this dismal cycle.

A final demographic characteristic determined for the various groups in the study was place of birth and community background. During the pretest it was determined that respondents were often unable to give a close estimate of the population of the town or city in which they had grown up. Generally, however, they were able to make a gross categorization of the population.

From these categorizations it is possible to determine that the respondents in the various groups came from somewhat different community backgrounds. Thus it appears that well over half of the Korean respondents grew up in cities of over one million population, while the majority of the Pilipino respondents grew up in smaller cities. Similarly, the Japanese immigrants and citizens appeared to have come from farms, villages, and small cities, while the background of the Chinese groups is somewhat more urban. In the case of the Japanese citizens, it should be remembered that 84% were born in the U.S. Therefore, the rural and small city background of the group may reflect the communities in which the Japanese citizens grew up before the internment camps and the forced resettlement after World War II.

Although the individual's community background may have some bearing on his adjustment to life in a large urban center, one should beware of facile generalizations. For example, "city living stress" was not often cited by any group as a problem associated with living in Chicago. The two groups which cited this problem most often (13.6% in both cases) were the Pilipinos, of whom only 13.1% came from rural backgrounds, and the Chinese, who were 37% rural. If community background influences adaptation and attitudes toward urban living, it seems likely that the interaction is complex, perhaps involving the length of residence in the city, educational level, the presence or absence of immediate family members, and English fluency. The findings of the present study suggest that the combined effect of these factors is relatively small, since the stress of city living was not frequently cited as a problem by any of the respondent groups.

Education, Employment, and Income Characteristics

Overall, the Pilipino group proved to be the most highly educated in the study, followed by the Korean, Japanese, and Chinese groups. While many respondents in both the Pilipino and Korean groups held advanced degrees, one can generalize that the Pilipinos are more likely to hold professional degrees—often in the medical area—while the Koreans tend to hold academic degrees. Contrary to the popular stereotype of the "foreign-educated professionals," most of the respondents who held advanced degrees had obtained at least part of their professional training in the United States. Thus, it seems clear that professional persons in Asian-American groups cannot be considered solely as persons who have immigrated in order to find job opportunities commensurate with their educational levels; many initially immigrated because of educational opportunities in the United States.

Compared to national norms (as reported by the 1970 decennial census) the Pilipino study group is markedly better educated than the average for Pilipino Americans, while the Chinese group in the study falls substantially below, and the Japanese group slightly above, the national averages for these groups. National figures for Korean Americans are not presently available for comparison purposes. In light of these findings, it appears that it would be advisable to assess local Asian-American populations in the course of planning social service delivery programs. In the present instance, highly educated Pilipino (and, probably, Korean) immigrants are drawn to the Chicago area by certain types of job opportunities while, conversely, many Chinese-American residents remain in the same area because they do not possess the education and training which would otherwise move them up the job ladder—and into the suburbs. Hence the need for local assessment.

In the Japanese and Chinese groups there is a tendency for the females to be less educated than the males. This, in turn, is reflected in the lower job levels of the female respondents. The Pilipino and Korean groups show a different pattern: the Korean women are very nearly as well educated as the Korean men, and the Pilipino female is often somewhat better educated than her male counterpart. Particularly in the case of the Pilipino group, this high female educational level is reflected in the respondents' job levels.

Unemployment did not appear to be a significant problem for any of the groups studied. In addition, many groups showed high levels of full-time employment for both males and females, indicating that both spouses are employed in many households in the study. The Japanese immigrants showed the greatest disparity between male and female full-time employment. But even in this group over a third of the women were employed full-time. Another finding of some interest is that, contrary to popular belief, few Asian Americans reported that they worked more than one job (only 4.3% of respondents and spouses who replied to this item).

While unemployment does not appear to be a major problem, there appears to be a certain amount of underemployment among the respondents. Underemployment is difficult to assess, but several findings indicate its existence. There appeared to be a moderate downward shift in the job categories of the respondents. In particular, a number of persons who had held professional or managerial positions were now found in white collar, clerical, or skilled labor positions. This shift was most noticeable in those groups with the highest educational levels (i.e., the Pilipino and Korean immigrants).

On a subjective level, the respondents tended to evaluate their present jobs as having fewer responsibilities than the jobs they had held before immigration. In many cases they also felt that their present jobs required less education than they actually possessed. It may also be indicative of the respondents' feelings about their jobs that, with the exception of the Japanese groups, few reported that they intended to keep their present jobs because of job interest; on the other hand, the Korean and Chinese immigrant groups were more likely to report that they would keep the job because it was "the best I could do, under the circumstances." Finally, there is evidence of some downward mobility between the respondents' fathers or male guardians, and the respondents themselves.

Overall, job levels varied considerably from group to group, with the Chinese citizens showing the lowest levels, and the Pilipino immigrants the highest. Only the Japanese citizens showed an appreciable proportion of respondents (13.8%) in the managerial category. In both the Japanese and Chinese groups there was a strong tendency for the females to be concentrated at the bottom of the job scale. Nearly half of the Pilipinos, and about a fourth of the Koreans, are in the professional category and in both of these groups females are represented about equally with males in most job categories.

Family income also varied widely from group to group, ranging from about $10,000 for the Chinese immigrants to about $18,000 for the Japanese citizens. This disparity is made even greater by the fact that the Japanese households are much smaller than the Chinese households, thus spreading this larger income over fewer persons. It was found that, in general, families with two incomes did not have total family incomes appreciably higher than families with only a single income. Therefore, it appears that in many cases both spouses are working because neither one has an income sufficient to support the family. A partial exception is the Japanese groups, where the pattern was for the husband to hold a well-paying job and the wife to hold a low level and/or part-time job only. In all groups, it must be remembered that the combined family income figure may conceal the substandard earnings of two or more persons.

In general, the respondents reported that they were satisfied with their income levels. For all groups in the study, an average of 69% said that their actual income was either equal to, or greater than, what they would consider to be an adequate income. This is obviously a highly subjective judgment. For example, the Chinese immigrants, who had the lowest income of any group, reported the highest level of income satisfaction.

Immigration Experience

The predominant reasons for immigrating varied from group to group and, within groups, by sex. Korean and Pilipino immigrants were especially likely to have immigrated for educational opportunities, while work opportunities were particularly important to the Pilipino and Chinese immigrants. Only the Pilipinos appear to have been attracted by job training opportunities, while the Japanese were the most likely to cite domestic motivations such as joining their families, or, in the case of females, to get married. In all groups, about one respondent in five cited a desire for a higher standard of living as a reason for immigrating. On the other hand, escaping political persecution in the home country was not a major reasons for immigrating.

Most of the immigrants had relatives in the U.S., and the majority had relatives living in the Chicago area. In most cases, these relatives were not the respondents' immediate family (parents and siblings), but other, less closely related persons. The Korean group was an exception, where siblings predominated.

It is not clear whether this family network is a major source of help to the new immigrant. In most groups, nearly half of the assistance received by new immigrants was rendered by non family members. The exception is the Chinese group, where one spouse tends to immigrate first and become established; the second spouse then immigrates and, consequently, receives most assistance from the established spouse. The Pilipino group, whose family network contains few immediate family members, tended to receive the majority of their help from non family members.

The assistance rendered to new immigrants by nonfamily members, who are from the same ethnic background, seemed generally to be basic support services: temporary lodging, help in finding housing and employment and, perhaps, a loan. In the Japanese and Korean groups it was fairly common for the newcomer to receive emotional support and encouragement; Chinese respondents were unlikely to receive this kind of assistance from nonfamily members.

The problem areas perceived in connection with immigration varied in relative importance from group to group. In all cases, however, language was seen as a major problem. This was even true of the Pilipino group, in which 45.2% cited language problems, despite the generally high fluency of this group. Lifestyle and cultural differences were also cited frequently as problems, and homesickness was also a substantial problem. For the Pilipinos, the

Chicago weather was a serious problem. Food differences and lack of contact with ethnic persons were not perceived as severe problems, presumably because of the presence of large ethnic communities in the Chicago area.

In all groups, females cited somewhat more problems than males. In the case of Japanese females, the problems reported must be adjusted for the large surplus of females in the immigrant sample. When this is done, Japanese female respondents appear to express about the same number of problems per capita as their male counterparts. The other groups have nearly even sex ratios, and therefore it appears that the females do in fact express more problems per capita. It is unclear whether this phenomenon results from cultural pressure on the males to restrain the expression of problems, or from greater problems actually experienced or perceived by the females.

Because of the predominance of language problems, respondents were asked whether they had ever taken English classes or lessons. Usage of classes was 59% for Koreans, 52% for the Japanese, 41.7% for the Chinese, and 24.2% for Pilipinos. In no case did the percentage of persons who had taken classes approach the percentage who had found English a problem. The unavailability of English classes seems to be the main cause for the lack of use, although in the case of the Koreans and Pilipinos it is also likely that the classes which are available would be inappropriate to the needs of these groups. These persons often have a reasonable level of English proficiency but are in need of more sophisticated English communication skills because of their professional-level jobs. These needs are not often met by classes which teach English as a second language.

Despite the various problems they have experienced, very few of the immigrant respondents had regrets over the decision to immigrate, or any plans to return to the home country. Overall, over half were definitely happy with the decision, and another fourth were happy, but with some reservations. The Korean and Japanese immigrant groups were the most ambivalent, while the naturalized Chinese citizens were the most completely satisfied.

These findings should help to dispel the time-worn stereotype of Asian-American immigrants as "adventurers and sojourners." Quite clearly, most of the study respondents feel they made the right decision in emigrating to America. As might be expected, some respondents are less satisfied than others, but very few are so discontented that they would consider returning to the home country. Many of these respondents have experienced severe disruption of their lives through immigration; some are unable to utilize their training and education in America, and nearly all have experienced moderate to severe problems in learning English. In spite of these difficulties, the respondents appear to be determined to make a success of the immigration experience.

Problems and Problem-Solving Activities

The respondents' perceptions of problems, and their strategies for solving problems, were approached from several different angles: problem perceptions were explored from the standpoint of both the individual and the community, while problem-solving strategies were approached in both hypothetical and experiential contexts. This multiple approach allowed examination of a greater variety of problem situations and was intended to make it easier for respondents to discuss sensitive issues. The success of this approach may be inferred from the fact that the interviewers reported relatively little overt subject resistance to these questionnaire items, and that relatively few respondents claimed to have no problems (16.1% of the total study sample).

When they were asked to name the major problems facing persons of their ethnic groups, all groups named "adjustment to language and cultural differences" more frequently than any other problem (42.3% of total sample). The other two problems most frequently named were "discrimination" (15.4%) and "city living stress" (11.0%), although the relative ranking varied from group to group. The other categories of problems—"interpersonal and psychological adjustment," "employment," and "ethnic community conflicts"—were cited with much lower frequencies. The large proportion of respondents citing adjustment to language and cultural differences confirms the importance of this problem area. On the basis of the evidence it appears that the relatively low level of English fluency shown by many respondents may in turn contribute to various adjustment problems.

A somewhat different pattern of problems was revealed when the respondents were asked what difficulties they had actually experienced. Again, adjustment problems due to differences in language and life style were cited by all groups, but some other problem areas were cited which did not appear in the respondents' enumerations of community problems. Most noticeably, insufficient income and difficulty in locating a job appeared to be problems that had been experienced by a number of respondents in all groups. Since this questionnaire item has a long implied time base, it may indicate that these are problems that are commonly experienced by newly-arrived immigrants. The same may be said of the other problem areas cited, such as "problems on the job," "getting medical service," and "locating housing." All of these problems were encountered by the respondents with moderate—but persistent—frequency. The problem area of "family conflicts" was cited with noticeably lower frequencies by the respondents. Still, the response rates on this item ranged from 6.6% to 12.7%, hardly negligible proportions, especially in view of the prevailing stereotypes concerning the rarity of family problems among Asian Americans.

Discrimination in housing and employment is a phenomenon which is often difficult to assess. As noted above, discrimination was cited by some respondents as an ethnic community problem; when asked about their personal experiences, as much as a fifth to a third of some groups reported that they had encountered various types of discrimination. Relatively few respondents felt that they had lost a job because of discrimination, but larger proportions reported that they felt they had been passed over for promotion or denied housing. Overall, the Japanese citizens reported the greatest amount of perceived discrimination, perhaps because of their experiences during and after World War II, or because this experience sensitized them to discriminatory acts. Conversely, the Pilipino respondents reported less discrimination than any other group, although they were also more likely to consider a discrimination to be a significant ethnic community problem.

Problem-solving strategies appear to differ somewhat from one ethnic group to another. For instance, when asked to name resources they would use in a hypothetical medical emergency, about two-thirds to three-fourths of all groups said they would go to a physician or hospital. However, twice as many Pilipino as Chinese respondents were able to name a specific doctor or hospital. Also, over a fourth of the Japanese respondents named private resources (such as friends or relatives) for solving a hypothetical medical emergency.

The Japanese sample showed a similar reliance on private resources for a hypothetical emergency involving mental illness. In the case of the psychiatric emergency, few respondents in any group specified a particular physician or hospital, and over a fourth of the Chinese respondents did not know where to go for help. Thus it appears that, although most respondents still chose a doctor or hospital as a resource, their responses to a psychiatric emergency were not as well defined as their strategies for finding help for a hypothetical medical emergency.

Help-seeking strategies in a hypothetical search for a job varied widely from group to group. The Pilipinos relied heavily on public resources such as classified ads and employment agencies, perhaps because of their command of English and their possession of marketable job skills. The Korean and Japanese groups showed a similar, but less extreme, trend. On the other hand, the Chiense groups relied heavily on ethnic friends while the Japanese cited both ethnic and unspecified friends to a moderate degree, and the Koreans and Pilipinos cited friends quite infrequently. These responses may also reflect differences in the amount of ethnic business present in the ethnic communities.

Responses to hypothetical job and housing discrimination were also varied; the one commonality in the data is that, in all groups except the Pilipinos, about half of the respondents would simply give up. The Pilipinos took an active approach to both job and housing discrimination, usually in the form of seeking help from a civil rights organization. The Japanese citizens adopted this approach to a lesser degree, but the responses of all groups showed a large amount of passivity, and a number of respondents who simply did not know where to turn. Apparently discrimination is a particularly perplexing and difficult problem to the respondents. The differences in the respondents' approaches to the two different types of discrimination (i.e., that related to housing or to employment) were slight, and varied from group to group.

When it came to solving hypothetical financial problems, all groups showed a tendency to cite private rather than public resources, although, again, there were differences from group to group. In the Pilipino group, for instance, 42.7% of the respondents cited private resources, while 68.4% of the Chinese groups made this resource choice. The most direct form of public resources cited was a bank or credit union: 36.9% of the Pilipinos, but only 8.7% of the Chinese, cited this resource. It is of particular interest that the usual social service forms of financial aid—unemployment compensation and public aid—were cited by very few of the respondents in any group. This may indicate that Asian Americans are reluctant to use social welfare services for financial problems, that they do not know about existing services of this type, or that they consider the services inappropriate.

All four nationality groups showed a marked tendency to avoid the use of outside resources for hypothetical marital problems. Between a fifth and a third said they would work out such problems by themselves, but each group showed concentrations of responses in various other categories. The Pilipinos cited family members and relatives, and marriage counselors or lawyers, as resources. The Japanese groups tended to cite friends as resources in marital difficulties, while a fair number of Koreans opted for separation or divorce. The Chinese groups cited few resources of any kind for solving hypothetical marital difficulties. No group cited ministers or priests with any great frequency; thus it appears that ethnic religious institutions cannot be expected to be a major channel of help for Asian Americans who are experienceing marital difficulties. Overall, marital and family counseling may be one of the most difficult areas in which to develop appropriate and acceptable services for Asian Americans.

In addition to the hypothetical situations enumerated above, the study respondents were asked whether or not they had actually experienced certain problems and, in the event that they had experienced them, whether or not they had sought help. The findings from this section indicate that, in general, Asian Americans do not routinely seek outside help in solving problems, although this tendency varies somewhat from group to group. Overall, the study respondents reported that they had experienced 1,136 problems, but had sought help for only 357 (or 31.4%) of these problems. The Pilipinos sought help most often (40.7%), followed by the Japanese (36.3%), the Chinese (29%), and the Koreans (25.7%). These differences may reflect the relative availability of social services to the different groups. In general, the respondents sought help most often for medical problems (53%), locating a job (47.8%), and for relief from insufficient income (34.3%). These three problem areas represent imminent difficulties which cannot be evaded through denying their existence or resorting to other coping mechanisms.

The problems for which help was sought with below-average frequency were on-the-job problems (30.8%), locating housing (24.6%), adjustment to the U.S. (19.0%), and family conflicts (12.6%). The low figures for seeking help in the case of adjustment problems and family conflicts are of particular interest, since these are areas which might be considered emotionally sensitive. While it is apparent that the Asian Americans in the study did not often seek help in these areas, one must be careful to place the significance of this finding in perspective. In the case of marital problems, it should be noted that these problems constitute only about 6.3% of all the problems reported by the respondents. Therefore, even though the respondents rarely seek help for marital problems, this may be of little perceived importance to the respondents since they rarely encounter such problems. On the other hand, it is possible that the respondents simply failed to report marital problems because of the sensitivity of this area, or because their definition of marital problems differs from that of the general population. For example, the tendency of the Korean respondents to cite separation or divorce as the preferred solution for hypothetical marital problems suggests that, at least in some groups, there may be hidden factors in this problem area. Among other things, the stress of immigration can create disruptions in the family structure and upset traditional role patterns. Few persons have the resources available to solve such problems effectively, but it may also be difficult for the individual to articulate the problem, since it lies outside of his or her previous experience.

In the case of the problem area of adjustment to life in the U.S., there may be a particularly large need for improved services and service delivery. Nearly a fourth of all the problems reported by the respondents were in this problem category, but few of the respondents who had experienced such adjustment problems had sought help. Stereotypically, this failure to seek help would be attributed to the sensitivity of the problem area. However, a simpler explanation may be that this problem area is an amorphous one for which there is no readily apparent source of help. At the present time, services specifically aimed at the adjustment problems of immigrants are not well developed in the repertoire of the social work profession. In the days of mass immigration from Europe, services of this type were developed by pioneering social workers such as Jane Addams. This work needs to be resurrected and reevaluated in the light of contemporary concepts of assimilation. When asked to rate the importance of several types of social services, the respondents gave high importance ratings to services— such as bilingual referral services and English conversation classes— that could be construed as being important to the adjustment of newly arrived immigrants. This may be a good indication that there is a need for a revival of the "settlement house" model for this service population.

To try to isolate the problem-solving strategies of the respondents in specific instances, they were asked to detail how they had located their first jobs in the United States, and how they obtained child care for their young children while the mothers were at work. Paralleling the respondents' strategies in the hypothetical job search, only the Korean and Pilipino groups had made extensive use of public resources such as employment agencies and classified ads. All groups made use of ethnic friends and organizations; in the case of the Chinese and Japanese groups these ethnic resources accounted for nearly half of the initial jobs in the U.S. Family and relatives were important resources for the Chinese and Japanese groups, but not for the Pilipinos or Koreans. Since the Chinese community in Chicago is well established, there is considerable opportunity for employment in ethnic business. The Japanese community, on the other hand, has a well-organized self-help system (i.e., the Japanese-American Service Committee) which, among other things, provides employment assistance to newcomers. The Korean and Pilipino communities, being much more recently established, have few resources of the sort to offer to newly arrived immigrants. It is worth noting that professional organizations provided very few of the respondents' first jobs, despite the fact that many of the Pilipino and Korean immigrants are members of the various professions. Overall, 11.6% of all first jobs had been pre-arranged before immigration.

The basic finding with respect to child care is that the Asian-American respondents appear to use everything—relatives, neighbors, the other spouse—except day care centers. In light of the booming popularity of day care centers in the United States, this finding raises a number of questions for the service provider. Stereotypically, it might be assumed that Asian Americans have an aversion to institutional (and probably non-Asian) care for their children. However, with the exception of the Japanese (who had few young children), the respondents gave fairly high priority ratings to child care services. This leads one to suspect that there is an acute shortage of child care facilities in the ethnic neighborhoods surveyed and that such services would be welcomed and utilized if they were available in an appropriate form. Both Pilipino and Korean community leaders have, in fact, voiced concern over the urgent need for expanded day care services in their communities.

As a final facet to the picture of problem-solving strategies, those respondents who had experienced problems but had not sought help were asked why they had not done so. For all groups, the reasons most commonly given were that the respondent had no problems or did not consider them serious enough to warrant seeking help, or that the respondent solved his problems by himself, or within the family. Among Korean respondents (especially males) there was a feeling that it was useless to ask for help because organizations were not really useful in helping one solve problems. Some Chinese respondents also felt this way; in both cases this mistrust of governmental and/or public agencies may be related to the respondents' experiences in their home countries, where such help was seldom provided. For many of these persons, most previous contacts with government agencies have been negative or punitive in nature. Chinese respondents were also inclined to cite the language barrier as a reason for not seeking help, and in both the Korean and Chinese groups there were many persons (especially females) who said they had not known where to go for help.

These last two problems—the language barrier and ignorance of available services—can be solved by direct action on the part of the service provider, through the provision of bilingual staff, referral services, and appropriate publicity within the ethnic community. However, the major reasons given for failure to seek help may require more imaginative solutions. For those persons who do not seek help because they do not consider their problems sufficiently serious, it is possible that services would appear more inviting if they were presented as being useful at a milder level of intervention. In other words, services should not be presented as being mainly for use in "worst case" situations; the services should emphasize "education" or "self-improvement," rather than being "problem oriented." Since many respondents declared that they solved their problems by themselves or within the family, services should perhaps be presented primarily as an aid to the individual's own problem-solving efforts. Many of the Asian-American respondents in the present study obviously prided themselves on their own resourcefulness and self-reliance; it seems clear that social services aimed at these persons should reinforce these individual traits, rather than attempting to impose external solutions to the individual's problems.

Service Characteristics and Priorities

The study respondents were asked to rate the importance of eight different social services which might be offered in an ethnic community. Both the relative importance assigned to individual services, and the overall level of importance given to the list of services, varied from group to group. Overall, the Chinese groups assigned the highest average importance levels (55.2%), and the Japanese the lowest (30.6%), while the Pilipino and Korean groups fell between these extremes (43.6% and 43.9%, respectively). These findings closely parallel the relative economic success of the various groups: the Chinese are the least successful and perceive social services to be most important, the Japanese are the most successful and assign the lowest importance to the services, etc. Table 99 presents the relative ranking of the eight social services by the groups in the study. It may seem anomalous that the respondents should give such high importance ratings to legal aid services when actual legal problems were almost never reported in the study. However, an interesting pattern emerges if one considers the three services which received the highest overall importance ratings from all the respondent groups. These three services—legal aid service, English conversation classes, and bilingual referral service—are all strongly related to cultural adjustment to life in the United States. The relevance of legal aid services in this connection may not be immediately obvious, but to most Asian immigrants the legalistic underpinnings of western culture are both strange and frightening. For many of these persons, life in America is their first encounter with a culture which is based primarily on *gesellschaft* rather than *gemeinschaft* relationships.[1] They are apparently coping adequately with this transition, since very few respondents reported having legal problems, but the availability of legal aid services would probably reduce the anxiety associated with this basic form of cultural adaptation.

The ratings given by the respondents to various characteristics of service agencies should be of interest to the social service provider, if only by way of dispelling another stereotype about Asian-American service usage. The two characteristics considered most important by the respondents were the helpfulness of the agency staff, and the availability of bilingual staff. Confidentiality—usually thought to be of overwhelming importance to Asian-American clients—was given top priority by only 8.3% of the study respondents. Convenient access to agencies was considered as important as—or more important than—confidentiality by all groups, while service fees were generally given little weight by the respondents. The implication of these findings is that the normal assurances of confidentiality will probably be satisfactory to most Asian-American clients. Conversely, if one wishes to increase social service utilization among these groups, the efforts of the agency should be directed toward providing bilingual staff and improving the attitudes and empathetic capacity of the staff.

Table 99

Importance assigned to various services by four respondent groups

Types of services	Korean immigrants			Pilipino immigrants			Japanese immigrants and citizens			Chinese immigrants and citizens			Totals	
	Rank order	N	%	Rank order	N	%	Rank order	N	%	Rank order	N	%	N	%
Child care centers	3	102	44.7	2	110	55.8	7	28	18.7	6	62	41.6	302	41.9
English conversation class	2	139	61.2	3	93	46.7	3	50	33.3	2	94	63.1	376	52.2
Mental health service	6	82	36.0	8	57	28.6	6	39	26.0	7	50	33.8	228	31.7
Employment service	7	74	32.5	6	82	41.2	4	45	30.0	4	83	55.7	284	39.4
Vocational training	8	71	31.1	5	83	41.9	5	43	28.7	5	80	55.7	277	38.5
Public aid	5	84	36.8	7	63	31.8	6	39	26.2	3	90	60.4	276	38.3
Bilingual referral service	4	98	43.0	4	87	44.2	2	55	36.7	1	105	70.5	345	47.9
Legal aid service	1	151	66.2	1	116	58.6	1	68	45.3	3	90	60.8	425	59.0
Size of responses		801			691			367			654		2513	

*Percentages on each cell were derived in relation to total respondents in each ethnic group, therefore, the percentage totals at the bottom of columns do not add up to 100%.

Conclusion: The Limitations of Generality

If there is one vitally important conclusion to be drawn from the results of this study, it is that the social service provider must bear the burden of closely examining the exact ethnic composition and characteristics of the Asian-American population he wishes to serve. The findings of the present study indicate that, even within a single urban area, Asian-American groups of different national backgrounds may differ sharply on various characteristics which influence service needs and service delivery preferences. For example, the basic English classes which would be useful to many of the Chinese respondents would be inappropriate for nearly all of the Pilipino respondents, who need more advanced communications skills. Likewise, the style of services that would appeal to the desire of Koreans for self-reliance would probably not appear very useful to the Pilipinos, who appear to have a more outward, activist orientation toward problem-solving.

The particular findings and conclusions of the present study should provide useful guidelines to service providers who are concerned with Asian-American service populations in urban settings similar to that of Chicago. In the individual chapters on the different ethnic groups, certain cautions are noted with respect to the various groups, and these cautions bear repeating here.

First, there are at present no reliable national norms for most Asian-American groups. The decennial census has traditionally aggregated some groups, and almost certainly has been ineffective in reaching Asian Americans in urban areas. It appears that the 1980 census will gather a great deal more useful information on Asian Americans, but until these results are available the service provider must rely on common sense and local data collection—however limited—to determine the particular characteristics of the local Asian-American service population.

Second, the results of the present study may not be readily generalizable to suburban Asian-American populations. Asian Americans—like most other Americans—tend to celebrate socioeconomic success by moving to the suburbs. Thus it is almost a foregone conclusion that most suburban Asian-American populations will enjoy higher levels of education, job category, and income than the urban populations surveyed here. The move to the suburbs may also signal that the individual has achieved a particular level of social and cultural assimilation. It follows that the service needs and problem-solving strategies of suburban populations may be quite different from those of urban ones.

Third, on the basis of available information, the Pilipino and Korean populations in the present study appear to depart from national norms. The study populations of these groups are younger, better educated, and come from more strongly urban backgrounds. Therefore, some adjustments must be made in transferring the study results to other settings. However, this transfer may not be as complicated as it seems at first sight, since the general cultural attitudes of these groups may be more consistent than their differing socio-economic status indicates. Also, although the study populations depart from national norms, conditions similar to those in the study groups are likely to be found in other urban, industrialized environments.

The final caution, then, is that there is no substitute for common sense, local observations, and intelligent use of existing data-based generalizations in establishing or modifying service programs for Asian-American groups. By way of summarizing the generalizations of the present study and relating them to the problems of practical service delivery, the final chapter which follows is devoted to a series of recommendations for services that might have particular relevance to Asian-American groups, as well as for modification of existing services to increase acceptability, appropriateness, and—ultimately—utilization.

NOTES TO CHAPTER VIII

1. For an elaboration of the distinction between *Gesellschaft* and *Gemeinschaft* see M. Gordon, *Assimilation in American Life,* New York: Oxford, 1964, 71. Briefly, Gesellschaft relationships are those which are based on explicit agreements; these might be termed "business" relationships. *Gemeinschaft* relationships are those based on implicit agreements. Examples of Gemeinschaft relationships in majority American culture would be most dealings between family members, or within such structures as the "old boy network."

CHAPTER IX

RECOMMENDATIONS

Cultural diversity is a theme which has been often repeated in the course of this study. Language, immigration history, socioeconomic and educational status, occupational level, and culturally-based attitudes toward seeking and receiving assistance—on all of these dimensions there are clear (but complicated) differences. For the service provider who must work with one or more Asian-American groups, the conclusion to be drawn from such a picture of diversity is this: *the style, content, and delivery mode of any service for Asian-American clients must take account of the nationality, origin, and generational position of the specific service population.*

In some ways, this may seem a disquieting conclusion: it does mean that there is no neat package of suggestions, on the basis of which it will always be possible to construct appropriate and effective service programs for Asian-Americans service populations. What this chapter seeks to do instead is to detail the various areas that the service provider must explore, with respect to the particular population for which s/he is attempting to provide services.

Reflection on the problems of dealing with any service population whose cultural background differs from our own should lead us to appreciate that, to some extent, it is *always* necessary (or at least advisable) to develop programs on the basis of the actual characteristics of the persons involved. This is neither more nor less true of Asian Americans than it is of, say, black Americans or native Americans. The only difference is that the term "Asian American" is rather larger and more indiscriminately inclusive as a semantic umbrella.

An additional problem is that, traditionally, service providers and public policy makers have both tended to view Asian Americans as a "safe" group (or collection of groups). The stereotype has it that either, (1) Asian Americans have no problems, or (2) they solve their problems within the ethnic community, or (3) in any case, their problems are unlikely to disrupt the fabric of the larger society, and hence may be safely ignored. Gradual changes in the social conscience of America over the last generation have—one hopes—finally made it untenable to decide priorities for filling human needs on the basis of social expediency. However, because of their "innocuousness," Asian Americans may well be the last major visible minority to suffer from this latent Machiavellian thinking on the part of those who decide social service priorities. The "safe" nature of these groups has probably also retarded progress toward detailed consideration of the diversity of their needs.

Dimensions of Diversity

It is clear, then, that the service provider must determine some of the exact characteristics of an Asian-American service population before proceeding with the development and implementation of programs for that population. In most cases it is equally clear that neither time nor resources permit anything like a thorough investigation. The question then becomes: What should the service provider try to find out about an Asian-American group, and how can the necessary information be obtained?

The first thing to be determined is the nationality group(s) to which the target population belongs. This may seem hopelessly elementary, but the present author has had all too many conversations with social service professionals that opened with the words: "Oh yes, we have quite a few Asian Americans in our community. . .I *think* they're Japanese." Whether these persons are in fact Japanese—or belong to some other group—will make a great deal of difference in both the kind of service they need and the style of services they are likely to utilize. In the case of Chinese American groups, it is also useful to determine the geographical origin of the local population, since this may determine their dialect and other important cultural characteristics.

It is also important to determine the immigration history and generational characteristics of the subject population. How recently did most members of the community arrive in America? Is the community divided into new immigrants and older settlers? Why did the immigrants immigrate? To escape dire poverty, to find job opportunities commensurate with a high level of education, to escape political persecution, to join family members, to get married, or as an act of adventure? In the case of Chinese- and Japanese-American communities, it is no longer possible to assume that all— or even most—of the members are either old immigrants or native born citizens. Recent immigration has considerably complicated the structures of these older Asian-American communities.

Investigating these topics will also lead one into the general area of demographic and socioeconomic characteristics. What is the age distribution of the community? What sort of jobs do the persons hold—and how many of the women are employed? How many children do most families have, and in approximately what age range? How large is the typical household, and in what kind of living quarters is it housed?

None of this information is particularly "sensitive," but it can be extremely useful in judging the approximate needs of a community. Formal survey techniques are usually unnecessary in gathering such information. In most cases, conversations with three or four community leaders will provide sufficient information to begin intelligent planning.

Examples of persons who might be contacted would be ministers of ethnic churches, officers of ethnic organizations, and ethnic persons who are engaged in retail or service occupations that bring them into contact with most of the ethnic community. One important caution: in the case of communities which are clearly divided into old settlers and new immigrants, be sure to contact members of both groups. Finally, never depend on a single informant; if two informants give contradictory information, look for other points of view until some sort of consensus begins to emerge.

This sort of informal surveying of the ethnic community can provide a valuable base of information to use in formulating a tentative appraisal of the community's characteristics and needs. At this stage, the most important use of such information may be negative: it allows one to eliminate certain types of services as unlikely to be important to the community. For example, a community composed mostly of middle-aged and elderly persons will be unlikely to need child care facilities. A community containing many young professional persons probably will not have a great need for assistance in procuring medical services. It is important, however, that the process of elimination be based solely on objective consideration of conditions in the ethnic community. It is all too easy to fall into the pattern of eliminating from consideration those services that are most likely to be expensive, difficult to provide, or bureaucratically "messy."

Problem-Solving Strategies

Once it has been determined that certain needs or problems are likely to exist in an Asian-American community, the next question to ask is this: In a "best of all possible worlds" situation, how would members of the community go about solving their problems? In other words, what are the characteristic *problem-solving strategies* in the community? An understanding of existing problem-solving strategies is essential to the design of appropriate styles and delivery systems for social services. It is not enough that the services address the needs of the subject population: services must be designed to complement and extend problem-solving activities in which the client would otherwise engage.

The first step in defining the problem-solving strategies of an Asian-American community is to determine the presence or absence of publicly visible resources within the community. For example, does the community have an ethnic language newspaper? Are there ethnic churches and, if so, do they appear to engage in social service activities? Does the community have active mutual-help societies, ethnic credit unions, an ethnic YMCA or YWCA? It will usually not be difficult to determine the existence of these community resources, either from informants or from a telephone directory. However, it may be quite difficult to determine the efficacy of the various institutions. Asking informants whether or not they have made use of such resources will probably evoke a defensive response. However, some objective criteria, such as size of membership, number of readers, or frequency of scheduled activities may indicate the importance of various institutional resources in the community.

Another approach is to question informants concerning their

knowledge of both ethnic and nonethnic resources in the community. In effect, this approach is much like the hypothetical problem questions which were asked in the questionnaire used in the present study. The informant is not asked whether s/he has actually experienced the problem, only what s/he would do *if* s/he were to encounter it. In questioning an informant, the approach is more impersonal yet, since one would generally put questions in the form: "What do persons in your community generally do when— (they need health care, are looking for a job, need child care. . .)?" It is important to phrase such questions to try to get at the informant's perception of what *most* persons in the community would do. There is a good chance that an informant who is a community leader will be better informed about available resources than most members of the community would be. Thus, the informant's *personal* knowledge, strategies, and preferences may be misleading as an indication of what really takes place in the community.

In addition to assessing knowledge of resources and strategies for their use, it is also important to try to gauge the community's attitude toward the use and nonuse of both ethnic and nonethnic resources. How does the community view persons who use resources from the "outside"? Is participation in the community self-help network viewed primarily as an individual or community activity? In other words, does community participation serve to mask the individual nature of problems? Perhaps most importantly, what is the community attitude toward the use of English, and is the monolingual nature of available social services seen as a major impediment to their use? Answers to questions such as these may be quite difficult to come by, not because the topic is "sensitive," but simply because few persons give much concious thought to their own attitudes in this area. When questioned about the attitudes of *other* people, the informant may quite literally have nothing to say. Nevertheless, these attitudes are important in planning social service content and style.

Building on Existing Resources

In the preceding sections we have discussed the various types of preliminary information that the social service provider may need to obtain within the ethnic community in order to be in a position to formulate appropriate and effective social service programs. To review, we need to know the following:

1) Problems perceived or experienced by community members
2) Existing resources within the community
3) Preferred strategies for problem solving
4) Attitudes toward the use of resources

Typically, what will emerge is a scenario in which the needs of the ethnic community sometimes do and sometimes do not mesh with the resources available in the larger community. Furthermore, the combination of strategies and attitudes will sometimes allow, and sometimes preclude, the use of nonethnic resources outside the community. The nature of the nonethnic resources—in terms of both style and content—will of course also have an effect on their utilization.

On the basis of the information collected, the following steps can be taken to develop services compatible with the needs, desires, and existing resources of the Asian-American community:

Identify the indigenous self-help network. Put simply, who helps whom, and within what institutional structures? It is necessary to sort out the organizations that have an assistance function of some sort from those which do not.

Develop an expanding network of personal contacts within the community. Beginning with initial informants, the outside social service provider needs to establish contact—and, hopefully, a working relationship—with potential leaders and workers in the Asian-American community.

Train primary care providers from within the community. Persons who have the potential to provide primary care within the community should be selected from the sphere of persons contacted. The principle is that it is easier to train an ethnic person in the technique of social service provision than it is to teach a social service provider an ethnic language and equip him/her with the broad span of cultural knowledge that may be needed in order to operate effectively.

Legitimize and establish the visibility of the primary care giver within the ethnic community. This usually means making certain that the primary care giver is an active member of ethnic community organizations, perhaps even attaining an executive position related to his/her community service work. In this way it may be possible to enlist the aid of the organization in carrying out social service work in the community. Likewise, the organization's self-help activities may be assisted by the presence and talents of the primary care giver.

Following a set of steps such as those outlined above cannot, of course, guarantee the successful establishment of appropriate and acceptable social services in an Asian-American community. However, following an approach such as this can at least provide an elementary reality base for deciding which services may be needed, and how they might be effectively delivered.

Service Needs of Asian-American Communities

The findings of the present study suggest that there are several general areas in which most Asian-American groups may be expected to have more or less severe problems. In this section, the various approaches are suggested. It should be emphasized again that the needs of an individual community may differ considerably from the norms found in the study and that, therefore, there is no substitute for individual, though informal, investigation within the local area under consideration.

Language. Except among the Japanese citizen groups, lack of English proficiency was a major problem for all of the Asian-American groups studied. It is quite likely that this problem will be found to some extent in almost any Asian-American community. Lack of English proficiency appears to have a definite effect on job level, income level, and several aspects of social interaction with the majority community.

However, while increased English proficiency plays a vital role in the process of social assimilation it also raises some difficult questions in other areas. For instance, at the same time that Asian-American immigrant parents equate fluency in English with attaining full social equality, they are anxious to maintain their children's knowledge of their native language and culture. In many cases, the two goals are simply incompatible.

Accepting for the moment that many Asian-American immigrants may have ambivalent feelings about learning English and retaining their ethnic culture, the fact remains that lack of English proficiency is one of the most severe problems of nearly all Asian-American groups. Traditionally, the response of the educational establishment has been to provide classes in "English as a second language," generally based on the immersion principle of language instruction.

Almost without exception, this is the wrong approach to improving the English proficiency of Asian Americans. In most cases, the instructor in such immersion classes is a member of the majority culture, and is probably not bilingual in the ethnic language of the students. These two factors will have a powerful inhibiting effect on Asian Americans, and will almost certainly lead to a low level of class participation and a high attrition rate. Because of cultural factors, a great deal more learning will probably take place in a less anxiety-producing class setting—meaning a class conducted by a bilingual ethnic person, with enough use of the ethnic language to provide verbal clarification of the class material.

A second problem is that few English-as-a-second-language programs provide a variety of levels of instruction, from basic "survival English" to courses intended to aid the professional person. Yet many Asian-American communities will contain persons representing this great span of needs. In most cases it will be necessary to assess the needs of the local community, and then develop English courses based on existing needs. One promising approach in developing such courses is to base them on subject matter that will be of immediate use to persons in the community. Examples would be employment-related English (how to conduct oneself in an interview, how to ask questions about job procedures), and orientation toward American life (how to use public utilities, obtaining social and health services, information about consumer's rights, civil rights, or legal obligations).

Orientation to American life. In addition to pursuing this topic as the subject matter of English classes, it may often be helpful to set up groups and forums within the ethnic community to promote the discussion of common problem areas. It may be possible to form these groups as adjuncts to English classes, church groups, alumni associations, or village and family associations. Appropriate discussion topics might include how to handle lowered self-esteem, reconciling value differences, handling increased modal choices, and how to relate to children who present a different outlook on life as a result of their contact with American culture.

It must be appreciated that these topics are often quite sensitive, and discussing them will be impossible for most participants except in the ethnic language. This is a case in which the organizer and leader of the group should definitely be an ethnic person from the local community, preferably one who has a sensitive and thoughtful appreciation of the difficulties of biculturality. It may be possible to assist such a person by providing resource materials and—if appropriate—some training in group process techniques.

Powerlessness and alienation. Many immigrants recognize that they have no impact on the majority society of America. They are continuously made to feel that they are outsiders, they often encounter both overt and covert hostility at the hands of the majority society, and they develop a keen sense of vulnerability. In several instances these feelings were evident from responses to the survey in the present study. There is, for instance, no other ready explanation for the overwhelming importance assigned by the respondents to legal aid service—in spite of the fact that few, if any, respondents had actually encountered legal problems. Likewise, many respondents took a fatalistic attitude toward discrimination, stating that "nothing can be done about it." Finally, it seemed desperately important to the respondents that social service providers be "helpful" toward the client, and that bilingual referal services be provided in order that ethnic persons might have a fighting chance of getting access to existing services.

The social service response to the alienation and vulnerability felt by many Asian-American immigrants will have to include several approaches. First, there is a need for informational and referral services to familiarize these persons with the American legal system. This is particularly important because the legalistic underpinnings of American society are such a peculiarly western institution. In many Asian cultures, even very large and complex business deals might be settled verbally, while in America renting a one-room apartment may entail signing a lease containing several pages of fine print.

It is probably safe to say that most American-born consumers have only a marginal understanding of their legal position in routine business dealings; however, they also have various cultural defenses, such as a generalized faith in the business and legal system, or a "family lawyer" to whom questionable matters can be referred. Asian immigrants usually lack such defenses and may also be handicapped by their low level of English proficiency: they may have difficulty understanding or communicating with a monolingual lawyer or consumer advocate. Thus it is important that legal aid services be bilingual, and that the persons providing them be able to explain legal matters in such a way as to bridge the cultural gap.

A second means of overcoming feelings of powerlessness and alienation is through the encouragement of civic and political participation. In most cases, this is best done through organizations in the ethnic community. Long-term resident aliens can be encouraged to apply for citizenship, and voter registration drives can be conducted to reach those who are citizens. Community organizations that can show that they represent substantial numbers of registered voters may then find themselves in the position of being able to bargain effectively with the leadership of the local political parties. If the ethnic community is small, it may be possible to form a minority coalition with other ethnic groups in the area, thereby amassing a sufficient block of votes to attain some political leverage. Another potential vehicle of political force is the PTA. While it is often a rubber stamp for the school administration, a well-organized PTA—or an organized and vocal group within it—can bring considerable pressure to bear on principals and teachers.

In all of these cases, the most important single element is the cultivation of political leadership within the Asian-American community. If the local political parties are of nearly equal strength and many elections are vigorously contested, then the political parties themselves may be interested in wooing the support of ethnic minorities. In other cases it may be necessary to establish a fairly substantial voter block before it is possible to impress the parties. Often, the social service provider will be put in the position of assisting the minority political leaders in learning how to manipulate the American political system—an activity that the service provider's superiors are likely to regard as subversive.

Downward mobility in employment. Several different measures in the present study suggest that many Asian-American immigrants are suffering from moderate to severe downward mobility in employment. There are probably several causes behind this phenomenon, among them, lack of English proficiency, inability to transfer skills, lack of appropriate continuing education opportunities, discriminatory licensing procedures, and employment discrimination in general. Because of these multiple causes, several types of assistance are needed.

There is a need for a clearinghouse for information on local, state, and federal programs for retraining. At present, these programs are widely scattered, little known, and generally inaccessible to Asian-American clients.

Licensing requirements are a thorny subject, since licensing agencies often have strong—but covert—ties with the professional organizations of the professions which they ostensibly license and regulate. In turn, professional organizations often find it desirable to limit the number of persons in a profession. Thus, although the refusal of many state agencies to license foreign-educated professional persons may be couched in educational terms, the real motivations may be more complex. The foreign-educated professional may also encounter a double bind due to the failure of American educational institutions to develop programs that would help him readily make up his supposed educational deficiencies.

Continuing education is a difficult area for many Asian Americans who are seeking to reverse their downward employment mobility through formal classwork. Continuing education is rarely—if ever—offered in a bilingual context. On the other hand, as noted earlier, few available English courses are appropriate for the Asian American seeking the skills to cope with educational and employment situations conducted in English. The approach to improving continuing education for Asian Americans is thus twofold: develop job-oriented continuing education programs in a bilingual context and, simultaneously, provide English instruction that will eventually aid Asian-American clients in dealing with monolingual continuing education experiences.

Underutilization of services. As has been pointed out several times in this study, it is difficult to know the degree to which Asian Americans underutilize social services compared to the general population, the difficulty being that there has been no adequate study of service utilization by the general population. However, it is clear from the study data that, for many types of services, various Asian-American groups are almost totally ignorant of available services, or claim that they would almost never—or do almost never—use such services. There is also evidence, however, that many Asian Americans would use certain services if they knew about them, or if the services were structured and presented differently from the way they are now.

One of the most pressing needs for social services in the Asian-American community is outreach. Like the USO's lonely soldier, many a social service provider has been driven to ask, "Does anybody know I'm here?" When the client group (as in the case of many Asian Americans) has only tenuous ties to the communications network of the majority society, this is more than an idle question. As Lee has shown, the most effective form of outreach to Asian Americans seems to occur when there is a confluence of formal and informal information about the social service.[1] Thus, while ethnic language brochures and articles in ethnic newspapers are an important form of publicity for social services, they must be supplemented by word-of-mouth for maximum effectiveness. Such informal endorsement may be secured through community leaders and the membership of concerned ethnic organizations.

Another important means of increasing social service utilization among Asian Americans is to establish advocacy-oriented referral services. What is meant by "advocacy-oriented" is that the client is not simply told "where to go" to obtain services, but is actively assisted in his/her dealings with the social service provider or agency.

Thus, the client may receive detailed instructions in how to deal with a certain agency, or may be accompanied by a bilingual ethnic person, who can provide assistance in communicating with monolingual agency personnel. These procedures not only fulfill certain informational needs, but also help overcome the Asian American's sense of powerlessness and vulnerability when confronted by an agency bureaucracy.

The establishment of advocacy-oriented referral services and the ultimate establishment of needed social services within the community are both dependent on the location and training of ethnic workers living in the Asian-American community. There are two possible approaches to attaining this goal. First, social service agencies can work to recruit workers from within the ethnic community. These persons are then part of the agency structure and can increase the visibility and utilization of the agency in the community through their bilingual capabilities and by helping to ensure that the agency's services are appropriate to the needs of the community. If it is not possible to train ethnic persons and integrate them into the agency structure, then a second approach is to locate and train part-time or volunteer para-professionals. These persons remain primarily identified as members of the ethnic community rather than becoming part of the agency structure. They can serve as a liaison link between the community and the social service agency.

It is not enough, however, to bring the existence of social services to the attention of the Asian-American community. In many cases it is also important to alter the style of service delivery to take account of the clients' cultural preferences. Generally speaking, the social services that appeal most to Asian-American clients are those which are relatively informal, have flexible hours, and involve a near-equal relationship between the social service worker and the client. These three factors are closely interrelated; all three are areas in which it is important to take account of the cultural predilections of the Asian-American client.

The concept of making an appointment at a specific hour is foreign to many Asian cultures. Hence it may often be necessary to conduct social service operations for Asian Americans on a "walk-in" basis. Also, because both spouses in many Asian-American families are employed full-time, it is mandatory that social services be available during evening hours, and on weekends and holidays.

Finally, it is important that an informal, nonthreatening atmosphere be established at the agency. The usual physical layout, which is based on the traditional business office, consists of receptionists, waiting rooms, and either private offices or large rooms full of endless rows of desks. This sort of environment can prove very intimidating to clients who are already reluctant to utilize social services. Privacy is essential, so that some sort of private, but informal and comfortable, meeting rooms should be available.

However, it is important to avoid the "private office" layout, with the service provider behind the desk and the client fidgeting on a straight chair. This arrangement introduces a superior/inferior relationship which will be deeply resented by most Asian-American clients. What is needed is a sort of "conference among equals," in the course of which the social service provider may give the client needed factual information, or offer suggestions for solutions. The social service provider who assumes the position of an "authority" vis à vis the Asian-American client will quickly find that s/he has been "tuned out."

Community participation. The failure of the social service professions to encourage active community participation in policy and program development is not limited to the case of Asian-American groups. However, in communities where there is a low level of service utilization and where there is much culturally-based misunderstanding of social services, community involvement is vitally important.

One approach to achieving this goal is to establish a policy and program development board within the Asian-American community. This body should include representatives of a broad spectrum of organizations and interest groups within the community. In turn, the policy and program development board should work with the entire range of social service agencies serving the Asian-American community. The board would provide the social service agencies with necessary information and guidance concerning community needs, would serve as a channel for evaluation of service programs, and could also serve in locating ethnic persons who could be trained for work in the social service agencies.

Ethnic language service directory. One of the most direct means of assisting Asian Americans in utilizing social services is to collect and publish information on what is available. At times, this may be easier said than done: In many communities, no such compilation is available in English. Thus it will usually be necessary to gather the information from whatever sources are available, edit the material into a useable form, and then secure the services of ethnic persons to translate the material and prepare it for printing (using either hand calligraphy or an ethnic language typewriter).

It is usually desirable to have the translation made collaboratively by two or more ethnic persons who have some familiarity with the services offered, and, if possible, a back translation should be made. These precautions should be taken because much of the terminology of social services has no exact equivalent in most oriental languages. Also, the aim of the ethnic language directory should be to provide clear, accurate descriptions of what the various services can—and cannot—provide. It is particularly important both to avoid raising the prospective client's expectations to an unrealistic level, and to avoid presenting the services in a way that makes them appear more threatening than they really are. Therefore, it is important to pay close attention to the wording of the directory descriptions.

There are two general uses to be made of the ethnic language service directory. One approach is to provide copies for general distribution in the community, usually through one or more ethnic organizations. If the directory is generally available, and read, it may serve as a formal reinforcement for the informal information that potential clients may have about available services. A second use for the directory is as a reference book for ethnic social service workers within the community.

In Conclusion: The Social Service Provider and the Asian-American Community

Much of the apparent underutilization of social services by Asian Americans has arisen from the cultural and structural separation that exists between the worker and the agency, on the one hand, and the real world of the potential client, on the other. In the preceding sections of this chapter we have discussed some ways in which this gap can be overcome, and we have detailed certain types of services—and service structures—that may be particularly appropriate for Asian-American communities.

It is to be hoped that the survey data presented earlier in this study will assist the service provider in selecting services and structures that are likely to be useful and acceptable to a particular community. After such a preliminary selection of alternatives, however, it is vitally important to test these alternatives in the community, using informants and other informal data-gathering techniques to tailor the service approach to the clientele.

NOTES TO CHAPTER IX

1. I. Lee, *A Profile of Asians in Sacramento*. U.S. Department of Health, Education and Welfare, Grant 1RO1MH21086-01, Final Report, 31–34, 1973.

BIBLIOGRAPHY

Abbott, K.A., and Abbott, E.L. "Juvenile delinquency in San Francisco's Chinese American community: 1961–1966," in *Asian Americans: Psychological Perspectives*, ed. S. Sue and N. Wagner. Palo Alto: Science and Behavior Books, 171–180, 1973.

Arkoff, A., Meredith, G., and Dong, J. "Attitudes of Japanese-Americans and Caucasian-American students toward marriage roles," *Journal of Social Psychology*. 59: 11–15, 1963.

Arkoff, A., Meredith, G., and Iwahara, S. "Male-dominant and equalitarian attitudes in Japanese, Japanese-American and Caucasian-American students," *Journal of Social Psychology*. 64: 225–229, 1964.

"Asian-America: Special issue," *Bulletin of Concerned Asian Scholars*. 4 (3): 1972.

Auerbach, F.L. *Immigration Laws of the United States*. Indianapolis: Bobbs-Merrill, 1955.

Barth, G. *Bitter Strength: A History of the Chinese in the United States, 1850–1870*. Cambridge, Mass.: Harvard University Press, 1964.

Beals, R. "Acculturation," in *Anthropology Today*, ed. S. Tax. Chicago: University of Chicago Press, 1962.

Bello, W.F., and Guzman, A. *Modernization: Its Impact in the Philippines*. Quezon City: Institute of Philippine Culture, Ateneo de Manila University Press, IPC paper 6, 1968.

Bennett, M. *American Immigration Policies: A History*. Washington, D.C.: Public Affairs Press, 1963.

Berk, B.B., and Hirata, L.C. "Mental illness among the Chinese: Myth or reality?" *Journal of Social Issues*. 29: 149–166, 1973.

Berrien, F.K., Arkoff, A., and Iwahara, S. "Generation difference in values: Americans, Japanese-Americans, Japanese," *Journal of Social Psychology*. 71: 169–175, 1967.

Breslow, L., and Klein, B. "Health and race in California," *American Journal of Public Health*. 61: 763, 1972.

Brigham, J.C. "Ethnic stereotypes," *Psychological Bulletin*. 76: 15–38, 1971.

Brown, T., Stein, K., Huang, K., and Harris, D. "Mental illness and the role of mental health facilities in Chinatown," in *Asian-Americans: Psychological Perspectives*, ed. S. Sue and N. Wagner. Palo Alto: Science and Behavior Books, 212–231, 1973.

Burma, J.H. "Current leadership problems among Japanese-Americans," *Sociology and Social Research*. 37: 162, 1953.

Caldwell, E. "Filipinos: A fast growing minority," *New York Times*. March 5, 1971.

Callao, M.J. "Culture shock: West, east, and west again," *Personnel and Guidance Journal*. 51: 413–416, 1973.

Catapusan, B.T. *The social adjustment of Filipinos in the U.S.* Los Angeles:

University of Southern California, 1940.

Cattell, S. *Health, Welfare and Social Organizations in Chinatown, New York City.* New York: Community Service Society, 1962.

Caudill, W. "Japanese-American personality and acculturation," *Genetic Psychology Monograph.* 45, 1952.

Caudill, W., and DeVos, G. "Achievement, culture, and personality: The case of the Japanese Americans," *American Anthropologist.* 58: 1102–1127, 1956.

Caudill, W., and Scarr, H.A. "Japanese value orientations and culture change," *Ethnology.* 1(1): 53–91, 1962.

Cayton, H.R., and Lively, A.O. *The Chinese in the United States and the Chinese Christian Churches.* New York: National Council of Churches of Christ, 1955.

Centers, R. "An effective classroom demonstration of stereotypes," *Journal of Social Psychology.* 34: 41–46, 1951.

Chang, F. "An accommodation program for second-generation Chinese," *Sociology and Social Research.* 18: 541–553, 1934.

"Changing scene in United States chinatowns," *National Council of Organizations.* 5 (April): 13, 1955.

Chen, J.C. *Handbook of Chinese in America* (in Chinese). New York: The People's Foreign Relations Association of China, 1946.

Chen, P.N. The Chinese community in Los Angeles, *Social Casework.* 51: 591–598, 1970.

Chen, P.W.-t. *Chinese-Americans View Their Mental Health.* Los Angeles: University of Southern California, D.S.W. thesis, 1976.

Chen, P.W.-t. *Cultural Conflict and Mental Illness: A Case Study of a Mentally Ill Chinese-American Patient.* Fresno: California State University, M.S.W. thesis, June 1968.

Cheng, D.T.C. *Acculturation of the Chinese in the United States: A Philadelphia Study.* Foochow China: Fukien Christian University Press, 1948.

Chin, R. "New York Chinatown today: Community in crisis," in *Roots: An Asian American Reader,* ed. A. Tachiki and others. Los Angeles: Asian Studies Center, University of California at Los Angeles, 282–295, 1971.

"Chinese exclusion," *New Republic.* 109 (Sept. 6): 323, 1943.

Chinn, T. (ed.) *A History of the Chinese in California: A Syllabus.* San Francisco: Chinese Historical Society of America, 1969.

Choy, W., and Wong, Y. "Survey needs of Christian Chinese." *Christian Century.* 72: 712, 1955.

Coleman, E. *Chinatown, U.S.A.* New York: John Day, 1946.

Conwell, R.H. *Why and How the Chinese Emigrate.* Boston: Lee and Shepard, 1871.

Coolidge, M.R. *Chinese Immigration.* New York: Henry Holt, 1909.

Cordova, F. "The Filipino-American: There's always an identity crisis," *Asian Americans: Psychological Perspectives,* ed. S. Sue and N. Wagner. Palo Alto: Science and Behavior Books, 136–139, 1973.

Daniels, R. "The Issei generation," in *Roots: An Asian American Reader,* ed. A. Tachiki and others. Los Angeles: Asian Studies Center, University of California at Los Angeles, 138–149, 1971.

Daniels, R. *The Politics of Prejudice.* New York: Atheneum, 1973.

De Vos, G. "A quantitative Rorscharch assessment of maladjustment and rigidity in acculturating Japanese-Americans," *Genetic Psychology Mono-*

graph, 52: 50–87, 1955.

DeWitt, H.A. *Anti-Filipino Movements in California*. San Francisco: R and E, 1976.

Dillon, R.H. *The Hatchetmen: Tong Wars in San Francisco*. New York: Coward and McCann, 1962.

Divine, R.A. *American Immigration Policy, 1924–1952*. New Haven, Conn.: Yale, Ph.D. thesis, 1954.

Dobie, C. *San Francisco's Chinatown*. New York: Appleton-Century, 1936.

Duff, D.F., and Arthur, R.J. "Between two worlds: Filipinos in the U.S. Navy," *American Journal of Psychiatry*. 123: 836–843, 1967. Reprinted in S. Sue and N. Wagner (ed.) *Asian-Americans: Psychological Perspectives*. Palo Alto: Science and Behavior Books, 202–211, 1973.

Duphiney, L. *Oriental-Americans: An Annotated Bibliography*. New York: Horace Mann-Lincoln Institute, Columbia University, produced for ERIC/ IRCD/EDRS Leasco Information Products, Bethesda, Md., Urban Disadvantaged series No. 26, 1972.

Ecclesine, M. "The church in Chinatown, U.S.A.," *Catholic Digest*. (Aug.): 57–62, 1960.

Fan, T.-C. *Chinese Residents in Chicago*. Chicago: University of Chicago, thesis, 1926. Reprinted, San Francisco: R and E, 1974.

Fenz, W.D., and Arkoff, A. "Comparative need patterns of five ancestry groups in Hawaii," *Journal of Social Psychology*. 58: 67–89, 1962.

Fong, S.L.M. "Assimilation and changing social roles of Chinese Americans, *The Journal of Social Issues*. 29 (2): 115–127, 1973.

Fong, S.L.M. "Identity conflicts of Chinese adolescents in San Francisco," in *Minority Group Adolescents in the United States*, ed. E.B. Brody. Baltimore: Williams and Wilkins, 1968.

Fong, S.L.M., and Peskin, H. "Sex roles and strain and personality adjustment of China born students in America," *Journal of Adnormal Psychology*. 74: 563–567, 1969.

Fong-Torres, B. "Foreword," in *"Chink!"*, ed. C.-T. Wu. New York: Meridian, ix-xiv, 1972.

Fujii, S.M. "Elderly Asian Americans and use of public services," *Social Casework*. 57: 202–207, 1976.

Fujimoto, I., Swift, M.Y., and Zucker, R. *Asians in America: A Selected Annotated Bibliography*. Davis, Cal.: Asian American Research Project, Department of Applied Behavioral Sciences, University of California at Davis, Working Publication 5, 1971.

Fujitomi, I., and Wong, D. "The new Asian-American woman," in *Asian Americans: Psychological Perspectives*, ed. S. Sue and N. Wagner. Palo Alto: Science and Behavior Books, 252–263, 1973.

Gilbert, G.M. "Stereotype persistence and change among college students," *Journal of Abnormal and Social Psychology*. 46: 245–254, 1951.

Glick, C. "Relation between position and status in the assimilation of Chinese in Hawaii," *American Journal of Sociology*. 48: 667–679, 1942.

Goffman, I. "Status inconsistency and preference for change in power distribution," *American Sociological Review*. 22: 275–281, 1957.

Gordon, M. *Assimilation in American Life*. New York: Oxford, 1964.

Green, D. *The International Role of the Korean Emigrant and Exile, 1905–1945*. Chicago: University of Chicago, unpublished dissertation, 1950.

Gurin, G., Veroff, J., and Feld, S. *Americans View Their Mental Health*. New

York: Basic Books, 1960.

Gutek, B.A., Katz, D., Kahn, R.L., and Barton, E. "Utilization and evaluation of government services by the American people," *Evaluation.* 2 (1): 41–48, 1974.

Hatanaka, H., Watanabe, B.Y., and Ono, S. "The utilization of mental health services by Asian Americans in Los Angeles area," in *Service Delivery in Pan Asian Communities,* ed. W.H. Ishikawa and N.H. Archer. San Diego: Pacific Asian Coalition Mental Health Training Center, 1975.

Haynor, N., and Reynold, C. "Chinese family life in America," *American Sociological Review.* 2: 630–637, 1937.

Haynor, N., and Reynold, C. "How American lives, Americans all," *Ladies Home Journal.* 60: 630–637, 1937.

Hodge, R.W., Treiman, D.J., and Rossi, P.H. "A comparative study of occupational prestige," in *Class, Status and Power: Social Stratification in Comparative Perspective,* ed. R. Bendix and S. Lipset. New York: Free Press, 309–321, 1966.

Homma-True, R. "Characteristics of contrasting Chinatowns: 2. Oakland, California," *Social Casework.* 57(3): 155–159, 1976.

Horinouchi, I. "Educational values and preadaptation in the acculturation of the Japanese-Americans," *Sacramento Anthropological Society.* 7: 1–60, 1967.

Hosokawa, B. *Nisei: The Quiet Americans.* New York: William Morrow, 1969.

Hsu, F.L.K. *Americans and Chinese: Two Ways of Life.* New York, Henry Schuman, 1953.

Hsu, F.L.K. *The Challenge of the American Dream: The Chinese in America.* Belmont, Cal.: Wadsworth, 1971.

Hsu, F.L.K. *Under the Ancester's Shadow.* New York: Columbia University Press, 1948.

Hurh, W.M., Kim, H.C., and Kim, K.C. *Cultural and Social Adjustment Patterns of Immigrants in the United States: A Case Study of Korean Residents in the Chicago Area.* Washington: Department of Health, Education and welfare, Grant R03 MH 27004. Final Report, 10, 19, 1976.

Ichihashi, Y. *Japanese in the U.S.: A Critical Study of the Problems of the Japanese Immigrants and Their Children.* Palo Alto: Stanford University Press, 1932.

Jew, C.C., and Brody, S.A. "Mental illness among the Chinese: Hospitalization rates of the past century," *Comprehensive Psychiatry.* 8: 129–134, 1967.

Jung, M. Characteristics of contrasting Chinatowns: 1. Philadelphia, Pennsylvania," *Social Casework.* 57(3): 149–154, 1976.

JWK International Corporation. *Identification of Problems in Access to Health Services and Health Careers for Asian Americans: Volume 2. Main Text.* Washington: Office of Health Resources Opportunity, Health Resources Administration, Department of Health, Education, and Welfare, 1976.

Kagan, L., and Kagan, R. "Oh say can you see? American cultural blinders on China," in *America's Asia: Dissenting Essays on Asian-American Relations,* ed. E. Friedman and M. Selden. New York: Vintage, 1971.

Kagiwada, G., and Fujimoto, I. "Asian American studies: Implications for education," *Personnel and Guidance Journal.* 51: 400–405, 1973.

Kalish, R.A., and Moriwaki, S. "The world of the elderly Asian-American," *The Journal of Social Issues.* 29(2): 187–209, 1973.

Kalish, R.A., and Yuen, S. "Americans of East Asian ancestry: Aging and the aged," *The Gerontologist.* 11: 36–47, 1971. Reprinted in Sue, S., and Wagner, N. (ed.) *Asian Americans: Psychological Perspectives.* Palo Alto: Science and Behavior Books, 236–251, 1973.

Kane, M.B. *Minorities in Textbooks: A Study of their Treatment in Social Studies Texts,* Chicago: Quadrangle, 1970.

Kaneshigi, E. "Cultural factors in group counseling and interaction," *Personnel and Guidance Journal.* 51: 407–412, 1973.

Katz, D., and Braly, K. "Racial prejudice and racial stereotypes," *Journal of Abnormal and Social Psychology.* 30: 175–193, 1935.

Katz, D., and Braly, K. "Racial stereotypes in 100 college students," *Journal of Abnormal and Social Psychology.* 28: 280–290, 1933.

Katz, D., Gutek, B.A., Kahn, R.L., and Barton, E. *Bureaucratic Encounters: A Pilot Study in the Evaluation of Government Services.* Ann Arbor: Institute for Social Research, The University of Michigan, 1975.

Keely, C.B. "Effects of the Immigration Act of 1965 on selected population characteristics of immigrants to the United States," *Demography.* 8(2): 157–169, 1971.

Kikumura, A., and Kitano, H.H.L. "Interracial marriage: A picture of the Japanese Americans," *The Journal of Social Issues.* 29(2): 67–81, 1973.

Kim, B.-L.C. "An appraisal of Korean immigration service needs," *Social Casework.* 57(3): 139–148, 1976.

Kim, B.-L.C. "Asian Americans: No model minority," *Social Work.* 18 (May): 44–53, 1973.

Kim, B.-L.C. "Casework with Japanese and Korean wives of Americans," *Social Casework.* 53: 273–279, 1972.

Kim, C.I.E., and Chee, C. "Aspects of social change in Korea," *Monograph Series on Korea, No. 5.* Kalamazoo, Mich.: Korean Research and Publication, 1968.

Kim, H.-C. "Some aspects of social demography of Korean Americans," *International Migration Review.* 8: 23–42, 1974.

Kim, H.-C. and Patterson, W. *The Koreans in America: 1882–1974.* Dobbs Ferry, N.Y.: Oceana, 1974.

Kimmich, R.A. "Ethnic aspects of schizophrenia in Hawaii," *Psychiatry.* 23: 97–102, 1960.

Kitagawa, D. *Issei and Nisei: The Internment Years.* New York: Seabury, 1967.

Kitano, H.H.L. "Changing achievement patterns of the Japanese in the U.S.," *Journal of Social Psychology.* 58: 257–264, 1962.

Kitano, H.H.L. "Japanese American crime and delinquency," *Journal of Psychology.* 66: 253–263, 1967.

Kitano, H.H.L. "Japanese-American mental illness," in *Changing Perspectives in Mental Illness,* ed. S.C. Plog and Edgerton. New York: Holt, Rinehart, and Winston, 257–284, 1969a. Reprinted in S. Sue and N. Wagner (ed.) *Asian-Americans: Psychological Perspectives.* Palo Alto: Science and Behavior Books, 181–201, 1973.

Kitano, H.H.L. *Japanese Americans: The Evolution of a Sub-Culture.* Englewood Cliffs, N.J.: Prentice-Hall, 1969b.

Kitano, H.H.L. "Mental illness in four cultures," *Journal of Social Psychology.*

60: 121–134, 1970.

Kitano, H.H.L., and Sue, S. "The model minorities," *The Journal of Social Issues.* 29(2), 1–9, 1973.

Knudsen, D.D., Pope, H., and Irish, D.P. "Response differences to questions on sexual standards: An interview-questionnaire comparison, *Public Opinion Quarterly.* 31: 290–297, 1967.

Konvitz, M.R. *The Alien and the Asiatic in American Law.* Ithaca, N.Y.: Cornell University Press, 1946.

Kramer, B.M. "Racism and mental health as a field of thought and action," in *Racism and Mental Health*, ed. Willie and others. Pittsburgh: University of Pittsburgh Press, 1973.

Kung, S.W. *Chinese in American Life.* Seattle, Wash.: University of Washington Press, 1962.

Kwoh, B.O. "The occupational status of American-born Chinese male college graduates," *American Journal of Sociology.* 53 (Nov.): 192–200, 1947.

Laki, V., and Murray, P. (ed.) *States' Laws on Race and Color and Appendices.* Cincinnati: Woman's Division of Christian Service, Board of Missions, Methodist Church Service Center, 1955.

Lasker, B. *Filipino Immigration to Continental United States and to Hawaii.* Chicago: University of Chicago Press, 1931.

Lee, C. *Chinatown, U.S.A.: A History and Guide.* Garden City, N.Y.: Doubleday, 1965.

Lee, I. *A Profile of Asians in Sacramento*, Sacramento: Sociology Department, California State University, submitted to U.S. Department of Health, Education, and Welfare, Grant 1 RO 1MH21086–01, Final Report, 1973.

Lee, R.H. *The Chinese in the United States of America.* Hong Kong: Hong Kong University Press, 1960.

Levine, G.N., and Montero, D.M. "Socioeconomic mobility among three generations of Japanese-Americans," *The Journal of Social Issues.* 29(2): 33–48, 1973.

Light, I.H. *Ethnic Enterprise in America.* Los Angeles: University of California Press, 1972.

Lin, T. "Study of the incidence of mental disorder in Chinese and other cultures," *Psychiatry.* 16: 313–336, 1953.

Ling, P. "Causes of Chinese emigration," in *Roots: An Asian American Reader*, ed. A. Tachiki and others. Los Angeles: Asian Studies Center, University of California at Los Angeles, 134–138, 1971.

Loewen, J.W. *The Mississippi Chinese: Between Black and White.* Cambridge, Mass.: Harvard University Press, 1971.

Low, R. "A brief biographical sketch of a newly found Asian male," in *Roots: An Asian American Reader*, ed. A. Tachiki and others. Los Angeles: Asian Studies Center, University of California at Los Angeles, 105–108, 1971.

Lyman, S.M. *The Asian in the West.* Reno: Desert Research Institute, 1970.

Lyman, S. "Red guard on Grant Avenue: The rise of youthful rebellion in Chinatown," in *Asian Americans: Psychological Perspectives*, ed. S. Sue and N. Wagner. Palo Alto: Science and Behavior Books, 20–44, 1973.

Lyman, S. "Strangers in the city: the Chinese in the urban frontier," in *Roots: An Asian American Reader*, ed. A. Tachiki and others. Los Angeles: Asian Studies Center, University of California at Los Angeles, 159–187,

1971.

Marden, C.F. *Minorities in American Society*. New York: American Book, 1952.

Maruyama, M. "Autobiography of Sansei female," in *Roots: An Asian American Reader*, ed. A. Tachiki and others. Los Angeles: Asian Studies Center, University of California at Los Angeles, 112–113, 1971.

Masuda, M., Matsumoto, G.H., and Meredith, G.M. "Ethnic identity in three generations of Japanese Americans," *Journal of Social Psychology*. 81: 199–207, 1970.

Matsumoto, G.M., Meredith, G.M., and Masuda, M. "Ethnic Identity: Honolulu and Seattle Japanese-Americans," in *Asian Americans: Psychological Perspectives*, ed. S. Sue and N. Wagner. Palo Alto: Science and Behavior Books, 65–74, 1973.

Mass, A.I. "Asians as individuals: The Japanese community," *Social Casework*. 57(3): 160, 1976.

Maykovich, M.K. *Japanese American Identity Dilemma*. Tokyo: Waseda University Press, 1972.

Maykovich, M.K. "Political activation of Japanese American youth," *The Journal of Social Issues*. 29(2): 167–185, 1973.

Meredith, G.M. "Sex temperament among Japanese-American college students in Hawaii," in *Asian Americans: Psychological Perspectives*, ed. S. Sue and N. Wagner. Palo Alto: Science and Behavior Books, 95–100, 1973.

Meredith, G.M., and Meredith, C.G.W. "Acculturation and personality among Japanese-American college students in Hawaii," in *Asian Americans: Psychological Perspectives*, ed. S. Sue and N. Wagner. Palo Alto: Science and Behavior Books, 104–110, 1973.

Miyamoto, S.F. "The forced evacuation of the Japanese minority during World War II," *The Journal of Social Issues*. 29(2): 11–31, 1973.

Miyamoto, S.F. "Social solidarity among the Japanese in Seattle," *University of Washington Publications in the Social Sciences*. 11(2): 57–130, 1939.

Morishima, J.K. "The evacuation: Impact on the family," in *Asian Americans: Psychological Perspectives*, ed. S. Sue and N. Wagner. Palo Alto: Science and Behavior Books, 13–19, 1973.

Munoz, A.N. *The Filipinos in America*. Los Angeles: Mountain View Publishers, 1971.

Murray, P. (ed.) *States' Laws on Race and Color*. Cincinnati: Woman's Division of Christian Service, Board of Missions, Methodist Church Service Center, 1950.

Myer, D.S. *Uprooted Americans: Japanese Americans and the WRA During World War II*. Tuscon: University of Arizona Press, 1971.

Nee, V., and Nee, B. "Long time Californ'," *Bulletin of Concerned Asian Scholars*. 4: 2–9, 1972.

Nelson, E.E. "Status inconsistency: Its objective and subjective components," *Sociological Quarterly*. (Winter): 3–18, 1973.

No, C.-Y. *Chae Mi Hanin Saryak (A Short History of Koreans in America)*. Los Angeles: v. 1, 1951.

Norris, F., and Shipley, P.W. "A Closer look at race differentials in California's infant mortality," NSMHA Health Reports. 86: 810, 1971.

Ogawa, D. "The Jap image," in *Asian Americans: Psychological Perspectives*, ed. S. Sue and N. Wagner. Palo Alto: Science and Behavior Books, 3–12, 1973.

Oh, T.K. "New estimate of the student brain drain from Asia," *International Migration Review.* 7: 449–456, 1972.

Okano, Y., and Spilka, B. "Ethnic identity, alienation and achievement orientation in Japanese-American families," *Journal of Cross Cultural Psychology.* 273–282, 1971.

Okimoto, D. "The intolerance of success," in *Roots: An Asian American Reader,* ed. A. Tachiki and others. Los Angeles: Asian Studies Center, University of California at Los Angeles, 14–19, 1971.

Olsen, M.E., and Tully, J.C. "Socioeconomic-ethnic status inconsistency and preference for political change," *American Sociological Reivew.* 37: 560–574, 1972.

Osgood, C. *The Koreans and their Culture.* New York: Ronald Press, 1951.

Owan, T. *Asian Americans: A Case of Benighted Neglect.* Chicago: Asian American Mental Health Research Center, 8–12, Occasional Paper, 1, n.d.

Palmer, A.W. *Chinatown: Orientals in American Life.* New York: Friendship Press, 1934.

Park, J.S. *A Three Generational Study: Traditional Korean Value Systems and Psychosocial Adjustment of Korean Immigrants in Los Angeles.* Los Angeles: University of Southern California, D.S.W. Thesis, 1975.

Paik, I. "That Oriental feeling: A look at the caricatures of the Asians as sketched by American movies," in *Roots: An Asian American Reader,* ed. A. Tachiki and others. Los Angeles: Asian Studies Center, University of California at Los Angeles, 30–36, 1971.

President's Advisory Council on Minority Business Enterprises. *Minority Enterprise and Expanded Ownership Blueprint for the '70s.* 1971.

Rabaya, V. "Filipino immigration: The creation of a new social problem," in *Roots: An Asian American Reader,* ed. A. Tachiki and others. Los Angeles: Asian Studies Center, University of California at Los Angeles, 188–200, 1971.

Reischauer, E.O. *Wanted: An Asian Policy.* New York: Alfred A. Knopf. 1955.

Riggs, F.W. *Pressures on Congress: A Study of Chinese Exclusion.* New York: Kings Crown Press, Columbia University, 1950.

Ryu, J.P. *Key Demographic Features of Korean Americans.* Chicago: Loyola University, working paper, n.d.

San Francisco. *Chinatown 1970 Census: Population and Housing Summary and Analysis.* San Francisco: Department of City Planning, 1972.

San Francisco. *Chinatown 701 Study Staff Report.* San Francisco: Department of City Planning, 1972.

Sata, L.S. "Musings of a hyphenated American," in *Asian Americans: Psychological Perspectives,* ed. S. Sue and N. Wagner. Palo Alto: Science and Behavior Books, 150–156, 1973.

Shin, L. "Koreans in America: 1903–1945," in *Roots: An Asian American Reader,* ed. A. Tachiki and others. Los Angeles: Asian Studies Center, University of California at Los Angeles, 200–206, 1971.

State of California. *Californians of Japanese, Chinese, and Filipino Ancestry.* Sacramento: Division of Fair Employment Practices Department of Industrial Relations, 1965.

Stehr, N. "Status consistency: The theoretical concept and its empirical referent," *Pacific Sociological Review.* 11: 95–99, 1968.

Strausz-Hupe, R. (ed.) *American-Asian Tensions.* New York: Frederick A.

Praeger, Foreign Policy Research Institute Series 3, 1956.

Sue, D.W. "Ethnic identity: The impact of two cultures on the psychological development of Asians in America," in *Asian Americans: Psychological Perspectives*, ed. S. Sue and N. Wagner. Palo Alto: Science and Behavior Books, 140–149, 1973.

Sue, D.W., and Frank, A.C. "A typological approach to the psychological study of Chinese and Japanese college males," *The Journal of School Issues*. 2(2): 129–148, 1973.

Sue, D.W., and Kirk, B.A. "Psychological characteristics of Chinese-American students," *Journal of Counseling Psychology*. 19: 471–478, 1972.

Sue, D.W., and Sue, S. "Counseling Chinese-Americans," *Personnel and Guidance Journal*. 50: 637–664, 1972 (a).

Sue, D.W., and Sue, S. "Ethnic minorities: Resistance to being researched," *Professional Psychology*. 3: 11–17, 1972 (b).

Sue, S., and Kitano, H.H.L. "Stereotypes as a measure of success," *The Journal of Social Issues*. 29(2): 83–98, 1973.

Sue, S., and McKinney, H. "Asian Americans in the community mental health care system," *American Journal of Orthopsychiatry*. 45(1): 111–118, 1975.

Sue, S., and Sue, D.W. "Chinese-American personality and mental health," in *Asian-Americans: Psychological Perspectives*, ed. S. Sue and N. Wagner. Palo Alto: Science and Behavior Books, 1973.

Sue, S., and Wagner, N. (ed.) *Asian Americans: Psychological Perspectives*, Palo Alto: Science and Behavior Books, 1973.

Sung, B.L. *Mountain of Gold*. New York: MacMillan, 1967. Reprinted as *Story of the Chinese in America*. New York: Collier Books, 1971.

Tachiki, A., and others. (ed.) *Roots: An Asian American Reader*. Los Angeles: Asian Studies Center, University of California at Los Angeles, 1971.

Tachiki, A. "An interview with L. Ling-Chi Wang," in *Roots: An Asian American Reader*, ed. A. Tachiki and others. Los Angeles: Asian Studies Center, University of California at Los Angeles, 275–281, 1971.

Tan, M.G. *The Chinese in the U.S.* Taiwan: The Oriental Culture Service, Asian Folklore and Social Life Monographs, 1971.

Tinker, J.N. "Intermarriage and ethnic boundaries: The Japanese American case," *The Journal of Social Issues*. 29(2): 49–66, 1973.

U.S. Commission on Civil Rights. *Asian Americans and Pacific Peoples: A Case of Mistaken Identity*. Washington: Author, prepared by the California Advisory Committee to the Commission, 1975.

U.S. Commission on Civil Rights. *A Dream Unfulfilled: Korean and Pilipino Health Professionals in California*. Washington: Author, prepared by the California Advisory Committee to the Commission, 1975.

U.S. Department of Health, Education and Welfare. *A Study of Selected Socio-Economic Characteristics of Ethnic Minorities Based on the 1970 Census. Vol. II: Asian Americans*. Washington, D.C.: Office of Special Concerns, Office for Civil Rights, Higher Education Division, prepared by Urban Associates, Arlington, Va., HEW no. US 75121, 1974.

U.S. News and World Report. "Success story of one minority group in the U.S.," 61(26): 73–76, 1966.

Wagner, N. "Filipinos: A minority within a minority," in *Asian Americans: Psychological Perspectives*, ed. S. Sue and N. Wagner. Palo Alto: Science and Behavior Books, 295–298, 1973.

Warner, W.L., and Strole, L. *The Social Systems of American Ethnic Groups.* New Haven, Conn.: Yale University Press, 1949.

Watanabe, C. "Self expression and the Asian-American experience," *Personnel and Guidance Journal.* 51: 390–396, 1973.

Weaver, J.L., and Inui, L.T. *Social Patterns of Health Care Problems of Asian Americans.* Paper presented at annual meeting of American Public Health Association, Chicago, 1975.

Weber, A.R. "The role of the U.S. Department of Labor in immigration," *International Migration Review.* 4(3): 44, 1970.

Weiss, M.S. "Division and unity: Social process in a Chinese-American community," in *Asian Americans: Psychological Perspectives,* ed. S. Sue and N. Wagner. Palo Alto: Science and Behavior Books, 264–273, 1973.

Weiss, M.S. "Selective acculturation and the dating process: The pattern of Chinese-Caucasion inter-racial dating," in *Asian Americans: Psychological Perspectives,* ed. S. Sue and N. Wagner. Palo Alto: Science and Behavior Books, 86–94, 1973(b).

Wu, C.-T. (ed.) *Chink!* New York: World Publishing, 1972.

Yamamoto, J.Q., and Palley, N. "Cultural problems in psychiatric therapy," *Archives of General Psychiatry.* 19: 45–49, 1968.

Yee, A. "Myopic perceptions and textbooks: Chinese American's search for identity," *The Journal of Social Issues.* 29(2): 99–113, 1973.

Yoneda, K. "One hundred years of Japanese labor history in the U.S.A.," in *Roots: An Asian American Reader,* ed. A. Tachiki and others. Los Angeles: Asian Studies Center, University of California at Los Angeles, 150–158, 1971.

Young, B.B.C., and Kinzie, J.D. "Psychiatric consultation to a Filipino community in Hawaii," *American Journal of Psychiatry.* 131: 563–566, 1974.

Yu, C.Y. "The Chinese in American courts," *Bulletin of Concerned Asian Scholars.* 4: 22–31, 1972.

APPENDIX A

Subject Pool and Sampling Rate

The subject pool for the immigrant samples consisted of all names reported on 1973 alien address report cards for the four ethnic groups in the Illinois files of the U.S. Immigration and Naturalization Service. According to Immigration and Naturalization Service estimates for 1973, there were 5,796 Chinese, 3,929 Japanese, 15,165 Pilipinos, and 4,806 Koreans registered in Chicago. Table A-1, below, gives the sampling rates and probabilities of selection for the four immigrant groups, based on systematic, random sampling.

The subject pool for the U.S. citizen sample was determined by using census information and community informants to delineate two highly concentrated areas of Chinese and Japanese persons in Chicago. For the Japanese sample, the area delineated was bounded by Howard St. (7600 N.) on the north, Belmont (3200 N) on the south, Ashland Ave. (1600 W.) on the west, and Broadway (600 W.) on the east. For the Chinese sample the delineated area was bounded by 19th Street (1900 S.) on the north, 26th Street (2600 S.) on the south, Canal St. (500 W.) on the west, and La Salle St. (150 W.) on the east. These two areas are inscribed on the map below (Figure A-1).

The sampling rates and selection probabilities for the citizen groups are given in Table A-2, below.

Table A-1
Sampling rates for the four immigrant groups

	Total Available	Selection Interval	Probability of Selection
Chinese	5,796	13.8	.0769
Japanese	3,929	4.0	.2500
Pilipino	15,165	16.8	.0595
Korean	4,806	5.0	.2000

CHICAGO AND VICINITY

Figure A-1: Citizen sample areas

Statistical Analysis Applied to the Study Data

The survey data collected in the study were coded in Fortran language and analyzed on the IBM 360 computer at Georgia State University using the Statistical Package for the Social Sciences (SPSS).[1] The SPSS is an integrated series of statistical programs developed around a basic data matrix, and makes use of an inter-active, semi-English language for performing statistical manipulations with the matrix. It is a convenient and relatively foolproof system for performing statistical processing of large data matrices without extensive or elaborate operator intervention.

Table A-2
Sampling rates for citizen groups

	Total Available	Selection Interval	Probability of Selection
Chinese	579	3.9	.256
Japanese	839	8.5	.117

In the present study, the principal use made of the SPSS matrix was to tabulate Ns and percentages for the large number of variables surveyed. Cross-tabulations were also performed on selected pairs of variables, but mulitvariate analysis was eschewed as being excessively sophisticated for the purposes of the study.

Dr. Kee Whan Choi of the Mathematics Department of Georgia State University supervised the keypunching of data and the running of the SPSS programs and his assistance is gratefully acknowledged.

NOTES TO APPENDIX A

[1] N. Nie, D. Bent and C. Hall. *Statistical Package for the Social Scineces.* New York: McGraw-Hill, 1970.

INDEX

Addams, Jane, 229
Adjustment to American life, 244;
Asian-American, 2; composite, 229;
Japanese, 124, Table 39; Pilipino,
161
Advocacy-oriented referral services,
247–249
Age, 214, Table 98; Chinese, 64, 65;
Japanese, 145–146; Korean, 178;
Pilipino, 145–146, Table 56
Alienation, 245–246
Asian-American communities, political participation in, 245–246;
strategies for helping, 241–243
Asian Americans, environmentally
induced diseases in, 31; geographical
distribution, 26; health care needs,
30–32; lack of data on, 13, 19–20,
23, 25, 32; naturalization and legal
protection of 5; population increase,
7, 29; problems of aged, 27, 32–33;
research difficulties, 34; self-help
network, 28, 37; service characteristics desired, 38
Assimilation, defined, 15n4

Bilingual staff in social service agencies, 232; lack of, 37; importance
to Chinese, 103

California Advisory Committee, 30
California, Asians in, 9
Census, aggregation of groups in, 25–
26, 41n18; data errors, 215; infor-
mation inadequacy, 60; Japanese
discrepancy in, 110; lack of block
data, 44; underreports Asian
Americans, 31, 39n2, 106n1
Census data, as research problem, 20
Center for Minority Group Mental
Health Programs (NIMH), 2
Chaemyun, 24

Chicago, 9, 34, 36, 37, 44, 63, 64
Chicago Japanese American Directory
(Shipmo, Inc.), 46
The Chicago Shimpo, Inc., 51
Child care problems, Chinese, 99;
composite, 230; Japanese, 134–135;
Korean, 203; Pilipino, 168, 170,
Table 72
Children, 217, Figure 5; Chinese, 66,
Japanese, 111, Table 29; Korean,
178–179; Pilipino, 146, Table 57
Chinatown areas, 28, 34
Chinese Americans, immigration
history, 3; mental illness, 27, 40n9
Chinese sample, composite, 206; bi-
lingual staff needed by, 103; sex
ratio, 64–65; urban background,
68–70; women's occupation level,
74
Churches, ethnic, 30, 34, 44–45,
179, 218
City living stress, 220
Composites: Chinese sample, 104–
106; Japanese sample, 139; Korean
sample, 206; Pilipino sample, 171
Confidentiality, in surveying, 47; in
services to Asian Americans, 204–
205, 232
Contact, Asian-American communities: ethnic churches and ministers,
30, 34, 44–45, 179, 218; local leaders, 239; through organizations,
113
Cultural norms, and service usage,
25; and interview response, 57
Cultural pluralism, in U.S., 213–214
Data, analysis, 59; mental hospitalization, 22; reduction, 58–59
Discrimination experience, job and
housing, Chinese, 92, Table 21;
composite, 226; Japanese, 128,